THE AMERICAN WAYS SERIES

🕊 AmericanWays

General Editor: John David Smith
Charles H. Stone Distinguished Professor of American History
University of North Carolina at Charlotte

om the long arcs of America's history, to the short timeframes that convey larger
ries, American Ways provides concise, accessible topical histories informed by the
st scholarship and written by scholars who are both leading experts in their fields and
ished writers.

Books in the series provide general readers and students with compelling introduc-
s to America's social, cultural, political, and economic history, underscoring questions
lass, gender, racial, and sectional diversity and inclusivity. The titles suggest the multi-
ways that the past informs the present and shapes the future in often unforeseen ways.

CURRENT TITLES IN THE SERIES

How America Gets the

How America Gets the News
A History of US Journalism

Ford Risley and Ashley Walter

ROWMAN & LITTLEFIELD
Lanham • Boulder • New York • London

Published by Rowman & Littlefield
An imprint of The Rowman & Littlefield Publishing Group, Inc.
4501 Forbes Boulevard, Suite 200, Lanham, Maryland 20706
www.rowman.com

86-90 Paul Street, London EC2A 4NE

British Library Cataloguing in Publication Information Available

Library of Congress Cataloging-in-Publication Data
Names: Risley, Ford, author. | Walter, Ashley, author.
Title: How America gets the news : a history of U.S. journalism / Ford Risley and Ashley Walter.
Description: Lanham : Rowman & Littlefield Publishers, 2024. | Includes bibliographical references and index.
Identifiers: LCCN 2024002598 (print) | LCCN 2024002599 (ebook) | ISBN 9781442235267 (cloth) | ISBN 9781442235274 (ebook)
Subjects: LCSH: Press--United States--History. | Journalism--United States--History.
Classification: LCC PN4855 .R45 2024 (print) | LCC PN4855 (ebook) | DDC 071/.3--dc23/ eng/20240117
LC record available at https://lccn.loc.gov/2024002598
LC ebook record available at https://lccn.loc.gov/2024002599

Contents

Prologue

When COVID-19 emerged at the beginning of 2020, the *New York Times*, like all news media in the United States, began reporting what would become the most significant event in a generation. The first story published in January told how China was racing to identify a dangerous new pneumonia-like illness in the country that was sickening people at alarming rates. Two months later, a video by the *Times* showed how the virus was threatening to overwhelm one New York City hospital's emergency room that was inundated with sick patients. For the rest of the year, the newspaper used podcasts, databases, interactive maps, and other reporting methods to show how the coronavirus was spreading globally, how US deaths were often linked to nursing homes, and how a lack of leadership helped the virus spread undetected for weeks, among other stories. When the number of US deaths reached 100,000, the newspaper devoted its front page to list every single person who had perished from the virus.

The coverage of the COVID-19 pandemic by the *New York Times* was not unusual. Many other American news organizations, big and small, went to great lengths to cover a story that impacted every corner of the country. But whereas news organizations in the past would have used traditional print and broadcast tools to report a major story, today they can employ an array of new digital tools to go into greater depth and have greater impact. Newspapers and magazines that for hundreds of years were limited to publishing stories and photographs on paper now can draw on audio, video, interactive maps, and other means to tell stories. At the same time, radio and television networks, as well as local stations, which for decades were limited in the length of time that could be devoted to reporting the news, now have unlimited space to do that. And new digital-only sources of news can use a variety of creative ways to explain what is happening.

American journalism has evolved from the first small, provincial publications to today's far-flung, hard-hitting digital media. A press that was once licensed by the government and largely a mouthpiece for political leaders has become a forceful watchdog for the public that often prods action. During its three-hundred-year history, the press helped push the colonists to revolt from the British and provided a forum to choose the shape of the country's new government. It debated the future of slavery and reported a tragic civil war that divided the country. It also uncovered everything from the treatment of mentally ill women and the unfair business practices of monopolies to the crimes committed by a president and abuses of children by the clergy. At the same time, it irresponsibly sensationalized the trivial, invented fictional events and characters, stoked public fever for a war, intentionally published erroneous information, crossed ethical lines, and too often failed to report the discrimination and violence faced by Black Americans and other minority groups.

Along the way, it grew from small publications turned out on hand-operated printing presses to multimedia organizations distributing information via the internet. It also expanded from an institution controlled by, and largely directed at, affluent, educated, white men, to one operated by and for all people, regardless of race, class, or gender. More recently, the press has undergone tremendous changes because of technological developments and economic forces. The internet has dramatically transformed how news is reported and presented. News now can be accessed virtually anywhere and anytime, often free of charge. Some venerable media organizations, unable to compete in the modern business environment, have ceased operating forever, while others have been forced to undertake deep and painful cuts. All have changed the way they operate and report the news in a 24/7, digital-first environment.

At the same time, the public's trust in the news media has sharply declined, while leaders at the highest levels question the honesty and integrity of journalists. Criticism of the news media is not new, and the media often makes serious mistakes that warrant condemnation.

However, when the criticism is done for partisan, political reasons—while making it difficult for citizens to distinguish what is truthful reporting from what is not—many consider it irresponsible and dangerous.

This book traces the history of US journalism to examine how America gets the news. It is a narrative and analytical survey that explores all forms of journalism: newspapers, magazines, radio, television, and digital media. The goal is to highlight the key institutions, events, individuals, technological developments, economic forces, and professional practices that have shaped the news media into the essential institution it is today. The term "press" originally referred to printed newspapers and magazines that were published on a printing press. It now includes all types of news media, from newspapers and magazines to radio and television, and the internet. In this book, the term is used interchangeably with the more modern term "news media." However, because this is a book about the history of journalism, the term press is often used.

Chapter 1 ("The Founding Press") examines the European roots of American journalism and the first publications in the 1700s. The press grew slowly in the colonies and the early newspapers had to learn to shake off the restrictions imposed by the British government. The trial of New York publisher John Peter Zenger, arrested for printing criticism of the royal governor, was a milestone in doing that. Colonial newspapers played a key role in spreading opposition to British rule. Chapter 2 ("The Political Press") discusses newspapers like the *Boston Gazette* and writers like Thomas Paine who helped inspire the colonies to revolt. Once America gained its independence, the press became a tool for the country's new political parties and leaders, largely funded by them.

Chapter 3 ("The Public Press") explores how during the mid-1800s the press took the initial steps into its modern form, one that depends on consumers and advertisers for financial support. The first mass-circulation newspapers sought to actively cover the news and that attitude was reflected in how the press reported the Civil War. Magazines became popular for the first time, showing the importance of the visual element in journalism. As America grew economically in the late 1800s, the press reflected the growing emphasis on being a profit-making enterprise, while also becoming a public watchdog. Chapter 4 ("The Commercial

Press") discusses the influence of publishers Joseph Pulitzer and William Randolph Hearst, who led this charge, while also revealing a side of journalism that sometimes seemed more interested in profits than acting responsibly. A group of investigative reporters, known as the muckrakers, showed that the press could be a force in exposing the myriad problems associated with the country's rapid growth.

Chapter 5 ("The Expanding Press") examines the growing news landscape in the twentieth century that included innovative magazines such as *Life* and *Time*. Radio and television became important sources of news during this period, seizing on technological developments to broadcast to a national audience for the first time. American journalists reported World War I and World War II, dealing with unprecedented levels of military censorship. After World War II, the press became increasingly aggressive and adversarial, seeking to cover a complex world. Chapter 6 ("The Alternative Press") discusses how the news media reported on key events in the last decades of the twentieth century, including the Cold War, the Civil Rights Movement, the Vietnam War, the women's liberation movement, and the Watergate scandal. Public broadcasting and cable television debuted during this time, providing alternative means of getting the news. Chapter 7 ("The Digital Press") explores the modern news media. Journalism increasingly became a big business at the end of the twentieth century, and the corporatization of the press affected how the press operated. The internet dramatically changed the way the news was reported and delivered. The news media continues wrestling with the impact, with varying degrees of success.

The press has a vital task in a democracy. It informs, analyzes, and explains. It investigates wrongdoing, holding individuals in positions of authority accountable. And it provides a forum for public comment and criticism. This book will discuss the times when the country's press performed that task responsibly and admirably, as well as the times when it didn't. The goal is for readers to gain an appreciation of American journalism history and be informed consumers of the news. Ultimately, we cannot understand the role of the news media today without knowing its history.

Our thanks to Mike Conway, John Dillon, Russ Eshelman, Teri Finneman, Gene Foreman, Carol Sue Humphrey, and Elliot King, who read portions of or all the manuscript and provided helpful comments. We are grateful to the financial support of Penn State's Bellisario College of Communications, which made this partnership possible. Special thanks to our spouses and families for their love and encouragement.

The Founding Press

1690 to 1765

THE MEN AND WOMEN WHO SETTLED THE NEW LAND THAT BECAME known as the United States prized news. Like humans for centuries, they had an insatiable appetite to know what was happening in their communities, as well as elsewhere. However, with no printing presses for decades, information in the colonies was initially exchanged mainly by word of mouth. That included everything from church sermons to tavern conversations. The first American newspapers were modeled after their European predecessors in content, appearance, and style. As had been the case in England, printers needed the approval of the British government to publish a newspaper or risk being shut down.

With the population of the colonies growing, printers began starting more publications. Publishing a weekly newspaper kept their presses working and provided another source of income. As the publisher of the *Pennsylvania Gazette*, Benjamin Franklin became one of the most influential early newspaper figures. The entrepreneurial Franklin established a network of printing shops throughout the colonies, setting up young men with equipment and supplies in exchange for a share of the profits.

By 1739, more than ten newspapers were published in growing colonial towns, including Boston, Philadelphia, New York, Williamsburg, and Charleston. Because they served the interests of the government, most newspapers initially were editorially neutral. However, as the colonies grew increasingly independent, newspapers became more censorious of the royal government. The trial of *New York Journal* publisher John Peter Zenger helped establish the principle that the press should be able to print criticism of the authorities.

EUROPEAN PREDECESSORS

The publishing of news in America had its roots in the same places the colonists emigrated from. Europeans had been exchanging news, or "intelligence" as it was often known, for hundreds of years before the newspaper was born. This was most often done via the newsletter, written by hand and exchanged haphazardly. The invention of the movable type printing press in 1455 revolutionized the process for spreading information. By the Protestant Reformation, the exchange of newsletters had become more systematized, and leaders regularly received news of what was happening elsewhere. By the mid-1500s, this exchange of intelligence had become a growing business in some European cities with dozens of newsletters distributed. The writing found in newsletters was generally terse and direct, with a businesslike tone. Newsletters also were organized in a way that the readers could distinguish one item from the next.

The prototype of the modern newspaper originated in Holland in the early seventeenth century. The country's capital, Amsterdam, had become an important trading and business center for Europe. The Dutch began publishing semi-regular commercial newsletters known as *corantos* ("currents of news") that grew to eventually contain local news. Within a few years, printers across Europe were imitating the *corantos*, and the first published newsletter in England appeared in 1621. Although the *corantos* shared some of the characteristics of newspapers, a good deal of the news was old, and they were not published on a regular basis. They also had a different look. Like a book, the first page contained the title; text did not begin until page three. They also ranged in size from eight to twenty-four pages.

The *London Gazette*, founded in 1665, was different. The newspaper was neatly printed on both sides of a half-sheet of paper, with the name and date at the top, and two columns of text below. The *Gazette* was full of news, much of it foreign. Nonetheless, it became widely read and inspired other newspapers in Britain that copied its appearance and approach to reporting the news. The *Gazette* was published on behalf of the English government and contained the important phrase, "Published by Authority," meaning that the newspaper was licensed and approved for publication.

English leaders had sought to control printing from its first appearance on the British Isles. The Tudor monarchs, beginning with Henry VII, who reigned from 1485 to 1509, understood the power of information. He authorized the publication of state communication in the form of occasional printed broadsides, making sure it was favorable to him. His successor, Henry VIII, went even further, issuing censorship rules and making sure they were enforced. Henry VIII, who famously wanted to divorce his first wife, Katherine of Aragon, challenged the authority of the Catholic Church and was established as head of the new Church of England. To maintain control, he imposed prior restraint, a system of prepublication censorship. Printers who didn't submit to censorship could be prosecuted for "seditious libel." Henry VII also inaugurated a system of licensing for printers so that only printers who supported his rule could publish. Later, under Queen Elizabeth, the secret Court of the Star Chamber prosecuted printers who challenged the Crown. Defendants were arrested and tried secretly.

The practice of licensing continued in the 1600s, but control of printing by the authorities became increasingly difficult as an unprecedented number of religious and political publications appeared throughout England. The spread of literacy created a demand for printed materials and intellectuals began to question the practice of licensing. In 1644, the poet John Milton wrote *Areopagitica*, a call for the pursuit of knowledge and freedom of expression. Milton, who had been threatened by punishment for expressing heretical opinions, pled with Parliament to end licensing. Requiring publications to be licensed, he argued, "hinders and retards the importation of our richest merchandise truth." Censorship prevented debate, which was essential to getting at the truth, he maintained. "Where there is much desire to learn, there of necessity will be much arguing, much writing, many opinions, for opinion in good men is but knowledge in the making," Milton wrote.

In the aftermath of the Glorious Revolution of 1688, prior restraint was clearly unpopular. In 1695, Britain's House of Commons refused to renew the licensing act, largely due to the belief that the system didn't work sufficiently to control the press. The monarchy still had avenues for seeking to control the press, but printers seized on the opportunity to start new publications. By 1704, nine newspapers were published in London alone, including a daily, and within a few years, newspapers appeared across England.

PRINTING IN BRITISH AMERICA

The early colonists immigrated from Europe for religious, political, and economic reasons. They also came from a variety of countries and spoke different languages. The colonists wanted to know what was happening in their new home, as well as in the places they left behind. Initially, news was exchanged largely by word of mouth. Most colonists were devout practitioners of their faith, so the clergy were particularly important in spreading information. They gathered news from public officials and shared it with their congregations in their weekly sermons. Letters and documents provided printed information, but most of it came from Europe.

Written news during this time depended entirely on transportation, and in the colonies that could be problematic. News was carried by ship or horseback and often was delayed by weather or accidents. For decades, the colonies also lacked a reliable postal service. New York, Massachusetts, and New Hampshire initiated mail service in 1692, and over the next several years, other colonies joined. In 1711, Parliament put the colonial postal service under government control. However, the southern colonies remained without postal service for more than ten years.

Printing began in the American colonies in 1638 with the arrival of the first press in Cambridge, Massachusetts. Sponsored by a new college that would later be named Harvard, the press turned out mostly educational and religious materials under the direction of Stephen Day. As in England, printers in the colonies had to be licensed, and authorities initially required that all printing be done in Cambridge. However, by 1700 there were three printers in the city. They published broadsides, gubernatorial proclamations, legislative resolutions, and commercial advertisements, as well as sermons, tracts, and religious writings of all sorts.

Printers learned their trade by working as apprentices. As with other trades, a young man agreed to work for a master for a set number of years while learning the craft. At the end of the time, the young man became a journeyman printer and perhaps later, a master printer, operating his own shop. Women were not admitted to the apprenticeship system, nor were people of color. Most printers were also merchants, selling books and other published materials. Some became prominent leaders in their communities.

None of the printers printed anything that resembled news until printer Samuel Green Jr. began reprinting the *London Gazette* in 1685. The first issue of the *Gazette* that came off his press in Cambridge reported the death of King Charles II and the ascension of James II to the throne. Green and others continued to reprint news from Europe, even though it was often months old. That included an earthquake in Naples, an English naval victory over France, and the coronation of a new pope. It had taken time, but printers were beginning to recognize that the American colonists wanted newspapers.

First Colonial Newspapers

Boston was the capital of the Massachusetts Bay province and the largest seaport in America. The city had a growing population of about seven thousand residents with most of its commercial establishments centered on the port. Ships brought goods from Britain and the West Indies, while fleets quartered at the port fished the waters of New England. Boston also was the center of religion and education in the colonies. All those factors made it the logical place for the first American newspapers to be founded.

On September 25, 1690, a new publication appeared in the city, *Publick Occurrences Both Foreign and Domestic*. The newspaper's publisher, Benjamin Harris, had immigrated to America from England, where he had a reputation for publishing materials that government authorities didn't like. He began as a printer and bookseller, gaining notoriety with the publication of the book titled *War with the Devil*. His London newspaper, *Domestick Intelligence*, included such sensational stories as a man who was found hanging with his head cut off and a priest who had an affair with a chambermaid. Harris also published a pamphlet, *Appeal from the Country to the City*, which was critical of Charles II. The authorities imprisoned him twice.

Looking for a place to start over, Harris arrived in Boston in 1686. He initially published almanacs and literary works, developing a prosperous business. But Harris soon decided to try his hand with another newspaper. As an experienced editor, he likely missed publishing the latest news and speaking out on issues. He also no doubt saw it as an opportunity to expand his printing business. The mission of *Publick Occurrences*, in the words of Harris, was to provide readers "with an Account of such considerable things as have arrived unto our Notice," in order that "Memorable Occurrents of Divine providence may not be neglected or forgotten, as they too often are." The September 25, 1690, issue contained stories about the state of the harvest, the plan of Native Americans to hold a day of thanksgiving, a fire, and a smallpox epidemic in Boston. It also had stories about the expedition of a Massachusetts militia and their Indigenous allies against the French in Canada, and the rumor that French King Louis XIV had intimate relations with his daughter-in-law.

Although the issue was labeled "Numb. 1," and intended to be the first in a series, *Publick Occurences* lasted just one issue. Less than a week after the newspaper was published, the Massachusetts governing council shut it down because Harris didn't have a license to publish. In its order, the council expressed concerns about "sundry doubtful and uncertain Reports" published in the newspaper. Although the council members didn't specify what they were, one likely was the story about the expedition in Canada, including Harris's reference to Native Americans as "miserable savages" with whom England should not be allied. The suggestion that Louis XIV was committing incest also no doubt angered the council.

Although Harris never published another issue of *Public Occurrences*, the controversy didn't adversely affect his fortunes in America. He went on to become one of Boston's most successful printers, eventually becoming the colony's official printer in 1692. Harris later returned to England, where he published at least three newspapers and continued to be controversial. He was arrested twice for printing materials that angered the authorities.

Fourteen years after *Public Occurrences* was published, John Campbell decided it was time for another newspaper in Boston. Campbell, who had emigrated from Scotland in the 1690s, had become the city's postmaster in 1702. As postmaster, he learned of news that arrived from letters, foreign newspapers, and the townsfolk who came in regularly to pick up their mail. For two years, Harris sent a handwritten newsletter to merchants, political leaders, and others in the city with news of government activities, commerce, shipping, and news from England. Some of the newsletters were posted in public places for anyone who wanted the news to read. Although he had help from his brother, Campbell eventually tired of writing the newsletter by hand.

On April 24, 1704, Campbell published the first issue of the *Boston News-Letter*. He hired Bartholomew Green to set the type and print it. He also arranged with a local bookseller to solicit advertising. Campbell patterned the *News-Letter* after English newspapers, such as the *London Gazette*, that he had been reading for years. The *News-Letter* measured about six by ten inches. The stories were arranged in two columns with the type size varying only slightly. It also prominently carried the notice "Published by Authority" at the top of the front page, signifying that Campbell was licensed to put out the newspaper.

Unlike Harris, Campbell wasn't going to endanger his prized government job by getting into trouble, so the postmaster was cautious in what he published. He filled the *News-Letter* with public announcements, commercial and local news, stories from London newspapers, and, occasionally, opinion pieces. Campbell didn't go out and search for news; most of it simply was given to him. However, the postmaster soon discovered that publishing the *News-Letter* was difficult. The newspaper had a paid circulation of only about three hundred, and many subscribers were habitually late in paying their bills. Advertising provided only a limited income. Campbell regularly published pleas to the public for support, but the newspaper always struggled financially. Campbell even had to stop publishing the *News-Letter* for most of 1709.

N. E. Numb. 1.

The Boston News-Letter.

Published by Authority.

From **Monday** April 17. to **Monday** April 24. 1704.

London Flying-Post from Decemb. 2d. to 4th. 1703.

Letters from *Scotland* bring us the Copy of a Sheet lately Printed there, Intituled, *A seasonable Alarm for* Scotland. *In a Letter from a Gentleman in the City, to his Friend in the Country, concerning the present Danger of the Kingdom and of the Protestant Religion.*

This Letter takes Notice, That Papists swarm in that Nation, that they traffick more avowedly than formerly, and that of late many Scores of Priests & Jesuites are come thither from France, and gone to the North, to the Highlands & other places of the Country. That the Ministers of the Highlands and North gave in large Lists of them to the Committee of the General Assembly, to be laid before the Privy-Council.

It likewise observes, that a great Number of other ill-affected persons are come over from *France*, under pretence of accepting her Majesty's Gracious Indemnity; but, in reality, to increase Divisions in the Nation, and to entertain a Correspondence with *France*: That their ill Intentions are evident from their talking big, their owning the Interest of the pretended King *James* VIII. their secret Cabals, and their buying up of Arms and Ammunition, wherever they can find them.

To this he adds the late Writings and Actings of some disaffected persons, many of whom are for that Pretender; that several of them have declar'd they had rather embrace Popery than conform to the present Government; that they refuse to pray for the Queen, but use the ambiguous word Soveraign, and some of them pray in express Words for the King and Royal Family; and the charitable and generous Prince who has show'd them so much Kindness. He likewise takes notice of Letters, not long ago found in Cypher, & directed to a Person lately come thither from St. *Germains.*

He says that the greatest Jacobites, who will not qualifie themselves by taking the Oaths to Her Majesty, do now with the Papists and their Companions from St. *Germains* set up for the Liberty of the Subject, contrary to their own Principles, but meerly to keep up a Division in the Nation. He adds, that they aggravate those things which the People complain of, as to *England's* refusing to allow them a freedom of Trade, &c. and do all they can to foment Divisions betwixt the Nations, & to obstruct a Redress of those things complain'd of.

The Jacobites, he says, do all they can to persuade the Nation that their pretended King is a Protestant in his Heart, tho' he dares not declare it while under the Power of *France;* that he is acquainted with the Mistakes of his Father's Government, will govern us more according to Law, and endear himself to his Subjects.

They magnifie the Strength of their own Party, and the Weakness and Divisions of the other, in order to facilitate and hasten their Undertaking; they argue themselves out of their Fears, and into the highest assurance of accomplishing their purpose.

From all this he infers, That they have hopes of Assistance from *France*, otherwise they would never be so impudent; and he gives Reasons for his Apprehensions that the *French* King may send Troops thither this Winter, 1. Because the *English* & *Dutch* will not then be at Sea to oppose them. 2. He can then best spare them, the Season of Action beyond Sea being over. 3. The Expectation given him of a considerable number to joyn them, may incourage him to the undertaking with fewer Men, if he can but send over a sufficient number of Officers with Arms and Ammunition.

He endeavours in the rest of his Letters to answer the foolish Pretences of the Pretender's being a Protestant, and that he will govern us according to Law. He says, that being bred up in the Religion and Politicks of *France*, he is by Education a stated Enemy to our Liberty and Religion. That the Obligations which he and his Family owe to the *French* King must necessarily make him to be wholly at his Devotion, and to follow his Example; that if he sit upon the Throne, the three Nations must be oblig'd to pay the Debt which he owes the *French* King for the Education of himself, and for Entertaining his supposed Father and his Family: And since the King must restore him by his Troops, if ever he be restored, he will see to secure his own Debt, before those Troops leave *Britain.* The Pretender being a good Proficient in the *French* and *Romish* Schools, he will never think himself sufficiently aveng'd, but by the utter Ruine of his Protestant Subjects, both as Hereticks and Traitors. The late Queen, his pretended Mother, who in cold Blood when she was Queen of *Britain*, advis'd to turn the West of *Scotland* into a hunting Field, will be then for doing so by the greatest part of the Nation; and, no doubt, is at Pains to have her pretended Son educated to her own Mind: Therefore, he says, it were a great Madness in the Nation to take a Prince bred up in the horrid School of Ingratitude, Persecution and Cruelty, and filled with Rage and Envy. The *Jacobites*, he says, both in *Scotland* and at St. *Germains*, are impatient under their present Straits, and knowing their Circumstances cannot be much worse than they are, at present, are the more inclinable to the Undertaking. He adds, That the *French* King knows there cannot be a more effectual way for himself to arrive at the Universal Monarchy, and to ruine the Protestant Interest, than by setting up the Pretender upon the Throne of Great *Britain*, he will in all probability attempt it; and tho' he should be persuaded that the Design would miscarry in the close, yet he cannot but reap some Advantage by imbroiling the three Nations.

From all this the Author concludes it to be the Interest of the Nation, to provide for Self defence; and says, that as many have already taken the Alarm, and are furnishing themselves with Arms and Ammunition, he hopes the Government will not only allow it, but encourage it, since the Nation ought all to appear as one Man in the Defence of

One of the problems was that the newspaper was invariably dull. Campbell believed foreign news was important, so he always printed it, even though the news often was weeks or months old. He also avoided controversial issues, acknowledging in one issue that his editorial philosophy was "to give no offence." Campbell believed that publishing the newspaper was simply part of his job as postmaster. However, he failed to report many of the major events that were taking place in a growing city, events that were of interest to readers.

The *News-Letter* was directed primarily at the political and business leadership of Boston. For this reason, it never enjoyed a large readership. Another problem was that the *News-Letter* was the organ of the unpopular royal governor of Massachusetts, Joseph Dudley. That meant it had to regularly publish official proclamations from the governor or the Crown. Boston's Puritan residents considered Dudley's administration to be corrupt and immoral, so the *News-Letter* was dismissed by many. The Reverend Cotton Mather called the newspaper "filthy and foolish" and said it provided only a "thin sort of diet." Mather and his brother, Increase, regularly published pamphlets attacking Dudley.

In 1718, William Brooker replaced Campbell as Boston postmaster. However, Campbell refused to give up the *News-Letter*, so Brooker started another newspaper, the *Boston Gazette*, in 1719. No longer feeling limited in what he could publish, Campbell livened up the *News-Letter*, adding essays and other material. Soon, the *Gazette* and the *News-Letter* were taking opposing sides on issues. The *Gazette* continued through a succession of postmasters before becoming one of the most important voices of the revolutionary era. Campbell eventually sold the *News-Letter*, and it continued publishing in various forms until the Revolutionary War.

New-England Courant

Anglicans made up the minority of residents in Puritan-dominated Massachusetts. Anglicans had generally remained publicly quiet about their religious beliefs, but under the leadership of Reverend John Checkley, they began to speak out more forcefully. They also wanted an outlet for their beliefs. With the support of affluent Anglicans, the *New-England Courant* was founded in 1721. The publisher was James Franklin, the young owner of a Boston printing establishment. Franklin was interested in the news happening in Massachusetts. He modeled the *Courant* after Britain's popular *Spectator*, making it a lively local newspaper that was not afraid to court controversy. He invited bright, witty writers to contribute essays, and they gladly delivered.

Noticeably, the *Courant* didn't carry the "Published by Authority" announcement, signifying that Franklin was going to publish what he saw fit. The first issue featured a stinging attack on Cotton Mather, who supported inoculation for smallpox. During this time, more deaths resulted from smallpox than any other cause. Boston had already experienced several outbreaks since its founding, and in 1721 another was raging. Although most Boston doctors opposed inoculation because they believed it was not scientific, the *Courant* did so because Mather supported it. Mather's supporters fired back in a broadside, and soon the opposing sides were trading insults.

The *Courant* was founded when the royal governor's power to license was in dispute. Among the governor's instructions from the British Crown had always been procedures for licensing. However, when the Massachusetts governor sought to secure approval for licensing, the House of Representatives refused to cooperate. As a result, publishers believed they had limited freedom to print what they saw fit. Franklin soon turned the *Courant's* sights on Governor Samuel Shute and learned that he didn't have as much freedom as he thought. Many residents of Massachusetts had become concerned about the presence of pirate ships off the coast. Piracy was hurting the economy of the region, and some believed the colonial government wasn't doing enough to combat the problem. The *Courant* published a story about one pirate ship operating in the area and sarcastically reported that the royal government was outfitting a ship to pursue it "sometime this month, wind and weather permitting." Outraged by the insinuation that he was remiss in his duty, the governor ordered Franklin jailed.

That didn't stop the publisher, who continued his criticism of the royal government. The court eventually ordered Franklin to stop printing the *Courant* altogether. He ignored the order and was jailed again. In his place, he substituted the name of his younger brother, Benjamin, as publisher of the *Courant*. Ben, who was only seventeen years old, had served as an apprentice for several years. In his first issue, published on February 4, 1723, the precocious Ben glibly described himself as a "man of good temper, courteous Deportment, sound judgment, a moral Hater of Nonsense, Foppery, Formality, and Endless Ceremony."

Franklin was the youngest son and the fifteenth child of Josiah Franklin. He attended grammar school and at the age of ten began working for his father's chandlery business, making candles and soap. Two years later, he became an apprentice in his brother's printing establishment, working for him and learning the trade. He also used the opportunity to read widely from the books available, beginning a lifelong love for self-education.

While an apprentice, Ben also got his first experience writing for a publication, penning the "Silence Dogood" essays published in the *Courant*. Ben, who was only sixteen at the time, patterned them after the essays of British writers Joseph Addison and Richard Steele, who shrewdly examined contemporary life. At the time, it was a common practice for a writer to use a pen name to protect the author's identity. Fearing that his brother would never publish anything he had written, Ben secretly put them under the printing house door. Silence Dogood was a prudish country widow, who styled herself as an "Enemy to Vice, and a Friend to Virtue," as well as a "mortal Enemy to arbitrary Government & unlimited Power." In the essays, Ben explored a variety of subjects, from drinking to marriage, often addressing the foibles of human nature. Ben wrote in his autobiography that it took his brother several months to discover he was "Silence Dogood." When James finally did, he was furious. The Franklin brothers had always clashed. Ben admitted he too often was "saucy & provoking." His brother, in turn, regularly used his fists to settle disputes. Tired of battling James, Ben fled Boston in 1724 and eventually made his way to Philadelphia.

James eventually resumed publishing the newspaper, but by that time it wasn't the same lively and outspoken publication. Still, the *Courant* in its brief life had left a mark on the journalism of early America with its outspoken essays. Whereas the *News-Letter* was cautious in what it published, the *Courant* was not afraid to court controversy. In 1726, James moved to Providence, Rhode Island, where he became the official printer and founded the colony's first newspaper, the *Rhode Island Gazette*.

Philadelphia Newspapers and Benjamin Franklin

Philadelphia, like Boston, was a seaport and commercial center with a sizable group of educated and wealthy residents. Andrew Bradford had founded the *American Weekly Mercury* in 1719 as the first newspaper published outside of Boston. Bradford's father, William, had been a leading printer in Philadelphia. He later set up a printing shop in New York City, and Andrew learned the printing business at his side. The *American Weekly Mercury* was aimed at the business community. As the name suggested, Bradford sought a circulation that was not limited to Philadelphia. He distributed the newspaper in New York, New Jersey, Delaware, Rhode Island, Virginia, and other colonies. The *Mercury* was similar in size and appearance to the Boston newspapers. A great deal of the content was European news copied from London newspapers.

A devout Anglican, Bradford generally avoided controversy and offending the authorities. He had also become the city's postmaster. That changed in 1729 when an essay in the *Mercury* by a contributor encouraged readers to "exert our Selves for Liberty and don't Tamely sit by and allow any Part of it to wrested from us by any Man, or combination of Men whatsoever." The essay was published on the eve of an election, and the governing council considered it an attack on the government. The council ordered Bradford arrested even though he hadn't written the essay but only printed it.

The *Mercury* gained a competitor in Philadelphia when the *Pennsylvania Gazette*, or the *Universal Instructor*, began publishing in 1728. Samuel Keimer, a rival printer in the city, had maintained a grudge against Bradford ever since a dispute over printing Quaker materials several years earlier. In announcing his plans for the newspaper, Keimer said the *Mercury* had been "not only a Reproach to the Province, but such a Scandal to the very Name of Printing, that it may, for its unparrellel'd Blunders and Incorrectness, but truly stiled *Nonsence in Folio*, instead of a Serviceable News-Paper." Eccentric and devoutly religious, Keimer wrote that his newspaper would contain "the Theory of All Arts, both Liberal and Mechanic, and the several Sciences both humane and divine, with the Figures, Kinds, properties . . . of Things natural and artificial." And, indeed, the first issue contained a lengthy essay on the letter *a*.

Keimer hired Ben Franklin as a journeyman printer. The astute Franklin recognized that Keimer likely wasn't going to be successful with his plan for the *Gazette*. He found a partner, and they purchased the newspaper in 1729. Franklin immediately shortened the title to *Pennsylvania Gazette*. He also stopped publishing the arcane essays that Keimer liked, saying that most readers do not think "such a Method of communicating Knowledge to be a proper One." In the first issue, he took a swipe at Keimer and Bradford, writing, "There are many who have long desired to see a good News-Paper in Pennsylvania." In one of the first issues of the *Gazette*, he explained what he considered the proper credentials for anyone who wanted to publish a good newspaper:

> The Author . . . ought to be qualified with an extensive Acquaintance with Languages, a great Easiness and Command of Writing and Relating Things cleanly and intelligibly, and in a few Words; he should be able to speak of War both by Land and Sea; be well acquainted with Geography, with the History of the Time, with the several Interest of Princes and States, the Secrets of Courts, and the Manners and Customs of all Nations.

Although he was only twenty-four, Franklin was already a talented writer and experienced printer. He immediately set about remaking the *Gazette*, and soon it was more interesting and informative than its rivals. What set the *Gazette* apart more than anything was the writing, much of it done by Franklin under pseudonyms. In one letter, he cleverly corrected a typographical mistake that noted someone "died" at a local restaurant, when the customer actually "dined." He used the letter to recount other amusing mistakes, such as one edition of the Bible quoting David as saying he was "wonderfully mad" rather than "wonderfully made."

After his partner departed in 1830, Franklin published the *Gazette* by himself for eighteen years. He put a great emphasis on selling advertising, and by 1835 advertisements made up about one-quarter of the

Figure 1.2 Benjamin Franklin *Source:* The White House Historical Association.

newspaper's total space. Franklin also won the job of being the official printer for the Pennsylvania Assembly. The Bradford family had enjoyed the lucrative contract for years, but when they bungled the governor's address to the Assembly, Franklin spotted his chance. He printed the message "elegantly and correctly," as he later wrote, and sent it to each member. The Assembly voted to give the printing contract to Franklin.

In 1732, Franklin began publishing *Poor Richard's Almanack*, which besides being another source of income, promoted his newspaper. Almanacs were popular reading during the time, offering weather predictions, astronomical information, household advice, and games. They were also reliable sources of revenue, because readers had to purchase a new copy each year. At the time, six almanacs were printed in Philadelphia alone. Franklin's version, which he described as "a proper Vehicle for conveying Instruction among the common People," included his collection of witty aphorisms and proverbs. He enjoyed hiding behind the veil of poor Richard Saunders to offer down-home wisdom such as:

"Haste makes waste."

"A good example is the best sermon."

"Eat to live and not live to eat."

"There cannot be good living where there is not good drinking."

"A friend in need is a friend indeed!"

"God heals, and the Doctor takes the Fees."

"Never leave that till tomorrow which you can do to-day."

Franklin invented some of the maxims, but many others were already known. He simply made them sharper. For example, he took the old saying "Three may keep a secret, if two of them are away" and reshaped it as "Three may keep a secret, if two of them are dead." *Poor Richard's Almanack* was published for twenty-five years and was one of the first bestsellers in the colonies, printing as many as ten thousand copies a year, far surpassing its rivals. Many of the sayings became part of popular American thinking.

As a printer, Franklin had always argued that he shouldn't be criticized for what he put out because the nature of the job required him to publish whatever was given to him. In response to several letters from readers who were angry about materials he had printed, Franklin published his "Apology for Printers" in 1731. "Printers," Franklin explained, "are educated in the Belief that, that when Men differ in Opinion, both Sides ought equally to have the Advantage of being heard by the Publick; and that when Truth and Error have fair Play, the former is always an overmatch for the latter: Hence they cheerfully serve all contending Writers that pay them well, without regarding on which sides they are of the Question in Dispute." In his view, the printer performed a valuable public service by publishing various points of view and nothing should be done to stop that. Historians have noted that this printing tradition carried over to newspaper publishing where newspapers gave equal treatment to both sides in issues. Of course, many newspapers still took sides. However, claiming neutrality helped shield them from attacks of being biased.

As his name became widely known, Franklin started a network of printers throughout the colonies. The first establishment was in South Carolina under the direction of Thomas Whitmarsh. The Assembly of South Carolina needed a colonial printer to publish laws and proclamations. In 1731, Franklin set up Whitmarsh with printing equipment and supplies in Charles Town (later to be renamed Charleston) in exchange for a share of the profits. Whitmarsh started the *South Carolina Gazette*, and the partnership proved successful. Franklin went on to set up other printers, many former apprentices and journeymen of his, in more than a dozen other locations throughout the colonies, including New York, Connecticut, Rhode Island, New Jersey, and Pennsylvania. The agreement bound the printers to Franklin for six years. At the end of that time, the printers had the option of continuing the partnership or purchasing the equipment from Franklin. The partners shared their newspapers with one another, helping to spread news that benefited them all. They also served as distributors of *Poor Richard's Almanack*.

While in the midst of his various publishing enterprises, Franklin was appointed postmaster of Philadelphia in 1837, replacing Bradford, who had failed to keep proper accounts. The enterprising Franklin was following in the footsteps of Harris and other newspaper publishers who recognized the benefits of being the chief postal official in a community. Although the financial rewards were modest, being postmaster also gave men like Franklin the inside track for lucrative government printing work. It also facilitated the exchange system in which publishers could send their newspapers to one another through the mail for free. Franklin recognized the benefits of the job that "facilitated the correspondence that improv'd my newspapers, increase'd the number demanded, as well as the advertisements to be inserted, so that it came to afford me a considerable income."

Franklin's various publishing and printing ventures allowed him to comfortably retire in 1748 when he was forty-two and devote his time to his other interests. "I flatter'd myself," Franklin later wrote, "that by the sufficient tho' modes fortune I had acquir'd, I had secured leisure during the rest of my life for philosophical studies and amusements." These included inventing the lightning rod, the Franklin stove, and bifocals. They also included helping draft the Declaration of Independence, serving as ambassador to France, and, at the age of eighty-one, being a delegate from Pennsylvania to the convention that drafted the US Constitution. Next to George Washington, the onetime printer's apprentice became perhaps the most admired American of his era.

PRINTING AND DISTRIBUTION

The newspapers published by Campbell, Bradford, Franklin, Whitmarsh, and others shared many traits. They were generally four pages in length and measured about six by ten inches in size. The copy was laid out in two columns and arranged for reading from left to right, just like a book. The newspapers contained a variety of news, opinion, and government notices, generally all mixed together. There were no headlines and no illustrations to break up the grayness, except for an occasional small woodcut. Advertisements appeared throughout each issue as small notices, stacked on one another. There was little to distinguish advertisements from stories.

The news was not arranged in order of importance but in chronological order. So, even if a fire had destroyed a public building the day before the newspaper went to press, that news would be put on the back page instead of the front page. The emphasis on chronological order also meant that the most important or interesting news in a story often was saved for the end. This can be seen in a story about the capture of the notorious pirate Blackbeard that appeared in the *News-Letter* on February 23, 1719, more than two months after the event:

> By Letters of the 17th of December last from North Carolina, we are informed, that Lieutenant Robert Maynard of His Majesty's Ship Pearl (Commanded by Capt. Gordon) being fitted out at Virginia, with two sloops mann'd with fifty Men, and small Arms but no great Guns, in quest of Capt. Teach the Pirate, called Blackbeard, who made his Escape from thence, was overtaken at North Carolina, and had ten great Guns and Twenty one Men on board his Sloop.

Nonetheless, the news that appeared in colonial newspapers ranged widely. Certainly, a good deal of it was European news. And there were also plenty of dry commercial and government reports. However, as David Copeland has shown, colonial newspapers also published stories about accidents, weather, agriculture, science, medicine, games, literature, and other subjects. Crime and court news was found regularly in newspapers, as was news of accidents and misfortune. Some of these stories could be graphic and gruesome. News about American Indians, as both friend and foe, was popular as were stories about slavery, including insurrections and attempts to end the slave trade. And in a land founded on religious freedom, stories about the church also were popular.

Most newspapers were published weekly and delivered on the morning of publication day. The publication schedule was keyed to the comings and goings of the mail because publishers depended on the colonial postal service for delivery. Some newspapers later shifted to market day, a weekly institution in many places when residents of the country visited town for the day. A single copy generally cost three pence. Subscribers could pick up their newspaper at the office or buy a copy from street hawkers. Newspapers were posted outside the printing office and in other public places so customers could peruse them.

With the exception of ink, most of the materials required to publish a newspaper had to be imported from Europe. The only material that was difficult to acquire was paper. Paper was made from cotton rags, and the raw material often was in short supply. Many printers made their own ink from a combination of lampblack, linseed oil, and tree sap. The quality of ink varied from printer to printer. In the mid-1700s, an American manufacturer began making presses, but for decades many printers continued importing presses.

The process for printing a newspaper was time consuming, tedious, and dirty. News, essays, and other content were written on paper in longhand. A printer standing at a high table read the material and set the type by hand. Using a small metal tray, called a "compositor's stick," the printer would select the individual letters of each word, one by one, until a line of type was filled. Then he would transfer the line to a shallow tray called a "galley." After the galley was filled, it was locked to hold all the type into place. The printer then applied ink to the chase using an "ink beater," which resembled a big ball on a stick. The ball was covered with leather. Sheets of paper were pressed down against the chase using a heavy, weighted platen. To lower the platen, the printer swung a horizontal bar and then raised it after the impression had been made. The paper was then lifted off the chase by hand and laid over a rope strung nearby in order for the ink to dry. The pages later were folded by hand and the newspaper was finally ready for distribution.

Newspaper publishing of the era was a small family business, often as a supplement to printing fliers, pamphlets, sermons, hymnals, almanacs, and other materials. Such "job printing" couldn't be counted on regularly in colonial America, so owners of printing presses liked to publish a newspaper because it was printed weekly and provided a regular source of income. The publisher of a newspaper put it out usually with the help of an apprentice, a teenager who was legally bound to the owner in exchange for being taught the trade, as well as a journeyman printer, a young man with experience but not yet possessing enough money to start his own business.

As was the custom of the time, women weren't admitted into the apprenticeship system. However, many women learned the craft of printing in the shops of their husbands or fathers. Moreover, women often were needed to help print and distribute the newspaper. In some printing families, the wife became as skilled as her husband at many tasks, particularly setting type. And in the event a husband became sick or died, wives often ran the publishing operation. After her husband died in 1738, Elizabeth Timothy published the *South Carolina-Gazette* for seven years. Sarah Goddard and her daughter, Mary Katherine, were heavily involved in the publication of the *Providence Gazette and County Journal*. Ann Catharine Green published the *Maryland Gazette* after the death of her husband in 1767. Anne Franklin, the wife of James Franklin, assumed management of the family newspaper when her husband died in 1735. Alongside their son, she continued working with the newspaper until her own death in 1763.

The postal system played an indispensable role in the development of American journalism. In 1673, William Penn started mail service connecting Philadelphia with the neighboring colonies of Delaware and Maryland. That same year, the governor of New York established a post between New York and Boston on what was known as the "King's Highway." The British Crown eventually took control of the primitive system and, by 1729, weekly mail was delivered to thirteen colonial post offices. The mail not only brought information that editors used to compile the news but also got publications into the hands of readers. More than that, as Richard Kielbowicz has noted, "the two institutions grew hand in hand, one stimulating advances in and shaping the other." Post offices were hubs of news in a community with townspeople sharing gossip and post riders picking up information while making their rounds. Newspapers were so dependent on post riders for news that some shifted the weekly day of publication when the postal schedule changed. And if the mail was late, newspapers often would delay publication by a day or two. Signifying the significance of the post office, some newspapers even incorporated the word "post" or "mail" in their names. (The *Connecticut Post* and the *Pittsburgh Post*, now the *Pittsburgh Post-Gazette*, are just two examples.)

Colonial newspapers were aimed primarily at professionals because it was assumed they were interested primarily in the content and could afford an annual subscription. Most readers were considered by publishers to be educated, politically active, and religious. They were also generally white men. But newspapers of the era almost certainly reached beyond this limited audience to include the working class. Newspapers provided readers with shared experiences of what was taking place in the new land. From newspapers, readers were becoming increasingly aware of what were often called their "neighboring provinces." Moreover, the news from other American colonies helped foster a sense of kinship.

JOHN PETER ZENGER TRIAL

A small but growing number of colonial newspapers were becoming outspoken supporters of press liberty. A free press, editors argued, was essential in a democratic republic. An essayist in the *New-York Weekly Journal* wrote in 1733 that "he is an Enemy to his King and Country who pleads for any Restraint upon the Press." Newspapers must be "a Curb, a Bridle, a Terror, a Shame, and Restraint to evil Ministers." However, British authorities in the colonies had other ideas. The issue came to a head in 1735 with the trial of John Peter Zenger, the publisher of the *Journal*.

Zenger, whose family had immigrated from Germany, had founded his newspaper two years earlier largely to express the views of a group of New York merchants who opposed many of the policies of the colonial governor, William Cosby. The *Journal* soon gained a reputation as a worthy opponent of the willful Cosby and his administration. One writer said of Cosby, "We see Mens Deeds destroyed, Judges arbitrarily displaced, new Courts erected with the consent of the Legislature, by which it seems to me Tryals by Juries are taken away when a Govenour pleases." Cosby was initially silent about the criticisms leveled at him. However, when the *Journal* published a series of stories in late 1734 implying that the governor had chosen his favorites over more qualified individuals for New York's governing council, Cosby had seen enough.

Zenger didn't write the materials that angered the governor, but as the publisher he was still responsible for the content of the *Journal*. The governing council ordered him arrested on charges of seditious libel for criticizing the king's officials, and copies of the *Journal* with the offending stories were burned. His bail was set at six hundred pounds. Although the newspaper's wealthy supporters could have paid the bail, the publisher was useful as a martyr and symbol of Cosby's heavy-handedness. While Zenger sat in jail for nine months awaiting trial, his wife, Anna, published the *Journal*.

English law defined seditious libel as any published material that criticized or subverted the government or its officials. The case against Zenger appeared to be open and shut: the material in the *Journal* was critical of Crosby, and Zenger had published it. James Alexander, one of Zenger's wealthy backers, planned to serve as his attorney and use the trial to challenge Cosby's rule. However, the governor managed to have Alexander disbarred before the trial began. To replace him, Zenger's supporters enlisted Andrew Hamilton of Philadelphia, the speaker of the Pennsylvania Assembly and one of the best trial attorneys in the colonies. Although he suffered from gout, Hamilton was brilliant, witty, and striking. He commanded a courtroom.

The trial began on August 4, 1735, and in his opening statement, the wily Hamilton surprised the court by acknowledging that Zenger had indeed printed the articles in question. The prosecution could have asked the court to stop the trial and return a guilty verdict, but for some reason didn't. Hamilton argued that in order to find Zenger guilty the prosecution had to prove the material "must be libelous—that is false, malicious, and scandalous." If it wasn't, he declared then he must be found not guilty. The judge wouldn't permit such an argument, so Hamilton made his appeal directly to the jury. He told them they should make their own decision regarding the truth of what the *Journal* had published. Hamilton also contended that the cause of liberty meant the truth should be published. Moreover, he said, a free press was essential to prevent government authorities from abusing their power. He proclaimed: "The question before the court and you gentlemen of the jury, is not of small nor private concern, it is not the cause of a poor printer, nor of New York alone, which you are trying," Hamilton argued passionately. "No! It may in its consequence affect every freeman that lives under a British government on the Main of America. It is the best cause. It is the cause of liberty, and I make no doubt but of your upright conduct this day will not only entitle you to the love and esteem of your fellow citizens, but every man who prefers freedom to a life of slavery."

Disregarding the judge's instruction about the meaning of the law, the jury returned with a verdict of not guilty. Zenger was freed. The chief justice and Governor Cosby didn't want to confront popular opinion, so they let the decision stand. The *Journal* carried no account of the verdict, nor did any other newspaper in the colonies. In fact, Zenger only published a brief note that said, "The printer, having got his liberty again, designs God willing to finish and publish the charter of the City of New York next week."

Although the trial established important precedents in libel law, it took more than fifty years before they were codified. Nonetheless, the trial of Zenger showed that colonial law didn't guarantee a guilty verdict for publishers if the published material could be considered controversial. It also helped spread the idea that the press had an obligation to criticize the government and leaders when it was necessary. Colonial newspapers would increasingly do that during the next four decades.

CHAPTER 2

The Political Press

1765 to 1833

BY THE MID-1700S, NEWSPAPERS WERE PLAYING A GROWING ROLE IN the life of colonial America. Most publications still had a paid circulation of only a few hundred, and for the most part, only the wealthy could afford a subscription. However, the reach of newspapers was greater than the small circulation figures might suggest. Americans of different social ranks were generally literate, and a single copy often was passed among numerous readers. Moreover, clergy, merchants, and community leaders related what they read to others. The spreading of information through newspapers helped bond colonists with varied backgrounds and interests into a group with a common cause.

During the revolutionary era, many editors spoke out forcefully against British rule and some became leaders of the patriot cause. They gladly printed the anti-British propaganda of writers such as John Dickinson and Thomas Paine. During the Revolutionary War, most editors sought to boost the morale of Americans, cheering victories and downplaying defeats. As a new government was being launched, newspapers provided a forum for the debate over what form the government would take. When new political parties emerged, editors became not only party spokesmen but leaders as well.

As America grew in size and population during the early 1800s, the number of newspapers increased. Newspapers were often among the first commercial establishments in a new community. However, the newspapers themselves changed little. Published on small hand presses, they still looked much the same as they had for decades, with two or three columns of dense text and a few small illustrations generally crammed into four pages. Political commentary and essays still constituted much of the content.

OPPOSITION TO BRITISH POLICIES

North America had been colonized by England, France, and Spain. Beginning in the late seventeenth century, these European powers repeatedly engaged in wars, and their colonies often were swept into the conflicts. Most of these colonial struggles were small in scale. The exception was the Seven Years' War (1756–1763), sometimes known as the French and Indian War. The long, costly war fought in North America left Great Britain with an enormous debt and more colonies to defend. The British believed Americans should be grateful to them for fighting the war and maintained it was reasonable for colonists to help pay the debt.

The Crown had previously enacted various financial measures that angered Americans, usually by regulating trade. However, the Stamp Act, passed in March 1865, was a new, and, to many, a more dangerous piece of legislation. The act required that all official papers, legal documents, books, almanacs, calendars, and newspapers be taxed. The British had been paying a similar tax for years. However, the colonists saw the Stamp Act as a threat to their liberties. They argued that only their elected representatives could enact such a measure and that, by imposing the tax, Parliament challenged the authority of local leaders who should have the power to raise and spend money.

A special Stamp Act Congress, with delegates from nine colonies, denounced the tax as an invasion of colonial liberties and endorsed a resolution opposing the act. Merchants organized boycotts of British imports. Protesters staged mock funerals in which liberty's coffin was carried to a burial ground. Groups of men calling themselves the Sons of Liberty organized in many colonies. In Boston, the Sons of Liberty regularly protested at the center of town near a large elm that became known as the Liberty Tree.

The Stamp Act hit the publishers of newspapers hard. Not only were the publications taxed but so was almost everything printed, even advertisements. Publishers wasted little time in using their newspapers to oppose the tax. One of the loudest voices of opposition was the *Boston Gazette*. "AWAKE—Awake, my Countrymen, and by a regular & legal Opposition, defeat the Designs of those who enslave us and our Posterity," a writer declared. "Nothing is wanting but your own Resolution." Some editors took creative measures to speak out. A German-language newspaper outlined its front page with black borders and a skull at the top, a sign that the newspaper would have to cease to exist. Other publishers copied the design in creative ways including the *Pennsylvania Journal and Weekly Advertiser*. Publisher William Bradford designed the front page to look like a tombstone topped by a skull and crossbones. Under the nameplate was the message: "EXPIRING: In Hopes of Resurrection to LIFE again." Before the Seven Years' War, Benjamin Franklin had created the illustration of a segmented snake, with the slogan "Join, or Die," to encourage the colonies to unite against the French. Editors revived the popular illustration in protest to the Stamp Act, and it became an icon of the revolutionary era. Some newspapers, such as the *Massachusetts Spy*, incorporated the image into their nameplate.

Some newspapers ceased publishing rather than pay the hated tax. Others continued to publish without the stamp. The *South Carolina Gazette* was started as a means of protesting the Stamp Act. In the first issue, published on December 17, 1765, Charles Crouch called for *"LIBERTY and PROPERTY and NO STAMPS."* He published an essay by a writer calling himself "Freeman," who declared, "Let us oppose them with all our might, even though death should be the consequence—we should die gloriously in our duty in the best of causes." Jonas Green, the publisher of the *Maryland Gazette*, found a clever way to get around paying the tax. He suspended the newspaper while the tax was in effect. However, he still wanted to put out a newspaper, so he published an issue he called the *Apparition of the Maryland Gazette, which is not Dead but Sleepeth*. Because it was a spirit, Green maintained, the newspaper did not have to publish with a stamp as a flesh-and-blood newspaper was required to do.

Figure 2.1 "Join or Die" Cartoon *Source:* Library of Congress.

With British merchants smarting from the boycott, Parliament grudgingly yielded to the protests and announced in March 1766 that the tax would be repealed on May 1, the following year. However, Parliament promptly passed the Declaratory Act to remind Americans that they "have been, are, and of right ought to be, subordinate unto, and dependent upon the imperial crown and parliament of Great Britain." They told the colonists that the king, and only the king through Parliament, had the authority to make laws for the colonies. Parliament also declared that "all resolutions, votes, orders, and proceedings" passed by colonial representatives were "utterly null and voice to all intents and purposes whatsoever."

The defeat of the Stamp Act was a major victory for the colonial press. Newspaper publishers had spoken out forcefully as a group against what they viewed as an unfair tax in editorials, which are brief articles that express the opinions of editors and publishers on current topics. As David Sloan and Julie Williams have written, the editorial protests against the Stamp Act helped the American press reach "a youthful, robust maturity." Editors realized they had the ability to influence public opinion. They would continue to wield that influence in the years ahead.

Britain still needed money to pay its debts, and the Crown was determined that Americans would have to pay their share. Colonists had complained that the Stamp Act taxed American products rather than products imported from Great Britain. The Townshend Acts, approved in the summer of 1767, set duties on tea, glass, lead, paint, and paper imported into America. British leaders believed that the tariff wouldn't infuriate the colonists the way the Stamp Act had. However, the fact that Britain was again levying any tax on the colonies angered leaders who viewed the measure as another threat to their liberties. One of the most eloquent voices of protest was John Dickinson, a Philadelphia lawyer who wrote a series of anonymous essays in the *Pennsylvania Chronicle* titled, "Letters from a Farmer in Pennsylvania." In the twelve essays, published in 1767 and 1768, Dickinson argued that Parliament didn't have the power to raise revenue by such means. Dickinson was no radical; he didn't call for American independence. Still, the letters were a forceful and reasoned argument against what Britain was doing. They were widely reprinted in other colonial newspapers and also as pamphlets.

Sensing that the situation in America was getting out of control, the British sent troops to Boston in 1768 as a show of force. Angry leaders decided to rally the colonists by spreading the news of what was happening in Massachusetts. Their vehicle was the *Journal of Occurrences*, a series of reports from 1768 to 1769 that detailed how residents of Boston were suffering under military rule. The reports were published in the Boston newspapers and reprinted throughout the colonies. From the *Journal*, Americans read time and again how British troops were cruel, violent, and could not be trusted. While some of the accounts were no doubt true, many others were exaggerated or even made up. The *Journal* was propaganda intended to inspire the colonists to continue their protests, and in many respects, it worked brilliantly.

The royal governor of Massachusetts was so incensed by the criticism being increasingly leveled at him that he tried to sue the publishers of the *Boston Gazette* for seditious libel. He demanded that Benjamin Edes and John Gill reveal the identity of writers who had been critical of him. The lawsuit was not successful, but the governor and the publishers continued to battle. The royal governor eventually was recalled to Britain, and, as he was departing, the *Gazette* dismissed him as "a Scourge to this Province, a curse to North-America, and a plague to the whole Empire."

Not all newspaper editors were opposed to British rule. Perhaps the most outspoken defender of the Crown's policies was John Mein, publisher of the *Boston Chronicle*. Mein had emigrated from Scotland in 1764 and became a successful bookseller in Boston. He and a partner founded the *Chronicle* in 1767. The newspaper's motto was "Be independent—your interest is intimately connected with this noble virtue—if you depart from this—you must sink from the esteem of the public." Mein soon began to criticize colonial leaders. When the *Gazette* attacked him in editorials, Mein demanded to know the identity of the writer. Edes and Gill refused. The next time Mein saw Gill on the street, he beat him with a club. Gill won a court judgment against Mein for the assault, but that didn't stop Mein's criticism of colonial leaders. In response, a mob hung him in effigy. Later, a mob attacked his home, and in defending himself, Mein shot a bystander. To escape prosecution, Mein fled Boston and eventually returned to Britain.

The tensions with British troops in Boston erupted on March 5, 1770, when angry protesters taunted soldiers at the city's Customs House. The troops fired at the crowd, killing five men. News of the "Boston Massacre," as it came to be known, was spread throughout the colonies by the press. Many of the accounts were sensationalized and left out the British side of what happened. The *Boston Gazette* accused the soldiers of causing all the trouble that led to the shootings. They reported that the soldiers "were seen parading the Streets with the drawn Cutlasses and Bayonets, abusing and wounding Numbers of the Inhabitants . . . they attacked single and unarmed persons until they raised much clamour . . . insulting all they met in like manner, and pursuing some to their very doors." The *Gazette* also published woodcuts of caskets that were meant to represent the colonists who were killed. But other accounts placed the blame for the massacre on the colonists. The *New York Gazette and Weekly Mercury* accused the mob of plotting to attack the British troops. "The 5th and 6th Instant was agreed upon for a general Attack upon the Troops, and great numbers came in with Arms from the Country, to join their Friends in town," the *Gazette* noted. "On the 5th in the Evening, two Soldiers were attack'd and beat, and Town's people . . . broke open two Meeting Houses, and rang the Alarm Bells, which was supposed to be for Fire."

Paul Revere, a silversmith and engraver who would become known for alerting the colonial army to the approach of British troops before the battles of Lexington and Concord, produced perhaps the most famous record of the clash. He showed the British soldiers firing in an organized manner with their commanding officer standing behind and issuing the order to fire. Revere didn't witness the massacre, and eyewitnesses gave different accounts of what happened. However, the engraving, which was made into prints and widely sold, no doubt influenced American perceptions of what took place. In the fall of 1770, the commanding officer and seven soldiers were put on trial for murder. Two of the soldiers were found guilty of manslaughter; the commanding officers and the five other soldiers were acquitted.

During the next three years, radicals opposed to British rule continued using the press to speak out. Leading the charge was the *Boston Gazette*, whose writers included such revolutionary leaders as Samuel Adams, James Otis, Josiah Quincy, and John Adams. The *Gazette's* office in many respects was a headquarters for the Patriot leadership. The men gathered regularly to discuss events and exchange ideas, while taking turns writing essays for the newspaper. Adams argued that the British were guilty of tyranny in their treatment of the colonies and, moreover, that Americans in many respects had become slaves of their mother country. "Is it impossible to form an idea of *slavery* more complete, more miserable, more *disgraceful*, than that of a people where justice is adminster'd, government exercis'd, and a standing army maintain'd at the expense of the people, and yet without the least dependence upon them?" he asked in one essay.

THOMAS PAINE AND *COMMON SENSE*
In 1773, Parliament passed another measure that angered Americans: the Tea Act. The goal was to help Britain's East India Company by allowing it to ship tea duty-free to America and thereby thwart Dutch trade in

tea. However, Americans viewed the measure as another attempt to prop up the sagging British economy by taxing the colonies. Colonial newspapers published a barrage of editorials criticizing the act. "Shall the island BRITAIN enslave this great continent of AMERICA which is more than ninety-nine times bigger, and is capable of supporting hundreds of millions of people?" Isaiah Thomas of the *Massachusetts Spy* asked.

Ships carrying tea docked in Boston in December. Local protesters, including Edes and Gill of the *Boston Gazette*, refused to let the tea be unloaded. The colonial governor threatened to seize the tea, and the protesters were determined to keep that from happening. On the evening of December 16, about sixty men disguised as Native Americans boarded the ships and dumped 15,000 pounds of tea into the harbor. A furious Parliament closed the port of Boston until residents repaid the East India Company. Parliament also revised the laws governing Massachusetts, taking away authority from the local citizenry. It gave the royal governor the authority to quarter more troops in the city to quell protests. Colonists soon began calling the measures the "Intolerable Acts."

Newspapers across the colonies protested the acts. They encouraged readers to support Massachusetts, arguing that the British measures could be used against other colonies. The *Georgia Gazette* published with a black border, the traditional newspaper symbol of mourning. The *North Carolina Gazette* adopted a new motto: "SEMPER PRO LIBERTE, ET BONO PUBLICO" ("always for liberty and the public good"). Loyalist editors, on the other hand, encouraged citizens to obey the laws. They said radical leaders were leading the colonists to their doom. "It is impossible to review the advantages we derive from our connection with Great Britain," one writer argued. "We are formed by her laws and religion; we are clothed by her manufacturers and protected by her fleets and armies. . . . In a word, the Island of Britain is the fortress in which we are sheltered from the machination of all the powers of Europe."

For years, radical leaders had been calling for a meeting of the colonies to join forces against British rule. After the Intolerable Acts, more argued that a meeting was needed. The First Continental Congress finally convened in Philadelphia in September 1774. It brought together many of America's most prominent leaders, including George Washington,

John Adams, Patrick Henry, Roger Sherman, Richard Henry Lee, and John Dickinson. The Continental Congress declared the British action against Massachusetts to be unconstitutional. It also called for trade with Great Britain to be halted and authorized local Committees of Safety to enforce the mandate. Local newspapers were encouraged to publish the names of violators.

The cause of liberty was spreading throughout the colonies. However, the British were determined to keep the colonists in line. On April 18, 1775, British leaders dispatched a force of soldiers to Concord to seize weapons stored there. Local militiamen took up arms, and fighting broke out at Lexington and Concord with an estimated forty-nine Americans and seventy-three British killed. For the first time, the colonists were in open rebellion against Great Britain, and the press immediately took sides. Ignoring the facts of what happened during the fighting, the *Massachusetts Spy* accused the British of atrocities and called on colonists to rally together: "Americans! Forever bear in mind the BATTLE OF LEXINGTON! – where British troops, unmolested and unprovoked, wantonly and in a most inhuman manner fired upon and killed a number of our countrymen, then robbed them of their possessions, ransacked, plundered and burnt their houses!"

Soon after the fighting began, the Second Continental Congress convened in Philadelphia. Delegates from twelve of the thirteen colonies promptly authorized the raising of troops and appointed Washington as the army's commander. The Virginian had earned a reputation for leadership and bravery during the French and Indian War. Members of Congress believed Washington's character would help him gain the respect of the troops under his command. Many newspapers praised the appointment and reported on the warm greeting Washington received upon taking command.

Despite their opposition to Britain's economic measures, many Americans didn't support the radical idea of independence. However, numerous writers again called on the colonists to unite. The most eloquent voice came from a recent emigrant, Thomas Paine. Born in England, Paine had tried his hand at various jobs, including tax collecting, but never found success. He became active in local politics and met Franklin, who was visiting England. Carrying a letter of introduction from the famous Pennsylvanian, Paine decided to make a new start in America. The thirty-seven-year-old Paine arrived in Philadelphia in 1774, planning to start a school. He began writing essays for the *Pennsylvania Magazine* and gained a reputation as an eloquent, forceful advocate for independence.

On January 10, 1776, Paine published *Common Sense*. The pamphlet directly attacked King George III and called on Americans to declare their independence from England. *Common Sense* was read throughout the colonies, going through numerous editions. Many newspaper editors reprinted all or parts of the pamphlet and endorsed the call. Paine wrote in a simple, straightforward style that the average reader could understand. His message was that the issues facing the colonists were neither transitory nor parochial, but timeless and universal. "The Cause of America is in great Measure the Cause of all Mankind," Paine wrote. "Many Circumstances hath, and will arise, which are not local, but universal, and through which Principles of all loves of Mankind are affected." As biographer Eric Foner has noted, Paine "forged a new political language. He did not simply change the meaning of words, he created a literary style designed to bring his message to the widest possible audience."

Although America was at war with Britain, it had not officially declared its autonomy. Then on July 4, 1776, the Continental Congress operating as a de facto government adopted the Declaration of Independence. Written by Thomas Jefferson and John Adams, the declaration began with the resounding words, "When in the Course of human events, it becomes necessary for one people to dissolve the political bands which have connected them with another." Newspapers throughout the colonies helped spread the historic news. Benjamin Towne was the first editor to do so, publishing the declaration on the *Pennsylvania Evening Post*'s front page. Newspapers also reported on the joyous reception the declaration received in their communities. When the residents of Williamsburg, Virginia, got the news a jubilant crowd celebrated at the courthouse. They also tore down the coat of arms of King George III and burned it, the *Virginia Gazette* reported.

Figure 2.2 Thomas Paine *Source:* Wikimedia Commons.

REPORTING THE REVOLUTIONARY WAR

During the Revolutionary War, newspapers filled their pages with news about the fighting. However, the news was often days or weeks late, and the accounts were generally incomplete. Without anyone to gather the news, editors relied on citizens and soldiers to provide brief accounts of battles and other events. Editors also reprinted the official reports of the fighting from General Washington and other commanders. In general, however, Americans did not get a complete or accurate picture of the war. On the other hand, newspapers played an important role in boosting morale. Editors cheered American victories and downplayed defeats.

They encouraged citizens to support the war, emphasizing time and again that it was absolutely necessary if America was to gain its independence.

The tireless Paine wrote the best-known essay encouraging Americans to remain steadfast. He joined the Continental Army in the fall of 1776 as an aide-de-camp to General Nathanael Greene and witnessed the fighting firsthand. In the first major battle after America declared its independence, the British defeated colonial troops at the Battle of Long Island and forced them to retreat through New Jersey. During the fall, the terms of enlistment were up for thousands of soldiers, and many were leaving the army. As the eventful year was drawing to a close, some believed the cause of American independence was lost. To help inspire his fellow countrymen, Paine wrote "The American Crisis" for the *Pennsylvania Journal*, and it was published on December 19, 1776. Washington was so moved by the essay that he ordered it to be read to his troops on Christmas Eve shortly before they secretly crossed the Delaware River to attack British forces in Trenton, New Jersey. "The American Crisis" began with the stirring words:

> These are the times that try men's souls. The summer soldier and the sunshine patriot will, in this crisis, shrink from the service of their country; but he that stands it now, deserves the love and thanks of man and woman. Tyranny, like hell, is not easily conquered; yet we have this consolation, the harder the conflict, the more glorious, the triumph.

Paine's call to stand with the army during the difficult winter was reprinted as a pamphlet and read by thousands of Americans. He went on to write six more "Crisis" essays during the next two years. Newspapers across the colonies published them.

During the next five years, Washington's resolute troops battled a far larger and better-equipped foe. They suffered numerous defeats, but with the economic help of France, the Americans eventually forced the British Army to surrender at Yorktown, Virginia, on October 17, 1781. Newspapers across the colonies reveled in the joyful news and reported the celebrations. In Newport, Rhode Island, the newspaper noted: "The Church Bell was set a ringing and continued nearly all that night and the next day . . . thirteen cannons were discharged in the morning and thirteen at noon."

Colonial life had been disrupted by the six years of fighting, and the press suffered along with everything else. Readership had increased as citizens sought to keep up with the war news. However, many newspapers struggled to publish in the face of shortages of paper, ink, and other printing materials. Only about half of the thirty-eight newspapers published when the war began survived. Although new publications were started during the war years, most did not last long. A scarcity of paper was a particular problem because of the lack of rags needed to make paper. As a result of the shortages, printers regularly reduced the size of their newspapers or suspended publication until materials could be secured. Finding enough help to put out a newspaper also proved challenging as many young men went off to fight.

Loyalist newspapers were reviled for their support of the British, and most sought the protection of the British army before eventually closing. Perhaps no loyalist publishers were more steadfast than brothers Alexander and James Robertson. The brothers emigrated from Scotland and established a printing business in New York City in 1768. They moved the business to Albany in 1771 but moved it back to New York City in 1771 to be closer to the British army. When the army evacuated the city, James moved around with the troops, briefly establishing a loyalist newspaper in each town that supported the British. After the war, James returned to Scotland.

FORMING A NEW NATION

Two years after the surrender, American and British negotiators signed the Treaty of Paris. It not only recognized American independence but also granted the new nation control of the entire region between Canada and Florida east of the Mississippi River. The United States of America became the first independent nation in the western hemisphere. However, the new country experienced significant problems during the ensuing six years. The Articles of Confederation, adopted after the British surrender, preserved the independence and sovereignty of the thirteen new states. The articles consciously established a weak central government, providing for a "firm league of friendship" among the new states. The national government consisted of a one-house Congress in which each state cast a single vote. Congress could maintain an army, make war, establish a postal service, and coin money, but it could not levy taxes or regulate commerce.

Newspapers provided a platform for citizens to express their frustration with the new government. A writer for the *Freeman's Oracle* in Exeter, New Hampshire, complained that the federal government "may DECLARE every thing but can DO nothing." An essayist in the *Connecticut Gazette* declared that the Articles of Confederation "presents a Comedy to the rest of the world" and "a Tragedy to ourselves." And a contributor to the *Providence Gazette* argued: "The American war is over, but this is far from the case with the American revolution; On the contrary, nothing but the first active of the great drama is closed. It remains yet to establish and perfect our new form of government, and to prepare the principles, morals and manners, of our citizens."

Eventually, leaders recognized that a more robust national government was needed, or the country was likely to dissolve into anarchy. In May 1787, the states sent delegates to Philadelphia for a convention to draft a new constitution. Beginning with an initial draft written by James Madison known as the "Virginia Plan," the Constitution was hammered out during the next four months. It significantly strengthened the federal government by creating a chief executive, legislature, and judiciary. But it also left much of the administration of government in the hands of the thirteen states. The delegates signed the Constitution and sent it to the states for ratification.

Newspapers across the colonies reprinted the Constitution. They also opened their pages for debate over whether it should be adopted. Hundreds of essays were published during the ratification debate and the overwhelming number supported adoption. Working together, Madison, Alexander Hamilton, and John Jay wrote the best-known arguments for ratification. The "Federalist Papers," as the eighty-five essays came to be known, were initially published in the *New York Journal* in 1787 and 1788, with each author signing his name "Publius." They were widely reprinted in newspapers throughout the colonies. The essays were later compiled in a book titled *The Federalist*, and they are still considered some of the most important works on America's constitutional form of government.

The opponents of ratification, known as the Anti-Federalists, argued that the Constitution lacked protection for the basic rights of citizens. The authors of the "Federalist Papers" maintained there was no need for a Bill of Rights because the new government would have only those powers granted to it by the Constitution. However, the Anti-Federalists, led by Thomas Jefferson, insisted that a check on government power must be spelled out. When the new Congress of the United States met in 1789, the House and Senate drafted a series of amendments to the new Constitution, and they were sent to the states for ratification.

The ten amendments were adopted on December 15, 1791, and became known as the Bill of Rights. The First Amendment addresses a variety of rights, including freedom of the press. It states: "Congress shall make no law respecting an establishment of religion, or prohibiting the free exercise thereof; or abridging the freedom of speech, or of the press, or of the right of the people peaceably to assemble, and to petition the government for a redress of grievances." The First Amendment prevents the federal government from shutting down the press. It doesn't mean there are not consequences for what is published. The First Amendment was a recognition that the press is essential to the proper functioning of the government. For people to govern themselves, they must be informed about what their leaders are doing. The press is a critical vehicle for doing that.

In 1789, Washington became America's first president. As a hero of the war, the Virginian represented national unity. However, political divisions soon emerged over Secretary of Treasury Hamilton's economic policies that included a controversial national bank. The founding fathers had hoped to avoid the development of political parties. Nonetheless, by the mid-1790s, two national parties had emerged: Federalists and Republicans (formerly Anti-Federalists). The Federalists, led by Hamilton and Vice President John Adams, favored a strong central government. The Republicans, led by Jefferson and James Monroe, argued that most authority should reside with the states.

During this time, many newspapers became voices for the two new political parties. The Federalists and Republicans needed to promote their political views, defend their policies, and attack rivals. Mass meetings, pamphlets, and correspondence could achieve these goals to some extent, but not in the same way as newspapers, political leaders believed. As Jeffrey Pasley has written, "the newspaper press was the political system's central institution." Party leaders worked hand in hand with newspaper editors to pursue political goals. As the election of 1800 approached, Jefferson urged Republicans to work with their party publications. "We are sensible that this summer is the season for systematic energies and sacrifices," he wrote to Madison. "The engine is the press." In exchange for that support, the two parties provided funding to supportive editors and patronage in the form of government jobs and printing contracts. The support was key for editors who, in many cases, struggled financially to make ends meet. Subscriptions and advertising still brought in relatively little income. Publishers who didn't have a large printing business needed support wherever they could find it.

In some cases, the political parties arranged with existing newspapers for their support. Other newspapers were founded simply to support a party. That was the case with the *Gazette of the United States*, a Federalist publication founded in 1789 by John Fenno. A former schoolteacher, Fenno had contributed to newspapers in his native Boston. He arranged with Federalist leaders to publish the *Gazette* in New York City, America's capital at the time, in exchange for government printing contracts. Fenno said the newspaper would "hold up the people's own government in a favorable point of light" and "impress just ideas of its administration by exhibiting FACTS." Two years later, Republicans established the *National Gazette*, edited by Philip Freneau. An accomplished writer, Freneau had been a roommate of Monroe at Princeton College and gained fame as the "Poet of the Revolution." Jefferson, who was secretary of state at the time, hired Freneau as a French translator for the State Department, even though he could not speak the language well. Republican leaders wanted Freneau to use the *Gazette* to combat his Federalist counterpart. Jefferson denied playing any role in founding the *Gazette*, but when it was revealed that he was subsidizing it, Federalists reveled in the embarrassment.

Party editors spared no words in attacking their political enemies. Perhaps no newspaperman was more abusive than William Cobbett, editor of *Porcupine's Gazette*, a Federalist publication founded on the day John Adams was inaugurated as the country's second president. Cobbett's nickname was "Peter Porcupine," and he was a master of political invective. He particularly enjoyed attacking Republican editors, describing one as a "public pest and bane of decency." Benjamin Franklin Bache, a grandson of the founding father and editor of the Republican *Aurora*, could be just as nasty. Bache was known as "Lightning Rod Junior," in honor of his grandfather's famous experiment and the fact that his prose often crackled like lightning. When Washington gave his eloquent Farewell Address in 1796, Bache wrote of the president:

> If ever a nation was debauched by a man, the American nation has been debauched by Washington. If ever a nation suffered from the improper influence of a man, the American nation has suffered from the influence of Washington. If ever a nation was deceived by a man, the American nation has been deceived by Washington. Let his conduct then be an example to future ages. Let it serve to be a warning that no man may be an idol.

ALIEN AND SEDITION ACTS

By the time Adams took office, relations between America and its ally France had deteriorated to the point where French ships were seizing American vessels carrying British goods. Adams, a Federalist, hoped to avoid a war through negotiations with France. However, the French sought a loan and other conditions before talks could begin. By 1798, war fever was running high. Republican leaders had long supported France, even after the French Revolution turned bloody with the use of the guillotine. Federalists were suspicious of how far Republicans would go in supporting the French, and they sought to silence their opponents and their publications. The result was the Alien and Sedition Acts.

The legislative package, passed by the Federalist-controlled Congress and signed by Adams, consisted of four laws. The Alien Act dealt with foreigners living in the United States. One increased the residency requirement for citizens from five to fourteen years, one permitted the deportation of legal aliens during wartime, and one allowed the selective deportation of undesirable aliens. The Sedition Act was designed to silence criticism of the government, and it was clearly aimed at Republicans, including newspaper editors who supported the party. It prohibited the publication of any "false, scandalous or malicious" writing against the government or Congress "with intent to defame . . . or to bring them . . . into contempt or disrepute." The measure required a trial by jury and truth was a defense. Those found guilty could be imprisoned for two years and fined $2,000.

Republicans attacked the Sedition Act as a violation of the First Amendment and argued that it was meant to muzzle the opposition. "The people have no other means of examining their [leaders'] conduct but by means of the press, and an unrestricted investigation through them of the conduct of the Government," John Nicholas declared. "Indeed, the heart and life of a free government, is a free press." Federalists claimed that the act only protected the government from unwarranted criticism, and they maintained it did not threaten freedom of the press. "Every independent Government has a right to preserve and defend itself against injuries and outrages which endanger its existence," Representative Otis Gray said.

As editor of the *Aurora*, Bache was a leading target of the Sedition Act, and he was arrested even before it became law. On the day the Senate began debate of the measure, Bache was charged with seditious libel. While he awaited trial, Bache continued publishing the *Aurora* and continued criticizing the government. However, he contracted yellow fever and died only a few days before the trial was set to begin. Another editor indicted was Matthew Lyon, editor of a publication with the unusual name *The Scourge of Aristocracy and Repository of Important Political Truths*. He had criticized the president's "continual grasp for power" and "unbounded thirst for ridiculous pomp, foolish adulation or selfish avarice." A jury found him guilty, and he was sentenced to four months in jail and fined $1,000.

In all, some twenty-five people, many of them editors, were arrested under the Sedition Act. Ten individuals were convicted, eight of them editors. Five of the six most influential Republican newspapers were prosecuted under the law. The legislation did not stop criticism of the Adams administration; if anything it encouraged the criticism even more. Republicans cited the Sedition Act as evidence that the Federalists could not be trusted with authority. Federalist leaders eventually recognized the damage that had been done and the legislation was allowed to lapse in 1801.

PARTY PRESS

At the turn of the century, the United States had a new president and a new capital. Jefferson defeated Adams in 1800 to become the country's first Republican president. He also was the first president to begin his term in the nation's new capital, Washington, DC. Jefferson wanted to dismantle as much of the new federal system as possible. He slashed the number of government employees and abolished all taxes, except the tariff. Nonetheless, Jefferson doubled the land area of the United States with the Louisiana Purchase in 1803. Several months later, he dispatched an expedition led by Meriwether Lewis and William Clark to explore the vast new territory and find a water route to the Pacific Ocean. Between 1790 and 1820, nine new states were added to the Union.

The number of newspapers grew steadily in the first decades of the 1800s. The overwhelming majority of publications still were identified as supporters of one of the political parties. When Jefferson took office, most newspapers were affiliated with the Federalists, so the president and his supporters worked to increase the number of Republican publications. One of the most important was the *National Intelligencer*, founded by Samuel Harrison Smith in 1801. Because its home was in the new capital, Jefferson used the *Intelligencer* to present his position on issues and policies. The *Intelligencer* also became something of the official record of government, providing detailed information about debates in Congress. Other newspapers reprinted the reports published in the *Intelligencer*. Although Smith retired in 1810, his successors as editor continued providing an official record of Congress for many years.

Jefferson's chief press critic was the *New York Evening Post*, founded in 1801 by his political archrival, Hamilton. Hamilton and a group of Federalists wanted to start a new party newspaper so badly that they donated money to start the *Post*. They selected William Coleman, a New York lawyer and regular newspaper contributor, as editor. The *Post* promised "to diffuse among the people correct information on all interesting subjects, to inculcate just principles in religion, morals, and politics, and to cultivate a taste for sound literature." However, under Coleman's direction, the *Post* soon began assailing the Jefferson administration, and he became known as "The Field Marshal of Federal Editors." Coleman admired Hamilton. The former treasury secretary regularly wrote for the *Post*, including a series of eighteen essays titled "The Examination" that sharply criticized Jefferson's attempt to overturn the Judiciary Act, which had created new federal courts and judgeships.

At a fundamental level, American leaders generally agreed about the necessity of a free press. However, when they or their policies were being attacked, their views often changed. Jefferson was a good example. The Virginian had once said that he would rather have "newspapers without a government" than "a government without newspapers." He also declared his support for freedom of the press and said it made no difference whether "the complaints or criticisms" against leaders were "just or unjust." However, during his presidency Jefferson lamented the party press, saying, "Nothing can now be believed which is seen in a newspaper." He also maintained that "the man who never looks into a newspaper is better informed than he who reads them." Once he retired from public life, Jefferson's attitude about the press softened. He wrote to a French correspondent that newspapers were "the best instrument for enlightening the mind of man, and improving him as a rational, moral and social being."

Starting about 1803, relations between Britain and America deteriorated. Britain was battling France and imposed naval blockades, often seizing American trading ships. America was also concerned about British influence in Canada, especially with the Indigenous population there, and saw that as a threat. On June 18, 1812, the United States declared war on England. Much of what became known as the War of 1812 was fought on the border with Canada and at sea. England was successful initially, capturing Detroit and Washington, DC. However, America fought back with victories at sea by the *USS Constitution* and on land at New Orleans. England eventually grew tired of the fighting and signed a peace treaty. Newspapers covered the War of 1812 in much the same way as the Revolutionary War. With no reporters, newspapers got most of their news from officials and private letters. Eyewitnesses to battles, including some soldiers, also provided firsthand accounts. Many editors went off to fight. Even so, the newspaper kept up a steady stream of editorial attacks on the British.

Federalists and Republicans battled over the need to fight the war. Republicans generally favored the idea, while Federalists opposed it. Federalist newspapers often were outspoken in their criticism and sometimes they paid a high price. Four days after Congress declared war, the *Federal Republican* in Baltimore carried a critical editorial. A mob destroyed the newspaper's office and burned the building. A month later, the newspaper resumed publication in a house stocked with ammunition and defended by supporters. After it published another editorial, a mob once again attacked the building. During the fight, several people were injured and one was killed. The authorities arrived and convinced the newspaper's supporters that they would be protected in jail. The mob, which had grown to more than one thousand people, then attacked the jail and a riot ensued in which several more people were injured and killed.

Jefferson served two terms and was followed in office by two more Republican presidents, his Virginia neighbors James Madison and James Monroe. By 1816, the Federalist Party had disintegrated. Republicans were left as the only political party but soon it began splitting into factions. During the presidential election of 1824, the four candidates—John Quincy Adams, Henry Clay, William Crawford, and Andrew Jackson—all had newspaper supporters in their corner. However, with so many candidates, no one received a majority of votes in the Electoral College. Even though Jackson received more votes, Clay threw his support to Adams, who became the president.

By the election of 1828, the country had divided again into two parties: Whigs and Democrats. Neither party had a real national organization, and personal campaigning by candidates was still frowned upon. That meant newspapers continued to play an essential function. To spread their views and attract members, the parties continued to line up supporters in the press. Editors also took on larger roles, organizing party operations, mobilizing voters, and actively campaigning for candidates. As Gerald Baldasty has written, editors in numerous respects directed their party's operations and were, in a real sense, the face of the party.

Candidates for office lined up newspaper supporters across the country. Determined to win the presidency that he believed had been stolen from him in 1824, Jackson established a network of editors who supported his candidacy. They helped Jackson win the election, and the new president rewarded many of his newspaper supporters with government jobs. In all, the first Democratic president appointed more than fifty editors to positions in the federal government. Jackson was criticized for appointing such a large number on the grounds that the press should be independent. However, he defended the practice, saying, "Why should this class of citizens be excluded from offices to which other, not more patriotic, nor presenting stronger claims as to qualifications may aspire?"

Amos Kendall, a lawyer and editor of the *Argus of Western America* in Frankfort, Kentucky, had been an early supporter of Jackson. He played a key role in Jackson's successful 1828 campaign, creating the slogan, "The world is governed too much," which became the guiding philosophy of the administration. The president brought Kendall to Washington, and he was appointed postmaster general. In that position, he worked to eliminate corruption, but he also permitted post offices in the South to refuse to deliver abolitionist publications. Perhaps no editor was closer to Jackson than Francis P. Blair, who followed Kendall as editor of the *Argus*. Blair was a circuit court clerk in Frankfort, and his editorials in the *Argus* attracted Jackson's attention. After the election, Jackson asked him to come to Washington to found the *Washington Globe* as an administration mouthpiece. He continued editing the *Globe* until 1845. Both Kendall and Blair were members of Jackson's "Kitchen Cabinet," a group of confidants who helped shape executive policy.

In many respects, the Jackson administration was the zenith of the party press period in America. Editors would continue to play an outsized role in the US political system in the decades ahead, actively supporting both parties and candidates. However, a new group of entrepreneurial editors in the largest cities recognized that in a growing country, newspapers needed to change. These editors wanted their publications to be widely read and sold. That meant they needed to focus more on news.

CHAPTER 3

The Public Press

1833 to 1865

BY THE 1830S, CHANGES IN AMERICAN SOCIETY, CULTURE, AND TECH-
nology set the stage for a new class of publications. American cities were
growing rapidly, home to both new immigrants and a growing middle
class. Thanks to free public schools, more Americans could read and
write. And developments in communications technology, most notably
the telegraph and the steam-powered printing press, were helping to
revolutionize journalism. In this setting, enterprising publishers founded
the first mass-circulation newspapers in New York City, and they gradually spread elsewhere. The "penny press," as it would be known, changed
journalism forever. Slowly, but increasingly, newspapers would be aimed
at the broad reading public.

At the same time the 1¢ papers were launched, publications cham-
pioning the end of slavery began to appear across the North. The abolitionist press had a different mission than mainstream newspapers. They
wanted to see an institution that enslaved millions of Black men, women,
and children abolished in a country dedicated to freedom. Despite criticism and even violence, unwavering abolitionist editors kept the issue
of slavery before the public throughout the Civil War until it was finally
ended by the Thirteenth Amendment. They were joined by the first
American newspapers published by and for free African Americans.

The press covered the Civil War to an extent never seen before.
Newspapers and magazines modernized to better cover the news, while

still maintaining the editorial role they relished. Illustrations and photography became an increasingly important means to provide a visual record of the news. No standards existed for what constituted accurate, trustworthy journalism. As a result, the quality of work produced in both the North and South varied widely. Nonetheless, with Americans fighting against Americans in a tragic war, newspapers and magazines became essential reading.

PENNY PRESS

The cost of a newspaper had always been beyond the means of most readers. Priced at 6¢ a copy and $8 to $10 for an annual subscription, newspapers were expensive. Moreover, much of the content of newspapers didn't interest readers. As a result, even the largest daily newspapers had a circulation of just a few thousand. Yet American cities were growing rapidly. A large untapped market of potential readers existed for a publisher with the right idea.

That publisher was Benjamin Day, who launched the *New York Sun* on September 3, 1833. Day had learned the printing business as a young man in Massachusetts. He moved to New York City where he worked at several publications as a printer. In his soul, Day was an entrepreneur, and he started the *Sun* because he thought it could outsell New York's existing newspapers. The *Sun*'s motto was "It Shines for All," and in the first issue, Day revealed his plan: "The object of this paper is to lay before the public, at a price within the means of everyone, ALL THE NEWS OF THE DAY, and at the same time afford an advantageous medium for advertising."

Day sold daily issues of the *Sun* on the street for a mere penny. The annual subscription price was $3, far less than that charged by his competitors. He also put an emphasis on selling advertising. Day didn't want to wait for the news to arrive at the newspaper's office; he wanted the *Sun* to uncover it. He wanted the news to be fresh, so he used any means, even carrier pigeons, to get the news as quickly as possible. The *Sun* reported a variety of news, especially local news. Day believed that readers wanted to know what was happening in a lively, growing city, especially human-interest news and news of crime. He hired reporters, men whose job was to find the news and then write it in an engaging style. No event was too small for the *Sun*, provided that readers might find it interesting, as in this police story:

> John Evans, brought up for throwing stones at the house of Eliza Vincent, who refused him admittance. The complainant, a watchman, said he advised the prisoner to desist—the prisoner called the watchman a rascal, and told him to clear out, or at some future time he would get a devil of a flogging; whereupon the watchman seized hold of him and walked him up to the watch-house—held to bail for appearance at court.

In 1835, the *Sun* published a sensational series of stories saying that life had been found on the moon. Titled "Great Astronomical Discoveries," the stories claiming an astronomer discovered that trees covered the lunar surface and flying creatures that looked like humans roamed the skies. The *Sun*'s competitors claimed the series was made up. The reporter, Richard Adams Locke, later confessed to a colleague that it was indeed faked. The *Sun* never admitted the series was phony and said the source for the story was a credible scientific journal. It also reveled in the attention that the "Moon Hoax," as the series came to be known, received.

Day soon purchased a new rotary press to publish the *Sun*, which could print about four thousand copies an hour. The *Sun* was on its way to becoming the most widely read newspaper in New York. With so many readers, the newspaper also became the place where merchants in the city wanted to advertise. By 1843, the staff numbered more than 150, and the *Sun* had joined the ranks of big businesses in the city.

James Gordon Bennett took notice of what the *Sun* was doing and decided to follow its plan for publishing. An immigrant from Scotland, Bennett had worked for newspapers since he was a young man. At one point, he was a correspondent for the *New York Enquirer*, at the time the largest newspaper in the city. But Bennett was outspoken and controversial and, as a result, never stayed at one place very long. Pulling together $500, he launched the *New York Herald* on May 6, 1835, putting the newspaper together in a basement office. Bennett modeled the

Figure 3.1 Hoe Press *Source:* Wikimedia Commons, History of the Processes of Manufacture, 1864.

Herald after the *Sun* in its cost, distribution, emphasis on advertising, and approach to covering local, human-interest news. In the first issue, he declared, "We shall endeavor to record facts, on every public and proper subject, stripped of verbiage and coloring, with comments when suitable, just independent, fearless and good tempered." Bennett wanted the *Herald* to be a newspaper for all readers and he seemed to instinctively know what would interest them.

Bennett was one of the first publishers to make extensive use of illustrations and maps. He developed the best financial section of any newspaper in New York, devoting attention to Wall Street. He also wanted the *Herald* to be the first newspaper to get the big new stories. To that end, he hired correspondents to cover Europe, Canada, and Mexico. He set up a bureau in Washington, DC, to cover news from the capital. He also began a section of the newspaper devoted to women's issues. And long before others recognized the appeal of the subject, the *Herald* was covering sports news. In many respects, Bennett redefined the concept of what news was.

Bennett was not afraid of controversy. He criticized other editors in print, so angering James Watson Webb, the editor of the *Enquirer*, that Webb attacked him on the street. Bennett liked frank language, including words that were generally avoided at the time, including terminology for women's undergarments. At one point, he goaded critics by writing, "Petticoats—petticoats—petticoats—petticoats—there—you fastidious fools—vent your mawkishness on that!" Outraged New Yorkers organized a boycott of the *Herald* and tried to persuade businesses to stop advertising in the newspaper. Bennett reveled in the attention the newspaper was getting.

A sordid crime in 1836 provided all the makings for sensationalizing by the penny press. A young prostitute named Helen Jewett was found dead in a bordello. She had been killed with an ax and her body left on a bed set on fire. The police soon arrested one of Jewett's patrons, nineteen-year-old Richard Robinson, who used an alias to disguise his visits. Recognizing the great interest in such a dramatic event, the *Sun* and *Herald* played up every aspect of the murder, arrest, and trial. The *Sun* published the first long account of the killing, but the *Herald* got a scoop when Bennett visited the crime scene while the body was still in the bedroom. Robinson's five-day trial gave the newspapers the chance to provide more breathless coverage. The prosecution could present only circumstantial evidence against Robinson, and after a short deliberation, the jury found him not guilty. The *Sun* and *Herald* showed creativity and enterprise in reporting the murder and trial. However, they were also guilty of exaggeration and tastelessness. The penny press would continue to mine crime as a means of boosting their circulation. It would also serve as a model for later publications that would exploit gripping stories.

The model of the cheap, popular newspaper soon was adopted by publishers in other cities. The *Boston Daily Times* was founded in 1836. That same year, William M. Swain and Arunah S. Abell launched the *Public Ledger* in Philadelphia. A year later, the two men founded the *Baltimore Sun*. In New Orleans, the *Picayune* debuted, consciously modeling itself after the *Sun* and *Herald*. In 1850, the *Richmond Dispatch* began publishing. That same year, the *Morning News* was founded in Savannah, Georgia.

New York was becoming the publishing center of America. In addition to the *Sun* and *Herald*, more than a dozen newspapers of various kinds were published in the city. The growing metropolis was becoming

Figure 3.2 The Murder of Helen Jewett *Source:* Wikimedia Commons.

a place where young men came to work and chart their own course. That included Horace Greeley. The son of farmers, Greeley was born in Amherst, New Hampshire, and learned the printing business as an apprentice. Greeley spent ten years working for various publications, including the *Log Cabin*, a Whig campaign newspaper that helped elect William Henry Harrison to the US presidency, and a weekly magazine, the *New Yorker*.

Seeing the success of the *Sun* and *Herald*, Greeley decided to launch another penny newspaper. With the financial backing of friends, he founded the *New-York Tribune* in 1841. The *Tribune* shared some of the characteristics of the other penny publications, most notably the price. However, Greeley, who was a reformer at heart, aimed his newspaper at a more educated, middle-class audience. The editor had no use for what he called "servile partisanship," but he also criticized strict neutrality in the political arena. He wanted to publish "a journal thus loyal to its guiding convictions, yet ready to expose and condemn unworthy conduct or incidental error on the part of men attached to its party."

Greeley hired an outstanding staff that included Henry J. Raymond, who would go on to start the rival *New York Times*. He also found correspondents to cover news across America and around the world. Among the reporters was Margaret Fuller, who had become recognized as a writer and editor of the transcendentalist magazine, the *Dial*. She reviewed books and wrote about social reform, women's rights, and the abolition of slavery. Fuller was probably the first female foreign correspondent when she covered the Italian revolution. The *Tribune* also became known for publishing reviews, book excerpts, and poetry.

But what set the newspaper apart more than anything else was the editorials. Greeley had a range of interests that he regularly addressed in the *Tribune*. At various times, he supported abolitionism, women's rights, and, for a time, socialism. He also believed that Western expansion was the answer to many of the country's problems and regularly touted the popular slogan, "Go West, young man." Taking advantage of the reduced postal rates available to newspapers, Greeley launched a weekly version of the *Trib*, as the paper was known. He wisely targeted readers in small towns and rural areas across the country that were only served by weekly publications with limited news coverage. By the middle of the century, the *Tribune* had become the most widely read newspaper in America. And Greeley became known as "Uncle Horace." As Greeley's biographer Robert C. Williams has written, "The *Trib* was not a newspaper, but an article of faith, faith in Uncle Horace, the philosopher of the paper."

TELEGRAPH AND ASSOCIATED PRESS

The development of the telegraph ushered in a new era of communication, and the press seized upon the technology. Inventors across the world had been experimenting with transmitting written messages across wires. In the United States, Samuel F. B. Morse developed and patented the electromagnetic telegraph machine in 1837. Working with his assistant, Morse also developed Morse code, an alphabetic system of dots and dashes to represent letters and numbers. Thanks to a subsidy from Congress, by 1844 telegraph wires had been strung between Washington, DC, and Baltimore. Morse was ready for a public display of the telegraph, and on May 24, he sat at a table in Washington and tapped out a message. His assistant in Baltimore decoded the biblical question: "What hath God wrought?"

In less than ten years, seventeen thousand miles of telegraph line were in use, linking all the nation's major cities except San Francisco. The demands on the telegraph were so great, in fact, that some cities were connected by multi-wire lines. Fourteen lines connected New York and Philadelphia, and seven lines linked New York to Baltimore and Washington, DC. Newspaper editors and publishers embraced the telegraph, publishing news faster than had ever been possible before. "The events of yesterday throughout the entire land will be given, as we now give the occurrences at home," declared the *Philadelphia North American.* The *Springfield Republican* proclaimed, "Nothing can be more evident to the public, and nothing certainly more evident to publishers of newspapers than there is a great deal more news nowadays than there used to be. . . . The increase of facilities for transmission of news brought in a new era."

Editors of the leading New York newspapers soon initiated joint ventures to cut the growing bills for telegraph usage by sharing news reports. The arrangements allowed them to avoid missing important news while splitting costs. The editors eventually decided that a more formal organization was needed and in 1846 the Associated Press, or AP as it came to be known, was born. The AP was founded as a nonprofit cooperative in which members agreed to share news with one another. The vehicle for doing this was the telegraph, which is why the AP is still sometimes called a "wire service." The members of the AP shared costs, appointed top management, and set policies. The AP also set up their own correspondents in key cities to supplement the news provided by members.

Because the stories from the AP had to satisfy the demand of its many press members, they needed to be free of personal views or political partisanship, as Richard A. Schwarzlose has noted. News stories had to be a collection of facts, arranged simply and directly. "My business is to communicate facts," Lawrence Gobright, the AP's first Washington correspondent, wrote. "I do not act as a politician belonging to any school, but try to be truthful and impartial." Of course, this was a sharp departure from the way that party press editors had operated. It was also different from the penny press editors, who declared their political independence but did not separate the news and opinion sections of their newspapers.

In 1854, Daniel Craig, the general agent of the AP, put forth his view of what stories should look like:

> We want *everything that is* IMPORTANT and everything that would be of General Interest in this City, State, or the country at large.

> In preparing dispatches for transmission, it is desirable always to bear in mind that we want only the material facts in regard to any matter or event, and those facts in the fewest words possible.

> All expressions of opinion upon any matters; all political, religious, and social biases; and especially all *personal feelings* on any subject on the part of Reporter, must be kept out of his dispatches.

GROWTH OF MAGAZINES

At the same time newspapers were growing, magazines were starting to gain a foothold. Magazines had been published in America as far back as the colonial era, but most struggled to find a readership, mainly because early magazines were expensive and contained little interesting material. Most simply reprinted articles taken from books, newspapers, and other magazines. Distributing magazines also was difficult. Readers received magazines in the mail, and postal rates were expensive. Not even Benjamin Franklin, who was successful with so many ventures, could find success in magazine publishing. His *General Magazine and Historical Chronicle* published for less than a year.

However, the obstacles didn't stop many publishers from trying. Among the magazines published in the 1700s were the *American Magazine, Philadelphia Magazine, United States Magazine, North-Carolina Magazine*, and *Columbian Magazine*. None lasted more than a few years, and many ceased publishing after only a handful of issues. In fact, magazines didn't find real success until the mid-1800s. Thanks in part to a growing group of American writers, a host of new magazines were launched that contained materials of interest to a wider group of readers. Much of the content initially was fiction and poetry.

Among the magazines founded during this time were the first aimed at specific groups of readers, a strategy that many publishers would continue to embrace. The *American Farmer* was launched in 1819 as a guide for farmers and published for more than seventy-five years. The *American Turf Register* was founded in 1830 as the first sports magazine. Several magazines for women also were started. The most successful was *Godey's Lady's Book*, edited by Sara Joseph Hale. The tireless Hale was not only an editor and writer—she penned the children's verse "Mary Had a Little Lamb"—she also founded the Ladies' Medical Missionary Society and was a leader in the preservation of Mount Vernon, George Washington's home. Under her direction, *Godey's* featured articles on fashion, etiquette, and manners, along with elaborate illustrations.

A group of general-interest monthly magazines also were launched, including *Harper's* and *Atlantic Monthly*. Priced at 25¢ per issue, both were aimed at a wealthy, educated readership, and they featured articles on biography, travel, science, and other subjects. *Harper's* began in 1850 as an offshoot of the Harper Brothers book publishing company. *Atlantic Monthly*, founded in Boston in 1857, featured commentary and fiction. Poet and critic James Russell Lowell served as the first editor. Its early contributors included Ralph Waldo Emerson, John Greenleaf Whittier, and Henry Wadsworth Longfellow, all of whom would go on to become among the century's most celebrated writers.

By the middle of the century, more than five hundred magazines were published in the United States. The great majority were local or regional publications, but the most popular specialty and monthly magazines enjoyed a sizable national readership. After a slow start, the magazine industry had finally established itself as a growing and important part of the journalism landscape.

ABOLITIONIST AND BLACK PRESS

During the early decades of America's history, slavery had become a firmly entrenched institution. Black slaves were brought to the country in the seventeenth century from Africa, and the use of slave labor became common throughout the American colonies. But while most Northern states began to outlaw slavery after the Revolutionary War, the South

Figure 3.3 Bathing Dresses from *Godey's Lady's Book*, July 1867 *Source:* Wikimedia Commons.

depended on slaves for its largely agricultural economy. By the 1830s, approximately three million slaves lived in the United States. Slavery had many supporters, certainly in the South, but also in the North where manufacturers and merchants benefited from their toil. Yet the institution also had a small but vocal group of critics known as abolitionists.

Taking their cue from other reform groups that sought to improve society through the press, abolitionists started newspapers dedicated to ending slavery. An estimated forty antislavery publications were started in the decades before the Civil War. Often founded by abolitionist groups, the newspapers provided an editorial platform for the movement's leaders, publicized the work of antislavery societies, and spread news about the treatment of Black Southerners. Abolitionist publications became one of the most important tools that abolitionists used in their fight to end slavery. At a time when most newspapers in both the North and South were opposed to the antislavery movement—if not supportive of slavery—the abolitionist press was for many years the only editorial voice of opposition.

The best-known and most controversial abolitionist editor was William Lloyd Garrison, the publisher of the *Liberator*. He considered several cities for his newspaper, but settled on Boston because he believed there was a greater need for a revolution in public opinion in a part of the country where "the curse of slavery" had been eliminated but "the curse of deep-rooted prejudice" still existed. Garrison wanted to launch his publication, as he wrote, "*within the sight of Bunker Hill and the birthplace of Liberty.*" He chose to name his newspaper the *Liberator*, despite the arguments of some that it was too inflammatory. When the first issue appeared on New Year's Day of 1831, the editor made it clear that the journal would be an uncompromising advocate for ending slavery immediately. "I *will be* as harsh as truth, and as uncompromising as justice," he wrote. "On this subject, I do not wish to think, or speak, or write, with moderation. No! no! . . . I am in earnest—I will not equivocate—I will not excuse—I will not retreat a single inch—AND I WILL BE HEARD."

Garrison made clever use of the newspaper exchange system, a popular practice in which editors around the country swapped newspapers with one another at no cost in order to publish news and opinion from elsewhere. Southern editors who received the *Liberator* were outraged at the editorials but reprinted them to show what they considered to be the North's view of slavery, often adding their own scathing comments. Garrison then would publish his original editorial with the response and add new comments. As angry responses poured in, Garrison basked in the infamous reputation he was gaining. Above the *Liberator's* front page nameplate, he added a woodcut depicting a slave auction in front of the nation's capitol. The image prompted a Southern senator to try unsuccessfully to ban from the mail any newspapers with "pictorial representations" of slavery.

Mob violence had always taken place in America, but during the 1800s it became an accepted way of dealing with the social, ethnic, and political strains facing the country. Abolitionist leaders, including publishers, bravely faced protesters who believed they were protecting the established order against dangerous and radical outsiders. In the summer of 1835, a mob in Boston protesting the appearance of an abolitionist lecturer turned their wrath on Garrison. As a threat, they erected gallows in front of the editor's home while he was away. The evening of the lecture, a group of protesters found Garrison, tied a rope around him, and marched him down the street presumably to tar and feather him. However, before they could get far, police warded off the attackers and Garrison was put in the city jail for safekeeping.

Mobs elsewhere wrecked the presses of abolitionist publications. Residents of Cincinnati, Ohio, marched to the office of the *Philanthropist*, broke in and destroyed an upcoming issue. Publisher James G. Birney vowed to continue publishing and argued that publishing his newspaper was a test of personal freedom. A mob returned two weeks later and broke into the office again. They tied a rope around the press, dragged it down the street, and pushed it into the Ohio River. Tragically, Elijah Lovejoy died defending his newspaper from a mob determined to stop him from publishing. Lovejoy, a devout Christian, founded the *Observer* in St. Louis, Missouri, in 1833, and over time he became an outspoken critic of slavery. His death shocked the country, and he became a martyr to the abolitionist cause.

One of the chief targets of the abolitionist press was the Fugitive Slave Law, part of the controversial Compromise of 1850, which allowed enslavers to recapture runaway slaves. The following year, the *National Era*, an abolitionist publication based in Washington, DC, began serializing "Life Along the Lowly," the fictional story of Tom, a slave torn from his family and later sold by the family that originally enslaved him. Written by Harriet Beecher Stowe, a prolific author who was the daughter of a minister, the story ran for some forty weeks in the *National Era*, far surpassing any series ever published in an abolitionist publication. In 1852, the novel was published under the title *Uncle Tom's Cabin* and became the literary sensation of the era, selling more than three hundred thousand copies in the first year.

Among the new publications launched during this time were the first newspapers published by African Americans. Samuel Cornish and John Russwurm founded *Freedom's Journal* on March 16, 1827, in New York City. Black leaders in New York for some time had been concerned about what they considered racist portrayals of Black individuals in the city's publications. "We wish to plead our own cause," Cornish and Russwurm declared in the first issue. "Too long have others spoken for us. Too long has the public been deceived by misrepresentations."

Although *Freedom's Journal* spoke out against slavery, the editors made it clear that the newspaper's chief goal was to be an advocate for free African Americans. Cornish and Russwurm believed that Black individuals must be able to publicly speak for themselves in order to dispel misrepresentations held by many white people. "Daily slandered, we think there ought to be some channel of communion between us and the public, through which a single voice may be heard, in defense of five hundred thousand free people of colour," they wrote. The newspaper published biographical sketches of successful Black Americans. It also constantly promoted education, arguing it was the best way for African Americans to advance financially and socially.

Frederick Douglass, a young Black abolitionist, took notice of the Black-owned publications and became determined to join the ranks of editors. Douglass had been born into a Maryland enslaved family but escaped when he was a teenager. He eventually settled in New Bedford,

Massachusetts, where he attended meetings of the local abolitionist society. The eloquent young Douglass became a popular antislavery speaker,
telling audiences moving stories of his experiences as a slave. Eventually,
Douglass decided he wanted other ways to spread his message. Using
donations from supporters, he set up a newspaper in Rochester, New
York. Rochester was the last stop on the Underground Railroad and
Douglass thought the city would support a Black-owned publication.

The first issue of the *North Star* appeared on December 3, 1847, and
in the lead editorial Douglass wrote that he had long wished to establish
a newspaper. It only made sense that "he who has *endured the cruel pangs
of Slavery* is the man to *advocate Liberty.*" Douglass extolled the cultural
significance of the newspaper's name for Black readers. "Of all the stars in
this 'brave, old, overhanging sky,' *The North Star* is our choice," he wrote.
"To thousands now free in the British dominions it has been the Star of
Freedom. To millions, now in our boasted land of liberty, it is the *Star of
Hope.*" Douglass pledged that the newspaper would fearlessly advocate
for the rights of free Black Americans, including the right to vote. He
preached the importance of education, temperance, and moral character
in order that Black individuals could achieve equality. The editor regularly
highlighted Black achievements in the *North Star*, and he encouraged
readers to use their God-given talents to be successful.

On the tenth anniversary of his escape from slavery, Douglass used
the *North Star* to publish an open letter to his old master. Douglass
boasted of his accomplishments since escaping slavery and described
the happy domestic life he enjoyed with his wife and four children. He
asked what had become of three sisters and a brother still owned by the
master, as well as a beloved grandmother who he claimed had been badly
mistreated. He also promised to continue making use of the master "as a
weapon with which to assail the system of slavery—as a means of concentrating public attention on the system." The editor closed the letter
with words that would become among his best known: "I am your fellow
man, but not your slave."

The press had always been a male-dominated institution. However,
that was gradually beginning to change and one of the areas where
women could work successfully was the abolitionist press. Women had

Figure 3.4 Frederick Douglass *Source:* National Archives, Collection FL: Frank W. Legg Photographic Collections of Portraits of Nineteenth-Century Notables.

long been active in antislavery circles, some in exclusively female organizations and others in societies that included both sexes. Because anti-
slavery publications were a focus of the organizations, it was natural that
women often would play a leading role.

Lydia Maria Child served as editor of New York's *Anti-Slavery
Standard* for a stint. She was already an accomplished writer of both
nonfiction and fiction. She had also started a children's magazine. Child
sought to attract a broader audience for the *Anti-Slavery Standard* by
adding literary and intellectual essays and commentary. She published
works by Charles Dickens, Alexis de Tocqueville, Nathaniel Hawthorne,
and other popular writers. She also started her own column, "Letters
from New-York," in which she explored social problems that crossed
racial boundaries, among them poverty and alcoholism. By the end of the
second year, the *Anti-Slavery Standard* had about five thousand readers,
twice the number it had when she took over.

Jane Grey Swisshelm founded the *Pittsburgh Saturday Visiter* in
1847. She was a Pittsburgh native who, while living in Kentucky for
several years, was horrified at witnessing slavery for the first time. In one
issue she wrote, "To see men running from a country that is not only
reputed to be free, but is extolled as the asylum of the down trodden of
all nations, and the only hope of freedom in the arms into another country . . . presents to the mind a strange perversion of ideas, principles and
common sense." Swisshelm later moved to St. Cloud, Minnesota, where
she took over a newspaper and renamed it the *St. Cloud Visiter*. Soon, the
outspoken editor ran afoul of local leaders who didn't like her criticism of
slavery. Swisshelm refused to back down and, in response, a group broke
into the newspaper office, wrecked the press, and left a note calling her
little more than a prostitute. Undaunted, Swisshelm rebuilt the newspaper and continued publishing, continually reminding readers of what was
done. The local leaders pleaded for an agreement that the *Visiter* would
not continue discussing what happened. Swisshelm responded, "The men
pledged their honor that the Visiter should not discuss the subject. We
pledged our honor that the paper we edit will discuss any subject we have
in mind."

REPORTING THE CIVIL WAR

By the mid-1800s, approximately 3,700 newspapers were published in the United States. That was twice the number published in Britain and about one-third of all the newspapers in the entire world. Virtually every community of any size had a least one or two newspapers, and many cities had three or more. Certainly, the press benefited from America's rapid growth in the mid-nineteenth century. Between 1840 and 1860, the country's population jumped from about 17 million to 31 million. Seven new states joined the Union. The growth of the press also was fueled by the fiery debate over the future of slavery. Hundreds of editors started publications because they believed they could help shape the view of readers on issues that were dividing the country, including the Dred Scott Supreme Court decision, the raid on Harpers Ferry, and Abraham Lincoln's election as president. "If we fail to notice the appearance of any new paper," one editor remarked, "it is not from an intentional discourtesy, but simply because we can scarcely keep up with the list, they increase so fast."

When the war began with the attack on Fort Sumter in Charleston, South Carolina, on April 12, 1861, the two regions were generally of two different minds about what it meant. As they had been doing for years, many Southern newspapers drew parallels in the Confederacy's struggle for independence with the patriots during the Revolutionary War. "Charleston has become to the South, in eighteen hundred and sixty-five what Lexington was once to the common country in seventeen hundred and seventy-five," declared the *Memphis Appeal*. "It is the scene of the first triumph which inaugurates the war of Southern independence." But in the North, many newspapers accused the Confederacy of starting the war and demanded that the Union respond immediately. "The confederate States are determined to have war, and war now exists by their act," said the *Boston Advertiser*. "It is now a question of life and death for the nation."

During the war, hundreds of reporters chronicled the fighting on land and at sea. No accepted standards existed for what constituted responsible journalism. The correspondents were guided instead by their backgrounds, education, talent, and personal standards. While some had

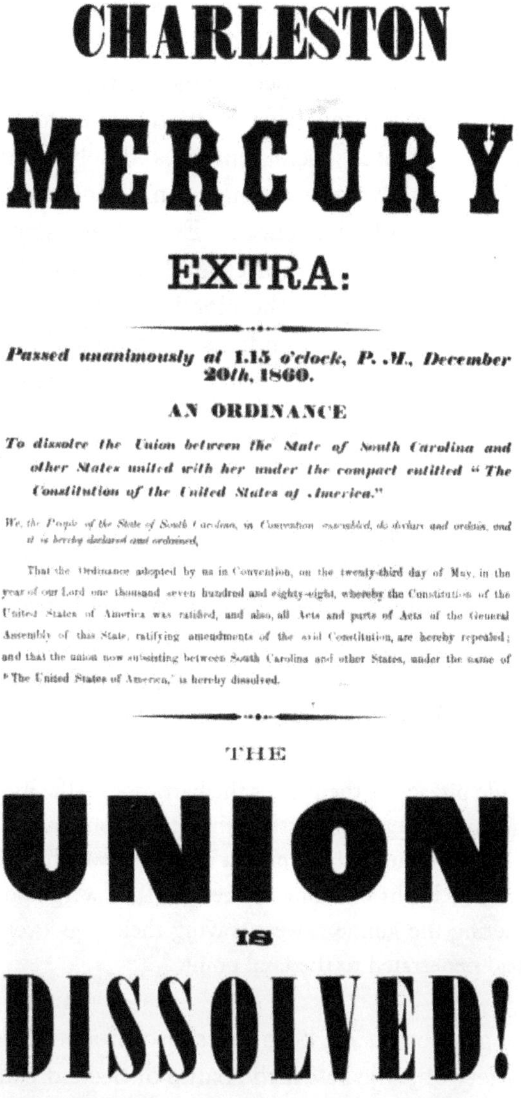

CHARLESTON

MERCURY

EXTRA:

Passed unanimously at 1.15 o'clock, P. M., December 20th, 1860.

AN ORDINANCE

To dissolve the Union between the State of South Carolina and other States united with her under the compact entitled "The Constitution of the United States of America."

We, the People of the State of South Carolina, in Convention assembled, do declare and ordain, and it is hereby declared and ordained,

That the Ordinance adopted by us in Convention, on the twenty-third day of May, in the year of our Lord one thousand seven hundred and eighty-eight, whereby the Constitution of the United States of America was ratified, and also, all Acts and parts of Acts of the General Assembly of this State, ratifying amendments of the said Constitution, are hereby repealed; and that the union now subsisting between South Carolina and other States, under the name of "The United States of America," is hereby dissolved.

THE

UNION

IS

DISSOLVED!

Figure 3.5 *Charleston Mercury Extra*: The Union Is Dissolved!

previous journalism experience, others included lawyers, teachers, clerks, and at least one poet (Walt Whitman). Not surprisingly, the overwhelming majority of correspondents were white men. Several women briefly reported during the war. Only one African American, Thomas Morris

Chester of the *Philadelphia Press*, is known to have been a correspondent for a daily newspaper during the war.

The best editors set high expectations for their correspondents, as J. Cutler Andrews has written. They wanted stories to be accurate and complete, and they wanted them sent in a timely fashion. Reporters for the *New York Herald* were instructed: "In no instance, and under no circumstances, must you be beaten. . . . Eternal industry is the price of success. . . . Remember that your correspondence is seen by half a million personal daily and the readers of the Herald must have the latest news." Many of the accounts by correspondents honestly and faithfully chronicled the war. Tireless newsmen went to great lengths to report stories on deadline and displayed considerable enterprise to describe the war in all its facets. Many of the biggest battles, including Shiloh, Antietam, Fredericksburg, and Gettysburg, seemed to bring out the best work by correspondents on both sides. The stories not only provided comprehensive views of the battles but also dramatic passages and colorful anecdotes. Perhaps none was more dramatic than the pivotal battle of Gettysburg. Whitelaw Reid of the *Cincinnati Gazette* reported from near the Union command on the fighting at Cemetery Hill, when Union troops turned back a furious Confederate charge:

> Up to the rifle pit, across them, over the barricades—the momentum of their charge, the mere machine strength of their combined action swept them on. Our thin line could fight, but it had not weight to oppose this momentum. . . . Right on came the rebels. They were upon the guns, were bayoneting the gunners, were waving their flags over our pieces. But they had penetrated to the fatal point.

Enterprising reporters on both sides also produced human-interest stories on a variety of subjects. At the battle of Second Bull Run, Southern correspondent Felix G. de Fontaine described the Confederate field hospitals thrown up after the fighting. "For nearly half a mile along the Warrenton turnpike, the forest presented a vast spectacle of human suffering," he wrote. "Here were the various temporary division hospitals. . . . The operating tables consisted of piles of rails, covered only with a few rough boards. . . . Arms and legs were lying around the half dozen surgical altars." Confederate correspondents who were outraged by mismanagement and poor treatment of the troops, reported on the problems. One story reported on the poor quality of shoes and clothing given to Confederate soldiers. Another exposed a quartermaster who stole from the army.

At the same time, numerous accounts by journalists mistakenly and, in some cases, irresponsibly reported the fighting. Reporters less concerned with the facts and more interested in rushing stories into print wrote damaging stories that hurt their side. Newsmen were guilty of everything from sensationalism and exaggerations to outright lies and conjecture. With little or no evidence, they accused commanders of a variety of mistakes and indiscretions. An even more serious issue were stories that revealed confidential military information. "Do not be deceived about the situation of affairs by the foolish dispatches of the papers," Union General George Meade wrote to his wife. "Be not over-elated by reported success, nor over-depressed by exaggerated rumors of failures."

In addition to the correspondents employed by newspapers, the Associated Press employed a staff of correspondents. Many newspapers in the North, particularly smaller ones, relied heavily on the wire service for war news. Editors published daily columns of telegraphic news, often on the front page. Southern publishers tried various cooperative news arrangements before settling on what became known as the Press Association of the Confederate States of America. The Press Association's superintendent hired correspondents to report from Richmond and Charleston, as well as the Confederacy's largest armies. He admonished his newsmen on the importance of "securing early, full, and reliable" news. He also ordered that stories should be free of opinion and to not send "unfounded rumors as news."

During the war people also wanted to see the news that they read about. Artists and photographers provided the images. Thousands of illustrations appeared, mostly in magazines. The printing technology of the time didn't permit photographs to be published, but they were shown in galleries. Most artists and photographers considered themselves reporters who worked with pictures instead of words. The best illustrations and photographs had a realism that captured the war in all its aspects. However, others simply glorified the war and were little more than propaganda.

The most popular magazines during the war were *Harper's Weekly* and *Frank Leslie's Illustrated Newspaper*. They emphasized material more common to magazines, chiefly features—which are longer-form pieces that use a narrative style to examine a person, event, or phenomenon—and illustrations. The magazines regularly devoted as many as half of their sixteen pages in each issue to illustrations, some of them covering a full page. An estimated thirty full-time sketch artists covered the war for the magazines. With a haversack hanging on his hip and a sketch pad and pencils in hand, an artist was immediately recognizable in the field. Being a successful sketch artist required sharp observational skills and a good memory as well as artistic talent. Artists also had to be hardy. They traveled mainly on horseback and often stayed up late finishing their sketches by campfire. The most prolific sketch artist was Alfred Waud, who sketched initially for the *New York Illustrated News* but switched to *Harper's Weekly*. He made sketches of most of the major battles in Virginia and also produced memorable pictures of camp life. Winslow Homer, who became one of America's foremost artists, acclaimed for his oils and watercolors, got some of his initial experience as a sketch artist during the war. He turned some of the war sketches into popular paintings.

The photographers who covered the fighting did some of the best reporting of the war. Because of the long exposure time required to take pictures, the majority of war photographs were posed. Individuals or groups were set up by the cameramen and instructed to simply look at the camera and not move while their picture was made. The more skilled and creative photographers did more, capturing subjects while they were at ease. Cameramen were unable to photograph the action of fighting, so they made pictures of the aftermath: dead soldiers, wrecked equipment, and devastated cities and countryside.

The most famous photographer when the war began was Mathew Brady. Brady had opened a studio in New York in 1844 and established himself as one of the city's leading portrait photographers. The ambitious

Brady wanted to make a complete photographic record of the war. He hired a staff of talented photographers that included Alexander Gardner, Timothy O'Sullivan, and James Gibson. The men followed the Union armies from campaign to campaign. While working for Brady, Gardner and others took many of the best-known photographs of the war, including those from the battle of Antietam. The Antietam photos were exhibited at Brady's gallery in New York. The *New York Times* enthusiastically praised the work, giving credit to Brady even though he took none of the pictures. "Mr. Brady has does something to bring home to us the terrible reality and earnestness of war," the newspaper said. "If he has not brought bodies and laid them in our dooryards and along the streets, he has done something very like it."

Press Censorship

A forceful press posed problems for the governments of both the Union and Confederacy. Newspaper correspondents were determined to report stories from the battlefield. Military and civilian leaders were just as determined to ensure they didn't reveal critical information. While editors wanted to voice their opinions on issues, political leaders wanted to ensure they didn't hurt the war effort. The result was censorship and newspaper closings never seen before during wartime.

At the same time, violence against the press rose to an unprecedented level during the war. Citizens and soldiers sought to silence newspapers they considered disloyal, often breaking into the offices and wrecking the presses. Few disputed the necessity of some press censorship during the war. However, in many cases, the restrictions imposed by both sides were haphazard. Journalists protested the censorship rules they considered unreasonable, and they spoke out against the mob violence. However, with little protection for freedom of expression, there was not much they could do.

During the first year of the war, administration of censorship in the North was passed from one department to another. Reporters and editors were understandably confused about the rules they had to work under. At the same time, Southern leaders also took steps to establish telegraphic censorship. Early in the war, the Confederate Congress approved a bill giving the president the authority to put government agents in telegraph offices to supervise the transmission of dispatches and to impose penalties of fines and imprisonment for anyone convicted of sending damaging news by telegraph.

The war departments of both sides also gave officers in the field leeway to deal with correspondents as they saw fit. Commanders barred reporters from their camps and took disciplinary action against journalists who they believed had published sensitive material. Union General William T. Sherman even went so far as to have one reporter court-martialed. A military panel found the correspondent not guilty, but he was ordered outside the army's lines. Officers believed the actions were necessary to deter reporters from publishing information valuable to the other side. Reporters complained that commanders acted arbitrarily and that too often newsmen did not know the rules they were expected to operate under.

Newsmen on both sides recognized that irresponsible correspondents were writing reckless stories that hurt their side. In a letter to the *Savannah Republican*, Peter Alexander, one of the most skilled Southern journalists, wrote: "The truth is there are correspondents who invariably magnify our successes and depreciate our losses, and who when there is a dearth of news will draw upon their imaginations for their facts. The war abounds in more romantic incidents and thrilling adventures than poet ever imagined or novelist described; and it would be well if the writers of fiction from the army . . . would remember this fact." But Alexander also argued for the necessity of a free press. "This is the people's war," he wrote. "Their sons and brothers make up the army, and their means, and their alone support it. And shall they not be allowed to know anything that is transpiring within that army?"

The other forms of press suppression during the war were the closing of newspapers considered disloyal, the arrest of editors, and the denial of postal privileges. John Nerone found that ninety-two newspapers were subjected to some form of restriction, and 111 were wrecked by mobs. The vast majority of the incidents took place in the North. Military commanders or political leaders, concerned about the effect of virulent editorials by the newspapers they opposed, ordered many of the closings. Others were the result of indignant citizens or soldiers acting on their own.

Opposition editors who were arrested or saw their newspapers closed had little opportunity for legal redress. Although the First Amendment in theory protected the press, journalists had limited legal defense during the mid-nineteenth century. At the same time, mobs generally were protected by the legal view that, in order to protect the citizenry, communities should have general control over ideas disseminated in their midst. Nineteenth-century law also left many regulatory responsibilities to local authorities. The experiences of abolitionist editors showed that local officials often were willing to let angry crowds do what they wanted to silence outspoken editors.

Many citizens in Ohio, Indiana, Illinois, and Iowa, not to mention the border states of Missouri and Kentucky, sympathized with the South. Numerous Democratic newspapers were closed in all of the states but particularly in Missouri. As a border state, Missouri had been bitterly divided before the war and that was reflected in its newspapers. General John C. Frémont put the state under martial law soon after the war began and used that authority to shut down newspapers considered disloyal. This included the *St. Louis News*, whose editor and assistant were arrested and charged with criticizing Frémont's military strategy. The editor of the *State Journal* also was accused of aiding and abetting the enemy for his editorials expressing pro-Southern sympathy. Troops seized the newspaper's office.

IMPACT ON THE PRESS

When Robert E. Lee and Ulysses S. Grant agreed to surrender terms at Appomattox Courthouse on April 9, 1865, the Civil War essentially ended. Five days later, John Wilkes Booth mortally wounded President Lincoln while he was watching a performance at Ford's Theatre in Washington. The four years of fighting had taken a devastating toll on the South's press. No sooner had the fighting started then newspapers and magazines in the Confederate states experienced shortages of materials and staff that made publishing difficult or impossible. The lack of suitable paper on which to print was particularly acute. During the war, editors were forced to reduce the size of the paper they printed on. When regular paper was not available, enterprising editors printed on whatever they could find, including colored paper, wrapping paper, and even the back of wallpaper. Circulation fell for newspapers, as many readers could no longer afford a subscription. Bowing to the pressures, many Confederate editors sold, merged, or closed their publications.

As more and more areas of the Confederacy fell, newspapers in the captured cities and towns either closed, fled, or were taken over by federal troops. In some cases, newspaper staffs managed to escape ahead of the Union forces, often with at least some of their presses and supplies. Refugee newspapers in Chattanooga, Tennessee, Huntsville, Alabama, Galveston, Texas, and other cities managed to escape and resume publishing in other locations, often doing so from train boxcars or abandoned buildings. The *Memphis Appeal* moved so many times that it became known as the "Moving Appeal."

At the same time, the war had a positive impact on journalistic practices. Reporting methods and writing styles changed to better cover a war of such complexity and scale. Although there were many problems, the standards for reporting and writing generally rose. The best editors set high expectations for their correspondents. They wanted stories to be accurate, complete, and sent in a timely fashion. The most talented newsmen for the North and South also showed considerable enterprise in providing interesting, informative, and insightful stories during the periods when the two armies were not fighting. The stories gave readers revealing pictures of entertainment, camp life, and religious ceremonies, as well as picket duty and military punishment.

Newspapers took advantage of technological developments to get war news into the hands of more readers and faster. High-speed presses allowed newspapers to print more copies and faster than ever before. The demand for news prompted some newspapers in big cities to begin publishing both morning and evening editions for the first time. Some publishers also initiated a Sunday edition for the first time, ignoring the traditional practice of not selling newspapers on the Sabbath. Many newspapers stepped up their use of "extras," special editions published to report big news events.

The American press changed significantly in the three decades between the launching of the first penny papers and the end of the Civil War. A new business model, relying on paid circulation and advertising sales, proved successful. In terms of content, many publications became more than simply partisan, political voices. They published news, and they sought to do it as fast as possible. Illustrations and photographs became a significant part of the news mix, even though photos could not yet be published. In the years ahead, the press increasingly focused on news and operated even more as a business.

CHAPTER 4

The Commercial Press

1865 to 1920

IN THE DECADES AFTER THE CIVIL WAR, THE AMERICAN PRESS BECAME truly commercial. Increasingly independent from political parties financially, daily newspapers relied on circulation and advertising as revenue sources. Publisher E. W. Scripps put together a chain of newspapers that stretched across the country, and others followed his lead to start groups of their own. Newspapers in big cities became prominent commercial enterprises, and their owners often erected large, ornate buildings that reflected their more visible role. New technology, including the linotype machine and photoengraving, improved the printing process, permitting newspapers and magazines to be printed faster.

A commercial press required news to attract readers and advertisers. Newspapers in the country's biggest cities competed to get the news first. Nowhere was that more evident than in New York City, where the newspapers of Joseph Pulitzer and William Randolph Hearst covered the news aggressively, and often in a sensational manner, while simultaneously pioneering creative page layouts and emphasizing illustrations. Pulitzer launched a new genre, the "stunt story," making reporters such as Nellie Bly household names. The boundary-pushing practices of Pulitzer and Hearst culminated in their often-reckless reporting of the Spanish–American War. At the same time, the *New York Times* and other newspapers sought to set themselves apart from the flamboyant brand of journalism practiced by Hearst and Pulitzer by taking a more serious approach to reporting the news.

A far different kind of journalism was practiced by a group dubbed the "muckrakers," investigative reporters for magazines who sought to expose systemic problems in American society, including municipal corruption, food safety, child labor, racial discrimination, and business monopolies. The muckrakers painstakingly researched their subjects, showing that the issues were not only serious but widespread. Their work helped lead to federal rules and legislation to address the problems.

NEWSPAPERS AND MODERNIZATION

In the last quarter of the nineteenth century, the United States underwent one of the most rapid and profound periods of economic growth any country has ever experienced. By 1913, America produced one-third of the world's industrial output—more than the total of Great Britain, France, and Germany combined. Between 1870 and 1920, almost eleven million Americans moved from farms to cities, and another twenty-five million immigrants arrived in the country. Many industrial workers labored at fifty- to sixty-hour-a-week jobs, receiving no pensions, compensation for injuries, or protection against unemployment. Driven by an intense pursuit of profits, American business increasingly engaged in ruthless competition. More corporations sought to control entire industries. Corporate leaders such as Andrew Carnegie and John D. Rockefeller accumulated enormous fortunes. Political corruption was widespread as elected officials and business interests often sought to get rich from one another. Political machines at the federal, state, and local levels plundered millions of dollars from the public coffers.

The changes initiated by the penny press—as evident during the Civil War—blossomed during this time. The daily newspaper came of age, as the number of dailies grew to about 1,500 by 1890. Much of the growth took place in the Midwest and West. Some of the best newspapers appeared in cities such as Chicago, Cleveland, Kansas City, Dallas, Los Angeles, and San Francisco. These newspapers were low-priced and easy to read. They believed that reporting the news was the primary obligation of the press and that editorial opinion should be independent of news. They also crusaded in the interests of the community.

The press in cities became increasingly independent of political parties, thanks in part to the growth of advertising. Many products once made at home, such as clothing, furniture, and food, were now being mass-produced. Manufacturers needed to market their products and they turned to advertising. Newspapers hired advertising managers and staffs to aggressively sell ads. By 1900, about 55 percent of daily newspaper income came from advertising. Advertising depended upon circulation, and in order to appeal to advertisers, newspapers needed to show they had many readers. Newspapers hired circulation managers and staffs to sell subscriptions. They also employed more newsboys and newsgirls—often called "newsies"—to sell individual copies on the street. Poor and homeless children famously shouted the headlines on street corners to attract customers.

That didn't mean newspapers were entirely neutral in reporting the news. However, more and more, newspapers limited their partisanship to the editorial pages. At the same time, publishing a newspaper was becoming seen as a moneymaking venture. "The newspaper is a private enterprise," wrote Charles Dudley. "Its object is to make money for its owner. Whatever motive may be given for starting a newspaper, expectation of profit by it is the *real one*."

James Scripps founded the *Detroit Evening News* in 1873. At the time there were already three morning newspapers in the city, and he wanted his to be different. In ten years, the *Evening News* had the largest circulation in the city. Edward W. Scripps joined his brother as the circulation manager. With financial backing from his family, E.W., as he was known, went on to establish a chain of newspapers in Cleveland, Cincinnati, St. Louis, San Diego, Los Angeles, San Francisco, and other cities. The Scripps newspapers were aimed at working-class readers. They featured aggressive news coverage, local crusades, and strong editorial opinion. Scripps kept newsroom expenses as low as possible, supplementing content with news and features provided by two wire services associated with the company, the United Press and the Newspaper Enterprise associations. By 1922, Scripps consolidated his more than forty newspapers in a new company, Scripps Howard, with a partner, Roy Howard. Other newspaper owners, including Samuel I. Newhouse, Frank Gannett, and Charles L. Knight, watched what Scripps and Howard were doing. They put together their own newspaper chains.

Wanting to promote their business role in the community, many newspapers erected fancy new buildings. The *Oregonian* in Portland built a new headquarters that was the tallest building in the city at the time. Built in the Romanesque Revival style, the building featured a large tower with a clock on four sides. The *Kansas City Star* erected an ornate, three-story building in an Italian Renaissance style. Designed by the renowned architect Jarvis Hunt, the building featured many Art Deco elements.

An explosion in communication technology played an important role in the growth of journalism. For decades, paper had been made from cotton rags. However, rags were expensive, and there were constant shortages. During the Civil War, a process for grinding and separating the fibers from wood was developed that permitted trees to be used to make cheap white paper, which became known as newsprint. By the mid-1880s, every newspaper in New York City was printed on newsprint, and other newspapers soon were doing so. The price of newsprint dropped over the next several decades, improving every newspaper's bottom line.

Setting type by hand had always been another big expense for newspapers. Large dailies required many compositors, and the process was cumbersome. The Linotype machine was invented, allowing someone sitting at a keyboard to set hot-metal type one line at a time, dramatically increasing productivity. Initially, only the largest newspapers could afford the expensive machines, but Linotypes were eventually adopted by virtually every printing establishment and were used through the middle of the twentieth century. At the same time, presses powered by electricity became faster. The new Hoe presses used stereotype plates and printed on both sides of a continuous roll of paper. They could print up to 72,000 copies an hour. Photoengraving was introduced in the 1880s, meaning that the growing number of illustrations could be printed more easily. At the end of the century, the halftone process permitted photographs to be reproduced in newspapers and magazines.

Alexander Graham Bell invented the telephone in 1876, transforming personal communications in unimaginable ways. The press embraced the telephone, most notably as a tool for reporting. Reporters working on stories no longer had to talk to sources in person. They could call them on the telephone. By the 1880s, reporters in large cities regularly worked as teams for breaking news stories. The "leg man" gathered news from the scene and phoned it to a "rewrite man" in the newspaper office who wrote the story.

As the press was actively reporting the news, journalism practices evolved. One important routine was the interview, the means by which a reporter gathered information from someone of interest or someone with knowledge of a subject. Reporters began talking to public officials during the penny press era, but the practice didn't become widespread until after the Civil War. At the same time, journalists wanted facts—the information gathered from interviews, public documents, and their own observations—to drive the stories they wrote. Theodore Dreiser remembered his editor at the *Chicago Globe* when he joined the newspaper in 1892. The editor told Dreiser that the first paragraph of the story had to tell readers the "who, what, how, when and where." When Dreiser turned in his stories, the editor would mark it up for changes, reminding the young reporters, "News is information. People want it quick, sharp, clear."

As Mitchell Stephens has noted, facts found their "true voice" with the arrival of the "inverted pyramid" style of composing a news story that became popular in the late nineteenth century. In the inverted pyramid, the most important information—a summary of the news event—goes into the first paragraph, known as the "lead" (often spelled "lede"). From there, the news value of the facts diminishes as one reads a story, much the way that the width of an inverted pyramid shrinks. Reporters were instructed to get the facts from different sources and write their stories in an inverted pyramid style.

Journalists also increasingly viewed their job as going beyond simply covering the news of the day to report on was considered the people's "right to know." This meant reporting stories that required more time and enterprise. Often these were stories about wrongdoing or malfeasance that people in positions of authority didn't want known. The idea that journalists should seek to be objective and not show any bias in their stories was not yet a creed. Moreover, maintaining high ethical standards was not always valued. The overriding goal was to "get the story."

The "new" journalism being practiced by the press came together in reporting on the Tweed Ring in New York City. The ring was a corrupt political machine that ruled New York City after the Civil War. Led by William Tweed, members used payoffs, kickbacks, extortion, and election fraud to seize power and make themselves rich. The Tweed Ring had some of the largest newspapers under its thumb, dispensing thousands of dollars in city advertising. Yet some in the news media recognized the Tweed Ring for what it was, and they were determined to show the public.

As an illustrator for *Harper's Weekly*, Thomas Nast gave a face to Tweed and his ring. Nast was born in Germany and immigrated to America with his family when he was a young boy. He studied drawing, and when he was only fifteen, he landed a job with *Leslie's Illustrated*. Nast traveled all over the country sketching for *Leslie's*. After the Civil War began, Nast moved to *Harper's Weekly*. *Harper's* encouraged Nast to use artistic talent to tell a story with a message. In his illustrations, Nast made Tweed the embodiment of political corruption. He used Tweed's ostentatious symbols of power—the diamond stickpin and the striped suits—to define his image. He mocked Tweed as bloated and gluttonous. Tweed himself recognized the power behind Nast's cartoons. "I didn't care a straw for the newspapers articles—my constituents didn't know how to read," he once said. "But they couldn't help but see them damned pictures."

Initially, the *New York Times* kept silent about the Tweed Ring. A member of the *Times* board of directors had received a large city contract and, after that member died in 1870, the *Times* became more critical of the ring. The *Times* started with editorials about the Tweed Ring. Then the newspaper found a whistleblower, a former Tweed crony, who turned over incriminating documents. The *Times* published a series of stories that exposed the corruption. All the time this was happening, Tweed tried bribes and other inducements to silence Nast and the *Times*. To their credit, both resisted. In fact, they turned up the pressure on

THE "BRAINS"

THAT ACHIEVED THE TAMMANY VICTORY AT THE ROCHESTER DEMOCRATIC CONVENTION.

Figure 4.1 Boss Tweed Cartoon *Source:* Wikimedia Commons, Harper & Brothers; illustration by Thomas Nast.

the Tweed Ring. The *Times* printed a special section summarizing the charges against the ring that was printed in English and German.

Nast continued his powerful cartoons, culminating in a drawing of the "Tammany Tiger" in the Roman Coliseum. Many of Tweed's cronies were voted out of office in 1871, and Tweed eventually was convicted and went to prison. Nast went on to draw illustrations for another fifteen years. His cartoons started the practice of using the elephant to represent the Republican Party and the donkey for the Democratic Party, and he also created the popular image of Santa Claus. The reporting by the *Times* established a benchmark for other newspapers to follow. Taken together, the work by Nast and the *Times* illustrated the power of the press as a watchdog over government.

FRONTIER PRESS

The growth of newspapers during the 1800s was due in part to the growth of the United States. The settlement of the West meant that more towns and cities were being founded. A newspaper was often one of the first commercial establishments in a frontier town. Hand presses and printing supplies, which had traveled in hundreds of miles in wagons, were set up any place a printer could find. As Barbara Cloud has written, publishers "often printed their first issues in canvas-covered shacks but, if they were successful in town building, went on to occupy fine buildings." Community leaders believed that a newspaper provided credibility and made their communities a "real" town, because any town back East had at least one publication. When gold was discovered in the Black Hills area of South Dakota in 1874, the *Black Hills Champion* began publication just three years later in the town of Deadwood City. Many of the frontier newspapers had colorful names; perhaps the best known was the *Tombstone Epitaph* in Tombstone, Arizona.

Because a newspaper's survival depended on the growth and prosperity of its area, editors typically were town boosters. Stories and editorials extolled a town's virtues to newcomers. The *Rocky Mountain News* was the first newspaper founded in what would become the state of Colorado. The second issue of the *News* featured a large map of the route to Denver and articles explaining the safest routes across the Kansas plains. Editors promoted cultural events and advocated for such issues as improved sewage disposal and treatment of the mentally ill. They were also sharp critics of the lawlessness that plagued many towns.

Many frontier newspapers did not last long. It's been estimated that ten newspapers in frontier towns were started for every one that survived more than two or three years. Nonetheless, some newspapers survived and played important roles in the growth of their cities. They included the *Deseret News* in Salt Lake City, Utah, the *Bismarck Tribune* in Bismarck, North Dakota, the *Los Angeles Times*, and the *Seattle Times*.

Newspapers on the frontier and back East sought to cover the Indian Wars when white Americans and Native Americans fought over control of the vast western lands. Fighting had taken place for decades, but it escalated after the Civil War when many Native Americans were assigned to reservations and the army's role was to keep them there. Editors used their own reporters and volunteer correspondents to report on the brutal fighting that took place across the West. Regrettably, newspapers and magazines often used sensationalism to depict the threat that Native Americans posed, exaggerating and, in some cases, faking stories. Racial hatred also colored many of the accounts published. Reflecting the racism of the times, Native Americans were often referred to in news stories as "savages," "animals," "demons," and other debasing terms. To be sure, Native American newspapers pushed back with news coverage of their own.

In early 1828, at the behest of the Cherokee Nation, Elias Boudinot printed the first issue of the *Cherokee Phoenix*, the first Native American newspaper. The paper, which printed in New Echota, Georgia, uniquely published in both English and Cherokee, attempting to attract Cherokee and non-Native readers. The newspaper fiercely advocated for Native American rights and eventually changed its name to the *Cherokee Phoenix, and Indians' Advocate*. It also published news articles on tensions between the Cherokee and US government, editorials, official notices, and statements from officials on land disputes. Eventually, the paper closed in 1834 due to financial issues. An attempt to reopen the paper a year later was quashed when the Georgia government seized the presses. That same year, in 1835, Boudinot and two of his relatives were assassinated for defying tribal leadership when he sold Cherokee lands to the US government.

Other Native newspapers and many tribal-owned presses emerged throughout the century, including the weekly bilingual *Choctaw Telegraph*, the *Muscogee Nation News*, and the *Arrow-Telephone*, all in Oklahoma. Notably, one Muscogee newspaper was owned by a Native woman named Myrta Eddleman, and by working with the Associated Press, she was able to gain a wider readership. While separate and distinct publications, each Native newspaper offered unique cultural perspectives and advocated for Native American rights.

Remarkably, as young Indigenous children were forced into boarding schools to assimilate into white culture, school newspapers could be places of resistance. Three young Native schoolgirl editors in 1880 used their paper, the *Hallaquah* at the Seneca Indian School in Oklahoma, to critique prejudicial representations found in larger newspapers, going as far to call the *Louisville Commercial* "a disgrace to respectable journalism." Of course, not all boarding school children were given this kind of editorial freedom. Other boarding school newspapers, such as the *Indian Helper* and the *Red Man*, were created by the Carlisle Indian Industrial School. The school's goal was to eradicate Native cultures, and the administration heavily censored the student publications.

Years later an important newsletter would emerge. The activist and physician Carlos Montezuma, who published *Wassaja*, in addition to founding the Society of American Indians, advocated successfully against the displacement of the Yavapai tribe in Fort McDowell, Arizona. In his newsletter, the Yavapai Native spoke out against the reservation system and land and water disputes. In one issue, Montezuma called for the abolition of the Bureau of Indian Affairs "on the ground that it is comprised largely of cheap, incompetent and immoral men."

The Battle of the Little Bighorn in 1876, during which about 265 US cavalry troopers led by Lieutenant Colonel George A. Custer were surrounded and killed by a force of two thousand Sioux, startled the nation and led to calls that Native Americans be subdued once and for all. The *Helena* (Montana) *Herald* declared, "The only proper monument to Custer's memory will be the extinction of the Sioux nation." However, some publications argued that the government mistreatment of American Indian tribes had led to many of the problems. *Harper's* said that if the Indigenous had been treated better, the nation would not have had to "contemplate the extermination of the Western tribes as the only means of protecting the settlers in the far West."

The best-known figure to emerge from the frontier press was a young man named Samuel Clemens. After serving an apprenticeship at the

Hannibal (Missouri) *Gazette*, Clemens worked for the newspaper owned by his older brother when he got a chance to write his first published stories. He later became a riverboat pilot on the Mississippi River and then moved to the West to become a miner. When it became clear he was not going to make a fortune searching for silver, Clemens took a job as a staff writer at the *Territorial Enterprise* in Virginia City, Nevada. Clemens was not a first-rate reporter. Rather than sticking to the facts, he was more interested in telling a good story and making readers laugh. One of his first stories, titled "Petrified Man," described the exhumation of a Paleolithic man. In reality, the story was made up and meant to embarrass the county coroner, who was notoriously closemouthed about deaths in the community.

While working at the *Territorial Enterprise*, Clemens began signing his stories "Mark Twain." (The pen name was from a river term indicating water two fathoms, or twelve feet, deep.) His brand of satiric humor became popular, and other publications reprinted his stories, including "The Celebrated Jumping Frog of Calaveras County." Clemens also began giving public lectures, spreading his name even more. After working at other newspapers, including the *Daily Union* in Sacramento, California, he eventually left journalism to devote all his time to writing fiction. But before Clemens wrote such classic novels as *The Adventures of Tom Sawyer* and *The Adventures of Huckleberry Finn*, he provided a fitting definition of what journalism increasingly had become in its focus on news, including the trivial. As with everything Clemens did, the account was written in his matchless satirical style:

> Our duty is to keep the universe thoroughly posted concerning murders and street fights, and balls, and theaters, and pack-trains, and churches, and lectures, and schoolhouses, and city military affairs, and highway robberies, and Bible societies, and haywagons, and a thousand other things which it is in the province of local reporters to keep track of and magnify into undue importance for the instruction of the readers of this great daily newspaper.

JOSEPH PULITZER AND WILLIAM RANDOLPH HEARST

Although various editors helped redefine newspaper journalism in the nineteenth century, perhaps none did more than Joseph Pulitzer. Born in Hungary, he left home as a teenager and moved to the United States. He served briefly in the Union army during the Civil War and afterward moved to St. Louis. Pulitzer joined the *Westliche Post*, a German-language newspaper, and eventually bought it. He later purchased the *Evening Dispatch* and merged it with the *Post* to create the *St. Louis Post-Dispatch*. Pulitzer announced, "The Post and Dispatch will serve no party but the people . . . will oppose all frauds and shams wherever and whatever they are; will advocate principles and ideas rather than prejudices and partisanship." Under Pulitzer's direction, the *Post-Dispatch* covered the news aggressively, crusading for solutions to the many problems that plagued the growing city. One of the first crusades addressed the issue of tainted milk, a problem that had led to many infant deaths in poor families. On its editorial page, the *Post-Dispatch* demanded reforms in the milk supply.

On a visit to New York, Pulitzer learned that the *New York World* was for sale. At the time, the *World* was owned by the notorious stock manipulator Jay Gould, who was losing money publishing it. Gould was asking far more than the struggling newspaper was worth, but Pulitzer eventually negotiated the price down, and on May 10, 1883, he acquired the *World*. In the first issue, Pulitzer promised to "fight all public evils" and "battle for the people." He declared, "There is room in the great and growing city for a journal that is not only cheap but bright, not only bright but large, not only large but truly democratic."

Pulitzer aimed the *World* at the city's working-class residents, especially the thousands of immigrants pouring into New York. More often than not, stories were about crime, sex, and tragedy. Readers were treated to headlines such as "An Insane Mother's Crime. Mrs. Moeller Throws Her Daughter and Herself from a High Window" and "A Ghastly Dream Realized. The Death of a Noted Grave Robber Recalls a Strange Episode in Body Stealing." The *World* also launched crusades, many on behalf of the poor and labor class. Perhaps the *World*'s best-known campaign was to show the terrible living conditions at the insane asylum for women on Blackwell's Island in New York. In 1887, a young reporter, Elizabeth

Cochrane, was assigned to get herself committed to the asylum and write about the conditions. Cochrane had worked as a journalist with the *Pittsburgh Dispatch*, where she mainly wrote about women's subjects under the byline Nellie Bly. (She took the name from the title character of a popular song by Stephen Foster.) However, the ambitious Bly wanted to do more, so she moved to New York and eventually landed a job at the *World*. To get herself committed, she moved into a boardinghouse for women and pretended to be mentally ill.

In a multipart series, Bly described awful food, wretched conditions, and cruel attendants. She called the asylum a "human rat-trap" where insanity was not cured but often created. "It is easy to get in," Bly wrote, "but once there impossible to get out." The exposé, which included illustrations, was widely read and reprinted by other newspapers. Just weeks after the series was published, a grand jury was empaneled to investigate conditions at the asylum. Before the end of the year, New York officials approved more funding to improve conditions at the asylum. And Bly went on to report more stories, posing as a working girl and being homeless, among other stunts. As biographer Brooke Kroeger has written, "Her assignments so often had the aura of mission, embracing the needs of the helpless or laying bare the schemes of scam artists and hucksters."

Pulitzer wanted the *World* to be visually eye-catching. The newspaper regularly used big, bold headlines to scream the news. It also used illustrations extensively, many of them spanning multiple columns. Pulitzer started pages devoted to sports news and women's news. He also began a Sunday edition combining news with entertainment that proved to be attractive to advertisers. Pulitzer believed that newspapers should not only inform, they should also amuse. "It is the Journal's policy to engage brains as well as to get the news," he once remarked, "for the public is even more fond of entertainment than it is of information."

The Sunday edition featured comics, and the *World* was the first to publish them in color. The most beloved comic strip was "Hogan's Alley," created by artist Richard Outcault. "Hogan's Alley" centered on life in the city's tenements and featured a raffish little boy with a shaved head who always wore a long yellow nightshirt. (Baldheaded kids were commonplace in New York's slums, where shaving a child's head was the

Figure 4.2 Nellie Bly *Source:* Library of Congress Prints and Photographs Division.

fastest way to get rid of lice. To save money, children often were dressed in cut-down nightshirts or dresses.) The character became known as the "Yellow Kid," and he was wildly popular with readers.

The *World* also pioneered the "stunt" story, pseudo-events that readers loved. The newspaper staged numerous events and assigned various reporters to them. The now-famous Bly was center stage for the best-known event, an attempt to beat the fictitious speed record for circling the world that the protagonist Phineas Fogg set in Jules Verne's novel, *Around the World in Eighty Days.* In 1889, Bly set off from New

York, dressed in a checkered coat and carrying a small bag. She traveled across the seas and continents on ships, trains, carts, and any form of transportation she could find. (In France, she visited Verne at his home.) Along the way, she filed stories that were eagerly awaited by the *World*'s readers. To sustain interest in Bly's quest, the *World* created a board game so that readers could follow her trip, and it held a contest asking readers to guess when she would arrive. On January 25, 1890, Bly arrived home to a ten-gun salute, seventy-two days after departing, and the *World* hailed the accomplishment. Critics decried a staged news event that was little more than an advertisement for the newspaper, but that didn't matter to the newspaper's leadership.

Pulitzer, a savvy businessman, priced the *World* at 2¢ a copy. That undercut other newspapers in the city, which had raised their prices over the years to 3¢ or more. The price also made a newspaper affordable to the working-class readers he sought. Pulitzer established advertising rates based on the newspaper's circulation, so that as the *World* reached more readers, he could charge higher rates. He went so far as to boast about the *World*'s circulation on the front page using "ears," little boxes on both sides of the nameplate on the front page. Breaking with the long-standing tradition of limiting advertisements to one column, his staff worked with merchants to design large, attractive advertisements that would catch the eyes of readers.

Pulitzer also recognized that lending a hand to causes made the *World* attractive to readers. The newspaper campaigned to raise $100,000 for a base for the Statue of Liberty, a gift from the people of France in honor of America's independence. Pulitzer encouraged the *World*'s readers to donate pennies, nickels, and dimes for the cause. The campaign not only succeeded in raising the money needed but helped build the newspaper's circulation among the city's new residents, many of whom were immigrants. Pulitzer's moves made the *World* the most widely read newspaper in New York. In just three years, the newspaper's circulation grew from a paltry fifteen thousand to an eye-popping 250,000. To mark the *World*'s success, Pulitzer built the newspaper's new home on Park Avenue, next to the *New York Sun*. Capped by a giant dome, it was the tallest building in the city when it opened in 1889. The symbolism of the *World*'s headquarters dwarfing the *Sun*, once the most widely read newspaper in the city, was evident to many.

Among the *World*'s readers was William Randolph Hearst. Hearst's father, George, had made a fortune in silver mining in the West. George Hearst aspired to a political career, and he purchased the *San Francisco Examiner* in 1880, hoping it would increase his name recognition. William attended Harvard, where he became business manager of the *Harvard Lampoon*, the college's humor magazine, and earned a reputation for hosting the best parties on campus. William became interested in the *Examiner* while in college, sending his father suggestions for improving the newspaper. They included relying on original reporting by its own correspondents and advertising itself widely. He dropped out of school in 1886, and the next year his father named him publisher of the *Examiner*. Hearst employed many of the same tactics that Pulitzer had used to be successful, publishing the kind of stories that readers loved, even if they were not exactly news. They worked for his newspaper, too, and the *Examiner*'s readership and profits grew.

The ambitious young Hearst wanted to publish a newspaper in New York, just like Pulitzer. In 1895, he purchased a struggling newspaper, the *Morning Journal*. With access to the family fortune—Hearst's father had died a few years earlier—William decided to take on the *World* head-on to see which would reign supreme in New York. Hearst hired away some of the *World*'s best staff members. Among the first was Arthur Brisbane, one of the top editors. Under Brisbane's direction, the *Journal* became even more aggressive than the *World*, especially in crusades and stunts. Hearst liked to call this approach "journalism of action." However, critics said the publisher was just sensationalizing the news to sell more copies.

Hearst spend lavishly to promote the *Journal*, putting up posters across the city and even hiring bands. He hired away Outcault, the creator of "Hogan's Alley," to draw his strip for the *Journal*. Hearst used the occasion to launch a big advertising campaign for the newspapers. Colorful posters featuring the Yellow Kid were plastered across New York. When Pulitzer learned that Outcault was leaving, he hired another artist to continue drawing the Yellow Kid. Pulitzer also responded to the

Journal's advertising blitz with one of his own. For a time, the Yellow Kid was seemingly everywhere in New York.

The new, sensationalistic style of reporting and writing became known as "yellow journalism," a term nearly always used scornfully. It also spread to other American cities. Soon after taking control of the *Denver Post* in 1895, the new owners transformed the newspaper, filling it with crusades, sensationalistic stories, stunts, big headlines, and cartoons. When the *Post* began gaining readers and advertisers, Denver's leading newspaper at the time, the *Rocky Mountain News*, started publishing the same kind of content.

REPORTING THE SPANISH–AMERICAN WAR

While the *World* and *Journal* were battling one another in New York, an international crisis was developing in Cuba. For three decades, America's neighbor to the south had struggled to gain its independence from Spain. At the same time, the United States was eager to flex its muscle with its Caribbean neighbor, just one hundred miles south of Florida. The United States was interested in Cuba because of the sugar it supplied, and American companies invested heavily in production equipment. Spain sought to meet the threat of Cuban independence by sending 150,000 troops under the command of General Valeriano Weyler.

The *World* and *Journal* reported the brewing crisis extensively. In 1897, a young Cuban woman named Evangelina Cisneros, the daughter of a jailed Cuban rebel, was thrown into jail for allegedly refusing the sexual advances of a Spanish army officer. The *Journal* reported the story with stories and illustrations. On the editorial page, the newspaper demanded her release and mounted a petition drive. When all that failed, Hearst sent a reporter, Karl Decker, to Cuba to plot her escape. With the help of others, Decker succeeded in breaking Cisneros out of jail. He brought her to New York, where Hearst had organized a giant public welcome. In a multi-deck headline, the *Journal* boasted:

MISS EVANGELINA CISNEROS RESCUED BY THE JOURNAL.

An American Newspaper Accomplishes at a Single

Stroke What the Best Efforts of Diplomacy

Failed Utterly to Bring About in

Many Months.

Early in 1898, rioting broke out in Cuba against Spanish rule. President William McKinley ordered the USS *Maine* to Cuba as a show of force. On February 15, 1898, an explosion on board the warship killed more than 250 American sailors and marines. The Spanish denied any role and expressed sympathy for the casualties. However, the *World* and *Journal*, with no evidence, declared that the explosion likely was the work of the Spanish. Both newspapers published front-page illustrations claiming to show what happened, even though no one working for the newspapers had seen the explosion. The *Journal* even went so far as to offer a reward of $50,000 for anyone who could find the "Perpetrator of the Maine Outrage." Critics were appalled. "Everyone who knows anything about yellow journals know that everything they do and say is intended to promote sales," the *New York Post* declared. "No one—absolutely no one—supposes a yellow journal cares five cents about the Cubans, the Maine victims, or anyone else."

By April, the United States had declared war on Spain. Most major newspapers and magazines sent reporters to Cuba to cover the fighting there. Reporters had to set up communications lines and cope with censorship. They relied on the US Commissary for food and supplies, but the Commissary was poorly organized and there were often shortages. The military had no policy for dealing with journalists, so commanders in the field or on the sea established their own rules.

No newspaper could match the resources that Hearst devoted to reporting the war. He leased a ship where *Journal* staff members could work. He even accompanied reporter James Creelman to the front lines of one battle near the town of El Caney. Creelman was wounded during a bayonet charge on the Spanish position. In his memoir, he recalled lying in a grassy area when Hearst approached him. The publisher expressed sorrow for his wound but said the battle had to be reported. According to Creelman, Hearst went on to say, "I'm sorry you're hurt, but"—and his

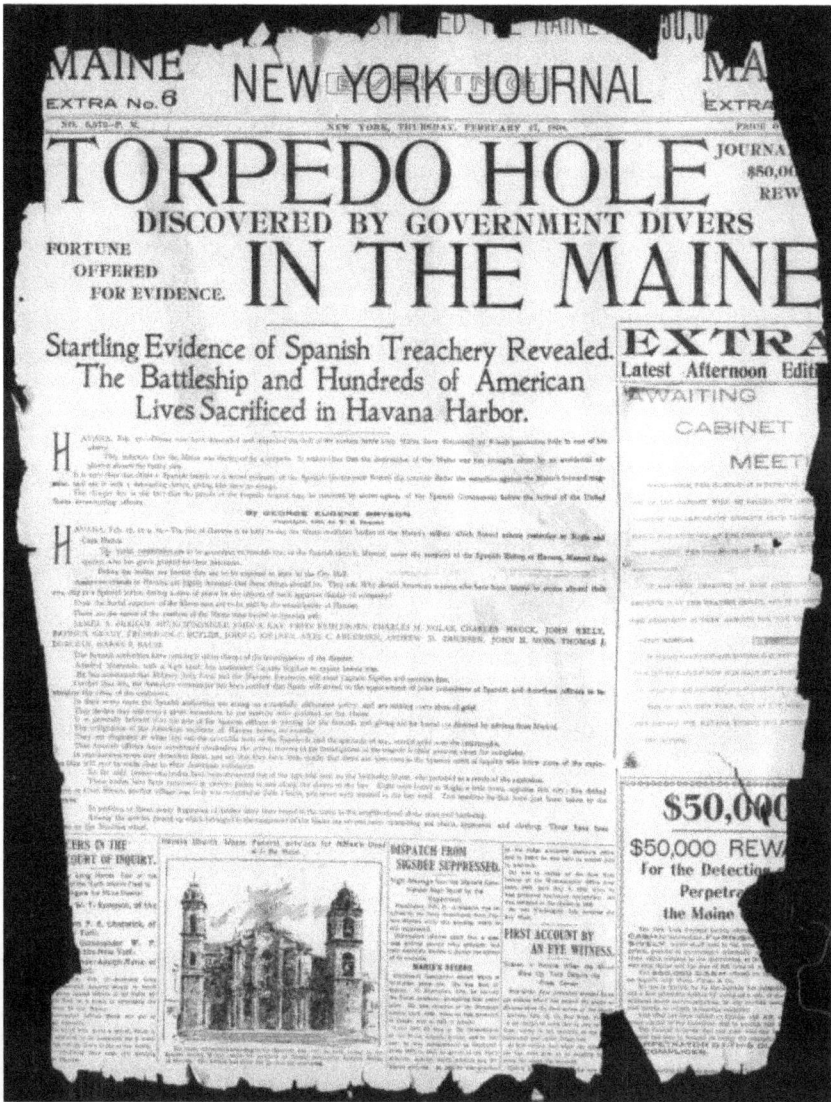

Figure 4.3 *The New York Journal*, February 17, 1898 *Source:* Library of Congress.

face was radiant with enthusiasm—"wasn't it a splendid fight? We must beat every newspaper in the world."

Perhaps the best-known correspondent during the war was Richard Harding Davis. He reported for the *New York Herald* and *Scribner's*

Magazine, often accompanying troops into battles. Davis was an outstanding writer who packed his stories with vivid, descriptive details. In a story for *Scribner's*, he ensured the reputation of Theodore Roosevelt, who helped command a volunteer cavalry unit known as the Rough Riders. During the decisive battle of the war at San Juan Hill, the Rough Riders were ordered to attack. The troops initially advanced slowly but Roosevelt, who was on horseback, galloped to the front and led the men ahead under withering fire. "No one who saw Roosevelt take that ride expected he would finish it alive," Davis wrote. "It looked like foolhardiness, but, as a matter of fact, he set the pace with his horse and inspired the men." The dispirited Spanish troops retreated.

The Spanish–American War lasted only three months. Even so, about 5,400 Americans and 10,000 Spanish were killed. At the war's end, Spain granted Cuba its independence and ceded the Philippines, Guam, and Puerto Rico to the United States as territories. By the time the war was over, many critics said "yellow journalism" had gone far enough. The *World* and *Journal* had not led the country into an unnecessary conflict, but the newspapers had contributed to the climate that made going to war possible. A political cartoon captured the view of many observers about the role of Hearst and Pulitzer. It depicted the two men, dressed in "Yellow Kid" garb, as spoiled children playing with building blocks that spelled "WAR."

NEW YORK TIMES

In the midst of the excesses often practiced by the *Journal* and *World*, the *New York Times* provided a more reasoned and serious alternative in the country's largest city. Henry Raymond, a former editor with the *New York Tribune*, had founded the *Times* in 1851. Under his leadership, it became a popular newspaper during the Civil War. However, by 1896, the *Times* had fallen on hard times, selling fewer than ten thousand copies a day. When the newspaper was put up for sale, an unlikely buyer, Adolph Ochs, purchased it for $75,000. Ochs's parents had emigrated to the United States from Bavaria and settled in Tennessee. As a boy, he sold newspapers for the *Knoxville Sentinel*, working his way up to journeyman printer. He bought the *Chattanooga Times* in 1878 and made

Figure 4.4 The Big Type War of the Yellow Kids *Source:* Illustration by Leon Barrit, from the Library of Congress Prints and Photographs Division.

the newspaper successful. Even though he was still in debt from that purchase, he managed to assemble the financing to get the far bigger *New York Times.*

Ochs pledged to publish the *Times* "without fear or favor, regardless of any party, sect or interest involved" and to make the newspaper "a forum for the consideration of all questions of public importance." He later settled on a motto—"All the News That's Fit to Print"—that was meant to serve as a response to what he viewed as the reckless journalism practiced by the *World* and the *Journal.* The motto became a fixture on the front page and still is today. Importantly, Ochs saw his role as guiding the business direction of the newspaper, and he left news coverage to his editors. Two years after buying the *Times,* he abruptly lowered the price from 3¢ to a penny. It was a bold move to get more readers, and it worked. Within a few weeks, the circulation climbed to more than 50,000, and within three years it had grown to more than 100,000. Ochs plowed the profits back into the newspaper, allowing it to devote more resources to journalism.

To distinguish the *Times* from the *Journal* and *World*, Ochs insisted that the newspaper cover the news in a serious and evenhanded manner. He put a great emphasis on business and financial news. He discouraged the publishing of photographs, a practice that earned the *Times* the nickname "the Gray Lady." He prohibited comics and instead started a weekly book review section. The *Times* also began publishing an annual index of stories published in the newspaper, a move that established its reputation as the "newspaper of record" and made it popular with libraries across the country. He also advertised the *Times* with the slogan, "It does not soil the breakfast cloth," contrasting it with the "yellow" journals of Pulitzer and Hearst.

In 1904, the *Times* moved to a stunning new headquarters on Forty-Second Street at Longacre Square. Ochs persuaded city officials to build a subway station there, and the area was renamed Times Square. Ochs had commemorated the opening of the *Times* building with a fireworks show on December 31, 1904, and continued the show annually. However, he wanted to do something more to draw attention to the newspaper. An electrician built a large lighted ball that was lowered from a flagpole atop the roof. It became the centerpiece of the city's New Year's Eve festivities, attracting thousands of revelers. The newspaper itself soon outgrew the location and, in 1913, moved to a larger building across Broadway. However, the area continues to be known as Times Square, and the New Year's Eve celebration is a New York City tradition.

The *Times* became known for its coverage of the sinking of the *Titanic* in 1912. The paper devoted fifteen of its twenty-four pages in one issue to the tragedy in which 1,500 people, some of them prominent New Yorkers, were killed. Just years later, the *Times* coverage of World War I was unparalleled, and the newspaper was awarded its first Pulitzer Prize in 1918 for outstanding reporting of the war. During the next thirty years, the *Times* won seventeen Pulitzer Prizes, more than any other newspaper.

Adolph Ochs and his wife had one child, a daughter, Iphigene. In 1918, she married Arthur Hays Sulzberger. Although he had no background in journalism, he immediately went to work for the *Times*. At first there was little for him to do, but over time, he assumed an increased role in the business side of the newspaper. When Ochs died in 1935,

Sulzberger became publisher. By the time of Ochs's death, the *Times* had become one of the most widely read and respected newspapers in the world.

REFORM JOURNALISM

A new generation of journalists sought to expose the growing problems of modern American life. The campaign took place against the backdrop of the Progressive Era, the period from the inauguration of President Theodore Roosevelt in 1901 until the United States entered World War I in 1917. It was a period of explosive economic growth, fueled by increasing industrial production, the expansion of the consumer marketplace, mass immigration, and the growth of cities. During this period, various efforts to solve the troubles that were becoming apparent in the country came together. Reform groups such as the Anti-Saloon League and the National Municipal Reform League were calling for changes in society. However, at the heart of the reform movement was a group of journalists who earned the title "muckrakers." As Richard Hofstadter has written, "It is hardly an exaggeration to say that the Progressive mind was characteristically a journalistic mind, and that it's characteristic contribution was that of the socially-responsible reporter-reformer. . . . Before there could be action, there must be information and exhortation. Grievances had to be given specific objects, and these the muckraker supplied."

The press had crusaded against corruption for decades, but the muckrakers drew nationwide attention to the problems. Most of the exposés were published in national magazines, such as *McClure's, Collier's, Munsey's,* the *Saturday Evening Post,* and *Cosmopolitan* which had the financial resources to devote time and attention to the issues. Unlike the expensive genteel literary magazines popular in the nineteenth century, the new breed of magazines, which were affordably priced at 10 or 15¢ a copy, had more in common with newspapers in their approach to reporting and writing. They also had a corps of bold, skilled reporters who knew how to do the digging that was required to uncover the stories. Journalism was becoming a profession that attracted educated men and women. Many had a strong social conscience and wanted to see the country's problems addressed.

Muckraking endeavored to show broad patterns that transcended one city or state. Many articles focused on business and political corruption. But they also examined the exploitation of child labor, the living conditions of the poor, racial discrimination, and lax standards for food and drugs. Muckraking reporters tended to view the concentration of wealth as dangerous. They also believed that corrupt politicians were destroying the country and political institutions should be more responsive to the popular will. Some critics believed that these reformers lacked the optimism that was needed by the country, or worse, wanted to overturn American society. Roosevelt bestowed the name muckrakers when he likened the journalists to the "Man with the Muckrake" in John Bunyan's book *Pilgrim's Progress*. However, the muckrakers denied the charge. "We 'muckraked' not because we hated our world but because we loved it," Ray Stannard Baker recalled. "We were not hopeless, we were not cynical, we were not bitter."

The muckraking era began in 1903 with a group of powerful, investigative stories published in *McClure's* magazine. S. S. McClure had founded the monthly magazine ten years earlier and had already been publishing stories about the country's new trusts and tycoons. McClure's talented staff of writers included three of the best-known muckraking writers: Ida Tarbell, Lincoln Steffens, and Baker. The January issue carried Tarbell's ongoing series about John D. Rockefeller's Standard Oil Company, an exposé by Steffens on municipal corruption in Minneapolis, and Baker's article on a violent coal-mining strike in Pennsylvania.

Tarbell, a Pennsylvania native who grew up where Rockefeller built his oil business, painstakingly researched what became a nineteen-part series about the giant monopoly. She used public documents, including congressional hearings and regulatory records, as well as interviews with current and former Standard Oil executives, to expose the unfair business practices Rockefeller used to squeeze out competitors. Told in an engaging, narrative fashion, with telling anecdotes, the series was wildly popular with readers. It was quickly published as a book. The series encouraged investigations into other monopolies, including the telephone and telegraph, liquor, and railroads.

Figure 4.5 *McClure's* for April 1895 *Source:* Library of Congress Prints and Photographs Division.

In other muckraking work, *Leslie's* magazine reported on the growing problems of railroad safety. *Ladies' Home Journal* exposed the fraudulent patent-medicine trade. In a series titled "Treason of the Senate," *Cosmopolitan* exposed how the problem of state legislators selecting US senators often lead to special interests having undue influence on the senators. *Colliers* ran a fourteen-part series titled "The American Newspaper," which exposed problems with the newspaper business. Will Irwin reported the ways some publications dodged controversial stories that might cause them to lose advertising and how sensationalism too often masqueraded as news.

Book authors also found subjects in the country's problems. Theodore Dreiser's *Sister Carrie* described how industrialization affected people. The main character is a young woman who tried to achieve the American dream but wound up becoming a prostitute in Chicago. Upton Sinclair's *The Jungle* described the unsanitary condition in slaughterhouses. He first investigated the food industry as a reporter for the *Appeal to Reason*, a Socialist newspaper. The series graphically described the unsanitary practices and terrible working conditions in Chicago's meatpacking houses.

The work of the muckrakers unquestionably had an impact. Two years after Tarbell's series, the Roosevelt administration filed a federal antitrust suit against Standard Oil that lead to the company's breakup. Publication of *The Jungle* led Congress to enact the Pure Food and Drug Act, which created a federal agency to ensure the country's food and drugs were safe. The *Cosmopolitan* series helped to galvanize support for the Seventeenth Amendment that provided for the direct election of US senators. Other legislative reform measures included child labor laws and civil service rules.

It would be going too far to give all the credit for the reforms to muckraking journalists. In most cases, they were not the first to uncover the problems. Nonetheless, the muckrakers demonstrated the power of strong reporting and writing. The muckraking era was another example of how the commercial press was evolving to become more enterprising and aggressive. That would continue through the middle of the century, at the same time the press scene expanded with the development of radio and television.

CHAPTER 5

The Expanding Press

1920 to 1950

AT THE BEGINNING OF THE TWENTIETH CENTURY, NEWSPAPERS CON-
tinued to dominate the American press landscape. The number of daily
newspapers was about to reach an all-time high, and weekly newspapers
were growing as well. The number of newspapers published by and for
Black Americans more than doubled in the early decades of the century.
The foreign-language press was growing too, thanks to the hundreds of
thousands of new immigrants moving to the country. Like their predecessors, the new publications served readers who had been generally
ignored by the mainstream press.

The news scene was expanding into other areas and new areas as
well. Popular new national magazines were launched, most notably *Time*
and *Life*. After years of technological experimentation, commercial radio
appeared over the airwaves, and for the first time, all Americans could
get the same information at virtually the same moment. Although news
on the radio was slow to develop, and initially limited to coverage of big
events, leaders of the radio networks recognized that radio's immediacy
made it ideal for reporting. Television emerged on the heels of radio,
although it would not become popular until after World War II. Television news required a bigger team of journalists, and many pioneering
radio journalists moved into the new medium.

All this took place against the backdrop of two catastrophic
world wars. American journalists covering World War I endured strict

censorship, and federal legislation made it a crime to publish disloyal or critical language about the government. As a result, Americans didn't get an accurate picture of the century's first modern war. With greater access to the fighting, the press reported World War II more completely. Photojournalists captured iconic images of fighting. Collectively, the two world wars revealed the tension that increasingly existed between the press and the military during periods of conflict.

TABLOIDS

Tapping into the public's interest in sensationalistic news had helped make the penny press popular, as it had for the newspapers of Hearst and Pulitzer. A new breed of newspapers known as the tabloids took it to new heights. The popularity of British newspapers such as the *Daily Mirror* showed that there was a market for smaller-sized publications that were a mix of scandal and crime news, with big headlines and photographs. Joseph Medill Patterson launched the first US tabloid, the New York *Daily News*, in 1919. The paper's motto was "New York's Picture News-paper," and the image of a camera was part of its nameplate. Readers liked the lurid, melodramatic content, as well as the compact size, which was easier to handle on the crowded subways. By 1925, the *Daily News* had a circulation of more than one million. Not surprisingly new tabloids soon followed, not only in New York but other major cities, including Phila-delphia, Chicago, Detroit, St. Louis, and Boston.

In many respects, the tabloids were ideally suited for the decades known as the "Roaring '20s." The best-known members of the news staffs of the tabloids often were the photographers who made pictures of the era's flappers, movie stars, and crime figures. In 1928, the *Daily News* published the most famous and controversial photograph of the 1920s. In a widely followed trial, Ruth Snyder and her lover had been convicted for the murder of Snyder's husband. Snyder was sentenced to die in Sing Sing Prison's electric chair. Tom Howard managed to sneak a camera in the prison by strapping it to his leg and hiding it under his pants. The moment that Snyder was put the death, he snapped a blurry image of the dramatic event. The *Daily News* published the photograph on the front page with headline that read simply, "DEAD!" Critics decried what they considered the garish coverage of Snyder's execution, but the newspaper sold a record number of copies.

The heyday of tabloid journalism was relatively brief. Some publications closed during the Great Depression, but the *Daily News* continued to be published. The tabloid size and lively approach to covering the news also continued to be popular with newspapers in some big cities that wanted to differentiate themselves from their more serious counterparts that published in the traditional broadsheet size. One of those is *Newsday*, a tabloid that serves Long Island, New York, but is sold throughout the New York metropolitan area. *Newsday* was founded in 1940 and for more than two decades largely copied the *Daily News* in its appearance and coverage of news. Starting in the late 1960s with new leadership, *Newsday* took a more serious approach to reporting the news. It has been popular with many readers for its mix of local and sports news, as well as commentary and criticism. In recognition of its outstanding journalism, *Newsday* has won nineteen Pulitzer Prizes.

The term tabloid continues to be used to describe a type of journalism that emphasizes sensational news that at its best is overly dramatized and at its worst is blatantly false. Tabloid journalism not only encompasses print publications but also television shows and online sites. Critics decry some of tabloid journalism's unethical practices, which can include paying for stories, but tabloid journalism remains unquestionably popular.

SUFFRAGE PRESS

For seven decades, the women's suffrage movement relied on journalism to help women gain the right to vote in the United States. As such, many female leaders campaigning for voting rights entered the public sphere for the first time. In addition to speeches and political stunts, suffrage leaders relied heavily on newspapers, periodicals, and pamphlets. They created their own publications, in addition to relying on mainstream press coverage. Suffrage groups differed in their approaches and strategy. Often, these strategies relied heavily on the press.

A key suffrage publication was the *Woman's Journal*, which was published from 1870 to 1931 with editorial support from Lucy Stone and her daughter Alice Stone Blackwell. The long-lasting publication was known as the "Suffrage Bible" and had close connections with the American Woman Suffrage Association. The *Woman's Journal* maintained a positive and moderate view of the women's suffrage movement, unlike more radical newspapers. Susan B. Anthony and Elizabeth Cady Stanton published the *Revolution* from 1868 to 1870. The publication focused on suffrage but also covered topics considered provocative for the period, including maternity, social inequities, divorce, and spousal abuse. While the two publications relied on traditional reporting, each suffrage press also published poetry and fiction appealing to readers' emotions about women's subordinate place in US society.

A controversial publication also emerged in 1870 with the creation of *Woodhull and Claflin's Weekly*. The newspaper, which was founded by Victoria Woodhull and her sister Tennie Claflin, championed sex education, free love, and legalizing prostitution. It also promoted Woodhull's 1872 presidential run. The newspaper rejected traditional marriage, and although Woodhull was an accomplished public speaker advocating for women's suffrage, other suffrage leaders opposed the content of her publication. *Woodhull and Claflin's Weekly* became infamous for exposing an affair between a married woman and the esteemed Reverend Henry Ward Beecher. The sisters were arrested for violating obscenity laws, and the newspaper closed in 1876.

At the heart of the suffrage movement was a bitter fight on race. Anthony and Cady Stanton initially supported the end of slavery. But, after the passing of the Fifteenth Amendment—which gave Black men the right to vote—the two women, who did not support the amendment, broke away from their suffrage communities to form the National Woman Suffrage Association. Groups like the American Woman Suffrage Association supported the amendment, and others were critical because it excluded women. As a result, many white suffragists and leaders espoused racist views. Some Black suffragists felt conflicted after the passing of the amendment but continued to fight for women's right to vote. Mary Ann Shadd Cary, a Black lawyer and suffragist, worked with Anthony and Cady Stanton and spoke at the 1878 National Woman Suffrage Association convention. She also published and edited the *Provincial Freeman* after fleeing to Canada. She was the first Black woman to run a newspaper in the North, and she fiercely advocated for the rights of Black men and women in America. According to her biographer Jane Rhodes, Shadd Cary risked her life by riding a horse across the border to collect subscriptions for her newspaper in the United States.

To be sure, not all citizens supported the rights of women. Anti-suffrage organizations—nicknamed the "antis"—began publishing their own political material during this period. One of these publications was the *Remonstrance*, which began printing in 1890. The publication advocated that women maintain order inside their homes and avoid the male-dominated public sphere. The publication often argued that women's suffrage would harm communities and imperil womanhood. In one 1909 issue, the periodical wrote that although women were capable of voting intelligently, suffrage would "come as an undesired burden." It argued that women were "overburdened with duties which she cannot escape and from which no one proposes to relieve her. If she is given suffrage, it is an added duty." The *Remonstrance* fiercely advocated against suffrage until it closed in 1919.

Before women were finally granted the right to vote in 1920 through the Nineteenth Amendment, new and more radical suffrage leaders emerged who relied less on their own publications and more on garnering headlines in the mainstream press. Lucy Burns and Alice Paul started the National Woman's Party and used what was then seen as extreme, flashy, and unladylike tactics to garner national media attention. This included hunger strikes, arrests, time spent in jail, and protesting outside of the White House. Another suffrage group hiked 170 miles from New York City to Albany in the cold during December 1912 to confront political leaders about voting rights. The protest became sensational news and exceptional free publicity for the movement. And although much of the coverage mocked the women, newspapers covered the hike for weeks.

Critics have argued that the passing of the Nineteenth Amendment granted just white women the right to vote. It wasn't until 1924 that Native Americans were granted citizenship. Additionally, Asian Americans weren't granted the right to vote until the Immigration and Nationality Acts of 1952 and 1965. Lastly, although Black men were technically allowed to vote following the Fifteenth Amendment, Jim Crow laws often excluded them from doing so. It wasn't until the 1965 Voting Rights Act that African Americans were better able to exercise their right to vote. Voting rights remained a political issue and newsworthy subject well into the twenty-first century.

BLACK PRESS

The number of Black-owned newspapers had grown in the years after the Civil War. Certainly, African Americans needed a strong press voice. More than six million Black Americans lived in the United States by the mid-nineteenth century. But despite the gains won during the war and the Reconstruction years, African Americans saw their rights slowly taken away by Jim Crow laws in the South, as well as by the racism that stubbornly persisted across the country. Sadly, the mainstream press routinely ignored these stories as well as the news of Black Americans in general. One reason was that few newspapers employed Black reporters or editors.

By the turn of the century, almost every big city—and many smaller ones—had a "race paper," as Black publications were popularly known. These newspapers had several features in common: they sought to unify the Black community; they educated African Americans about white society; and they fought for equality and civil rights. These goals were expressed by the *Colored Tribune* in Savannah, Georgia, founded in 1875 with the slogan "With Charity for All: With Malice Toward None." The *Colored Tribune* pledged to help "the advancement and elevation of the colored race"; teach "their duty as Christians and as citizens" and demand "all the rights secured to them by the laws of God and the country"; and provide a much-needed "organ of communication" for the Black community.

Black newspapers were among the few publications that reported on the lynchings that tragically took place regularly across the South and other parts of the country as well. However, it took a remarkable woman named Ida B. Wells to turn it into a national issue. Born into an enslaved family in Holly Springs, Mississippi, during the Civil War, she took over the family affairs as a teenager after her parents died in a yellow fever epidemic. Wells became a teacher in a rural school and later made her way to Memphis, Tennessee. While teaching, she began writing for a number of Black publications, including the *Memphis Free Speech*, and her work was widely praised. When she wrote a story about the disgraceful condition of the city's Black schools, including the one where she taught, her school fired her.

Wells joined the *Free Speech* as a full-time editor, and by 1889 she was attacking the horror of lynchings. She insisted that Black men and women must resist the killings any way they could, even if it meant responding with violence. In one story, she praised Black Americans in Georgetown, Kentucky, who burned white-owned buildings after a Black man was hanged. Carrying a pistol in her purse, she began visiting the sites of the killings and discovered a pattern: the cases usually involved a white woman who consented to have sex with a Black man and then, to protect her reputation, later accused him of rape. Her outspoken editorials on lynchings and the role that white women played eventually led the *Memphis Commercial* to declare that Wells must be silenced. While she was out of town, a mob of angry white people wrecked the *Free Speech* office and destroyed the press.

Wells decided it was not safe to return to Memphis, and she became part owner of another Black newspaper, the *New York Age*. She launched another anti-lynching campaign, using the newspaper to chronicle the killings she investigated. The first story, published in 1892, took up the entire front page of the *Age* and sold ten thousand copies. She said the country's mainstream newspapers could no longer be silent and must condemn the lynchings. Wells later published booklets such as "Southern Horrors: Lynch Law in All Its Phases."

During this period, the *Chicago Defender* and the *Pittsburgh Courier* were started, both achieving a size and status that far exceeded any previous Black publications. Robert Abbott founded the *Chicago Defender* in 1905. Born to former slaves, Abbott attended Hampton Institute, where he trained to be a printer. He helped publish a newspaper in his hometown of Savannah, Georgia, then decided to pursue a law career. At the Kent College of Law in Chicago, he was the only Black student in his class. At one point, a prominent Black attorney told Abbott that he was too dark-skinned to make any impression on a jury. He tried

Figure 5.1 Ida Wells *Source:* Barnett, public domain, via Wikimedia Commons.

unsuccessfully to start a law practice and then returned to printing. Chicago already had three Black publications, but Abbott was convinced that he could be successful with his own. He called his newspaper the *Defender* because he wanted it to be an outspoken advocate of equal rights for Black Americans.

The *Defender* almost failed because of a lack of money, and at one point Abbott moved his office into the dining room of his landlady. Abbott soon adopted the slogan "World's Greatest Weekly," a takeoff on the *Chicago Tribune*'s slogan "World's Greatest Newspaper." He also decided to model the *Defender* after the yellow journals in its approach to presenting the news. Headlines such as "Aged Man is Burned to Death by Whites" denounced the racism and violence often directed at Black individuals. The *Defender* also argued that Black men and women must fight back. Critics accused him of being sensationalistic, but the newspaper's circulation grew steadily.

Looking for more readers, Abbott turned to the South. He used Black train porters to deliver the *Defender* to newsboys waiting in southern cities. Abbott encouraged Black Southerners to move to the North where there were greater opportunities and they would be better off. "If ever there was a time to strike for freedom in its broadest sense, that time is right now," he wrote. "If we fail to reap the benefits of the golden opportunity, we have but ourselves to blame." He touted the number of African Americans leaving their homes, believing more would move if they saw themselves as part of a mass movement. A photo on the front page of the *Defender* showed a railroad yard in Savannah, Georgia, filled with hundreds of Black individuals waiting to board the next train. The headline said, "THE EXODUS." The *Defender* tapped into this new group of residents and helped them adjust to life in a big, new city. It answered their questions, encouraged them to better themselves, and stood up for them when they were poorly treated.

During World War I, the *Defender* generally supported the war effort. However, the newspaper repeatedly called for integration of the armed forces and for Black citizens to be appointed officers. The *Defender* said Black Americans deserved to prove themselves in combat and not just be relegated to positions of support. By 1918, the *Defender* had a circulation of more than one hundred thousand, making it the country's largest Black publication, and Abbott was a millionaire.

Following Abbott's death in 1940, his nephew John Sengstacke became the publisher. By this time, the *Defender* had begun devoting more attention to the arts, sports, music, and other subjects. Sengstacke played a role in encouraging the Roosevelt administration to allow Black reporters to cover the White House. He also developed a chain of Black newspapers in Detroit, Memphis, and Louisville.

The *Defender's* longtime rival was the *Pittsburgh Courier*, founded as a weekly in 1910 by a group of men who billed it as "Pittsburgh's Only Colored Newspaper." Robert Vann, who was an attorney in Pittsburgh, drew up the incorporation papers, for which he received shares of stock. He also wrote articles for the *Courier*. The newspaper struggled initially, and before the end of the year, the editor quit. Vann was offered the position and he accepted. Besides Vann, the *Courier's* staff included a reporter, sports editor, secretary, and errand boy. The newspaper was produced from a small office over a funeral home and then sent to a local printer.

Vann initially eschewed the sensationalistic practices of the *Defender* and some other Black newspapers. The newspaper published a series of articles by columnist George Schuyler based on his visit to every town and city with more than five thousand Black residents in thirteen Southern states. The series described the racial conditions in the communities and included biting satire. The *Courier* covered sports extensively. Starting in 1934, it reported on the rise of popular boxer Joe Louis, known as the "Brown Bomber," and continued doing so exhaustively until he became heavyweight champion of the world in 1937. Reporter William Nunn described Louis as "the answer to our prayers, the prayers of a race of people who are struggling through dense clouds of prejudice." By this point, the *Courier* was publishing four national editions and had become the most widely read Black newspaper in the country.

FOREIGN-LANGUAGE PRESS

The colossal wave of immigration at the end of the nineteenth century and the beginning of the twentieth century led to the founding of many new foreign-language publications. Between 1870 and 1920, an estimated 25 million new residents arrived in the United States, settling in ethnic communities across the country. Many spoke little or no English, so the mainstream US press was of no use for information about their new homeland. Next to the church and the school, ethnic publications were the most significant educational and social institution in immigrant communities. The publications helped immigrants adapt to life in a new country, preserved sociocultural heritage, and played a political role. Because they were aimed at a limited audience, most of the ethnic press had a small number of readers and struggled financially. However, that didn't stop hundreds of editors from launching foreign-language newspapers and magazines.

Newspapers and magazines were published in many languages, including French, Spanish, Italian, Polish, Scandinavian, Czech, Japanese, and Chinese. But German publications accounted for the largest number. The first German-language newspaper in America had been founded before the Revolutionary War, and by 1885 there were about 650 German newspapers and magazines. The center of the German-language press in the United State was Chicago, a city that teemed with immigrants, many from Germany. By the turn of the century, Chicago had three German daily newspapers and several other German publications. Some of the publications were founded by radical editors who had emigrated to the United States after anti-Socialist laws in Germany made it impossible for them to remain. The weekly *Der Vorbote* was founded in 1874, and five years later the daily *Arbeiter-Zeitung* was started. By this time, Chicago was becoming a major center of radical labor organizations. The union movement was strong in the city, even though a minority of workers were not union members.

Many workers at the time had to work long hours in order to keep their jobs. Unions fought for an eight-hour workday, and their efforts were fanned by radical German publications. On May Day of 1886, the *Arbeiter-Zeitung* proclaimed: "Bravely forward! The conflict has begun. . . . Capitalism conceals its tiger claws behind the ramparts of order. Workmen, let your watchword be: No Compromise!" Two days later, police attacked a group of striking workers, and the next night police marched into Haymarket Square to break up another protest. A bomb exploded, and more than seventy police and workers were killed. Chicago authorities arrested the protest leaders, including three editors.

Some foreign language continued to be published well into the twentieth century and beyond. The *Decorah-Posten* was one of the longest-running foreign language newspapers in Iowa and one of the largest Norwegian language newspapers in the United States. It was founded in 1874 in Decorah, Iowa, where large numbers of Norwegian immigrants began settling in the 1850s. The newspaper focused on local news as well as news from Norwegian communities across the United States, and the circulation grew to twenty thousand. It later absorbed other Norwegian newspapers before closing in 1972.

REPORTING WORLD WAR I

The Great War, or World War I as it came to be known, began in 1914 when a Serbian nationalist assassinated Archduke Franz Ferdinand, heir to the throne of the Austro-Hungarian empire. Austria-Hungary declared war on Serbia, and within a month the military alliances in Europe squared off against one another. On one side were Britain, France, Russia, and Japan, and on the other were Germany, Austria-Hungary, and much of the Middle East. President Woodrow Wilson initially declared America to be neutral. Subsequent events drew the United States into the war. In 1915, a German submarine sank the British liner *Lusitania*, killing more than one thousand passengers, including 124 Americans. In 1917, Germany stepped up its submarine warfare and sank several American merchant vessels. That same year, British spies intercepted and made public the so-called Zimmerman telegram, a message by the German foreign secretary calling on Mexico to join in a war against the United States and promising to help it recover the territory lost in the Mexican War. In April 1917, Wilson asked Congress for a declaration of war against Germany, saying, "The world must be made safe for democracy." Congress voted for war.

The US government believed it was necessary to sell a war being fought across the Atlantic Ocean to the public. It created a new federal office, the Committee on Public Information (CPI), headed by George Creel, a former journalist, which provided war news ready for publication in newspapers. The CPI launched the government's first daily newspaper, the *Official Bulletin*, which was distributed free to newspapers. It coordinated the distribution of war news from the army and navy, released lists of casualties, and published interviews with high-ranking military officials. The CPI hired photographers, advertising executives, and motion-picture producers to create war propaganda. It also produced a regular piece for publication titled "The Daily German Lie." In a report for the president after the war, Creel boasted, "There was no part of the great war machinery that we did not employ. The printed word, the spoken word, the motion picture, the poster, the signboard—all these were used in our campaign."

The government enacted new laws to prevent interference with military operations by discouraging insubordination or disloyalty. The Espionage Act of 1917 provided for prison sentences of up to twenty years and fines as high as $10,000 for making statements in violation of the act. Publications found in violation of the law could be withheld from the mail or have their second-class mail permits revoked. The next year, the Sedition Amendment expanded on the scope of the act, making it a crime to write or publish any "disloyal, profane, scurrilous or abusive language about the form of government of the United States, the Constitution, military or naval forces, the flag or the uniform, or to use language to bring those ideas or institutions into contempt or disrepute." Not surprisingly, German and Socialist publications were particularly targeted.

The Supreme Court upheld the Espionage Act in 1919 in one of its most significant rulings on free expression, *Schenck v. United States*. Charles Schenck, a leader of the Socialist Party, had sent fifteen thousand leaflets urging men who faced the draft to refuse to serve in the military. Schenck and his codefendants were convicted of violating the Espionage Act, and the Supreme Court upheld their convictions. Writing for a unanimous court, Justice Oliver Wendell Holmes Jr. said that freedom of expression was not absolute. "The character of every act depends on the circumstances in which it is done," Holmes wrote. "The most stringent protection of free speech would not protect a man in falsely shouting fire in a theatre and causing a panic." Holmes said Schenck was guilty of inciting readers of the leaflets to action against the government. "The question in every case," he continued, "is whether the words are used in such circumstances as to create a clear and present danger that they will bring about the substantive evils that Congress has a right to prevent." The ruling upended the unqualified language of the First Amendment and declared that the safety of the government during wartime trumped the right of citizens to speak out in protest.

During the war, American reporters seeking accreditation to report from the field had to swear "they would convey the truth to the people of the United States" and refrain from publishing information valuable to the enemy. They were required to post a bond that was subject to forfeiture for violating the accrediting rules. They also had to wear uniforms with the letter "C" on armbands designating them as correspondents. In all, only about thirty American reporters were accredited to report on the war. Dozens more were considered "visiting" correspondents and briefly reported on the fighting. Four journalists had their credentials suspended for violating rules.

Even with all the hurdles they had to overcome, American journalists provided some outstanding reporting of the war. Richard Harding Davis, perhaps the best-known American correspondent at the time, reported on the entrance of the German army into Brussels in 1914. He likened the marching troops to a "river of steel" and went on, "At the sight of the first few regiments of the enemy we were thrilled with interest. But when hour after hours passed and there was no halt, no breathing time, no open spaces in the ranks, the thing became uncanny, inhuman. . . . It held the mystery and menace of fog rolling toward you across the sea." *Chicago Tribune* reporter Floyd Gibbons wrote an eyewitness account of a German submarine sinking the British cruise liner *Laconia* in 1917. Later, he was hit by gunfire while crossing a field with American troops. He lost his left eye and was easily recognizable for the rest of his career by the eye patch that he wore. Peggy Hull, a reporter for the *El Paso* (Texas) *Morning Times*, became the first woman correspondent to receive accreditation from the War Department. She often wrote personal stories about soldiers, making her work popular with readers. Hull not only reported news from Europe but traveled to Serbia with the American expedition at the end of the war.

In general, however, readers of newspapers and magazines did not get an accurate picture of World War I. Americans did not learn about the horrific trench fighting or deadly gas attacks until after the war ended. The press was hobbled by the government's effort to promote the war effort, suppress any criticism, and censor virtually all news. Moreover, except in rare cases, editors capitulated. World War I was a conflict of unprecedented proportions, a total war. All resources were mobilized to achieve victory. It also required one of the greatest propaganda campaigns in history.

Henry Luce and New Magazines

World War I marked the end of the Progressive Era. Republican Warren G. Harding, campaigning on a "return to normalcy," won the election of 1920. The Eighteenth Amendment, banning alcoholic beverages, took effect the same year, along with the passing of the Nineteenth Amendment, granting women the right to vote. The decade that followed, known as the "Roaring '20s," was marked by a popular revolt against the moral rules of the nineteenth century. Speakeasies sold liquor in violation of Prohibition, jazz music became popular, and sexually liberated young women dressed as flappers. American businesses boomed and the stock market soared. Calvin Coolidge became president after Harding died of a heart attack in 1923, just two years into his term of office. "The chief business of the American people is business," Coolidge declared.

On March 3, 1923, Henry Luce and Brit Haden launched a new magazine, *Time*, that reflected the era in many ways. The two young men believed there was a market for a weekly magazine that summarized the news while also providing color and context. People too busy to read a daily newspaper could still keep up with the news with such a publication. Luce and Haden had met while staff members at the *Yale Daily News*. After graduating, they both worked briefly at daily newspapers before putting together a prospectus for their magazine and seeking investors. When they had raised $87,000, they decided to make a go of it. The magazine would be organized into departments: National Affairs, Foreign News, Arts, Sports, and People. Each issue would have about one hundred articles, none more than four hundred words in length. The working title for the magazine was "Fact," but they eventually settled on *Time* to reflect its dual purpose of chronicling the passage of time while saving readers' time.

The challenge for Luce and Haden was how to make old news look fresh. With no staff to do additional reporting, they had to use creative writing techniques to liven up the stories. Led by Haden, the staff created what became known as "Timestyle." Writers packed as much information as possible into stories, finding new ways to use words. Compound adjectives such as "snaggle-toothed" and "bandy-legged" described people. Haden encouraged writers to use vivid words ("whacked," "ogled," "bumbled," and "ousted"). Some of the words that *Time* used regularly—"kudos," "socialite," and "pundit," to name a few—became lasting parts of modern English. The approach struck a chord with readers, and circulation grew steadily. After just five years, *Time*'s revenue topped $1 million. Sadly, the hardworking and heavy-drinking Haden died suddenly in 1931. Borrowing money, Luce bought Haden's shares in the magazine and became the largest stockholder. Before he turned thirty-five, Luce was a millionaire.

With Haden's death, *Time* increasingly reflected the conservative political viewpoint of Luce. Although the magazine didn't publish editorials, his views often could be found in the news stories. As he once told a friend: "Listen, I don't pretend this is an objective magazine. It's an editorial magazine from the first page to the last, and whatever comes out has to reflect my view, and that's the way it is." Luce was fascinated by powerful men. Beginning in 1927, *Time* selected a "Man of the Year" every January. The first was aviator Charles Lindbergh. Other early winners included Walter Chrysler, Mahatma Gandhi, Franklin Roosevelt, and Joseph Stalin. Notably missing were women. During the magazine's first fifty years, only two women—the socialite Wallis Simpson and Queen Elizabeth II—received the honor of being "Women of the Year." In 1999, the title was changed to "Person of the Year," and since then, more women have been recognized.

The success of *Time* led Luce to start other magazines, including *Fortune, Sports Illustrated,* and *Life,* a weekly picture magazine. Luce had always been fascinated by photographs, and he wanted to bring together the world's best photographs in one place. Photographic technology had come a long way in the past five decades. Many news photographers used what was known as the press camera, which had a folding-bellows design and used sheet or roll film. However, photographers increasingly preferred the smaller thirty-five-millimeter camera, which was introduced by Leica in 1924. Various mass-circulation magazines were making extensive use of photographs, but no American publication was making pictures the principal subject. Luce wanted his magazine to take on serious issues, but at the same time not shy away from the frivolous.

Figure 5.2 *Time* Cover *Source:* William Oberhardt (1882–1958), public domain, via Wikimedia Commons.

He wanted it to be a magazine for everyone. Luce laid out his plans for *Life* in a prospectus:

> To see life; to see the world; to eyewitness great events; to watch the faces of the poor and the gestures of the proud, to see strange things—machines, armies, multitudes, shadows in the jungle and on the moon; to see man's work—his paintings, towers, and discoveries . . . to see and to take pleasure in seeing; to see and be amazed, to see and be instructed.

Life was launched in 1936, and it was an immediate hit. The press run of the first issue—466,000 copies—sold out. The cover featured a photograph of Fort Peck Dam in Montana taken by Margaret Bourke-White and was tied to a photo essay on the community of workers in the boomtown of Fort Peck. The first issue also contained a portrait of Brazil, an account of a French hunting party, a two-page spread of black widow spiders, and a full-page picture of a doctor in a delivery room holding a newborn baby. Readers loved it. By the end of 1937, *Life* had a circulation of 1.5 million—more than triple the first-year circulation of any magazine in American history.

Life's editors soon learned that buying photographs from suppliers such as the Associated Press couldn't meet the magazine's needs. They built their own staff of photographers that include Bourke-White, Alfred Eisenstaedt, Eugene Smith, and Gordon Parks. The enormous readership of the magazine helped *Life*'s photographers achieve national fame. *Life* popularized the photo essay, stories told primarily with pictures instead of words. One of the most widely acclaimed was the "Career Girl," an essay that chronicled the work and life of twenty-three-year-old Gwyned Filling. Photographed by Leonard McCombe, the twelve-page essay showed how smart and ambitious women like Filling were transforming the American workforce while, at the same time, trying to balance their professional and personal lives.

NEWSPAPER SUCCESS AND INTROSPECTION

In terms of financial success, newspaper publishers had many reasons to boast. The number of daily newspapers was reaching an all-time high, and the number of weekly newspapers was growing as well. The biggest cities had several daily newspapers; New York City had more than a dozen. Newspapers had become a big business, and publishers wanted to attract as many readers—and advertisers—as they could. Pursuing this goal, newspapers published a wider variety of news that was more appealing to readers.

At the same time, there were calls for more insightful and meaningful reporting by the daily press. Facts-only reporting remained the rule, but critics said readers needed help in understanding an increasingly complicated world that was still reeling from a shattering war and devastating depression. "Because the contemporary world is so complex and because the average man has neither the time nor the facilities to apply the proper tests to determine the significance of current events, mere reporting of the 'what' by newspapers is insufficient," Curtis McDougall, author of *Interpretative Reporting*, wrote in 1938. "The 'why' must be explained in terms of factual background and general principles which make the immediate understandable in terms of the general."

The nationally syndicated political columnist was a means of interpreting the news. News syndicates, which packaged material from writers for distribution and sale to newspapers, dated back to the nineteenth century. They had become a popular means of providing ready-made work that editors could drop into a hole in the newspaper. Syndicate material was especially popular with smaller newspapers that didn't have the same kind of in-house talent as their larger counterparts. Moreover, the syndication rates were tied to circulation figures, which made them affordable. William Randolph Hearst founded the Newspapers Feature Service and later the King Feature Syndicate to sell political commentary, advice columns, serial fiction, and cartoons to publications. The arrangement made many writers and artists household names with readers across the country.

Columnists expressing their perspective on issues gave newspapers a strong, visible voice. The 1930s and 1940s were a heyday for syndicated columnists as many newspapers regularly published several columnists each week. They provided publishers a diversity of opinion and helped newspapers examine key issues. As Philip Glende has written, "Editorial page editors could use columns to try to find that middle ground that appealing to a mass audience required, creating a de facto public sphere of sorts, albeit for a commercial purpose." Popular columnists such as Walter Lippmann, Dorothy Thompson, and others were published in more than one hundred newspapers each, reaching millions of readers. Publishers recognized the economic value of providing a variety of columnists because each appealed to different groups of readers, depending on their views.

Lippmann has been called one of the most influential Americans to never hold political office. His syndicated column, "Today and Tomorrow," was published in hundreds of newspapers for more than fifty years. Born into an affluent family, Lippmann attended Harvard, where he became a radical. He became a research assistant for the muckraker Lincoln Steffens and later joined the staff of a magazine that would be called the *New Republic*. During World War I, Lippmann was recruited to join a new intelligence unit that was creating propaganda to be dropped behind enemy lines to encourage German soldiers to desert or surrender. From the experience, Lippman came to believe how easy it was to manipulate public opinion. After the war, he published *Public Opinion*, which examined the differences between perception and reality. He argued that in the modern world most people get their information from mass communication (news, advertising, and entertainment). Moreover, most people did not make a real effort to inform themselves and, as a result, leaders were able to manipulate public opinion.

Lippmann became editor of the *New York World* and wrote many of the unsigned columns on the editorial page. In 1931, he joined the *New York Herald Tribune*, the newspaper founded in 1924 from the merger of the two pioneering penny publications. He wrote four columns a week, as well as several popular books. "Readers turned to Lippmann, not for solutions, but for dispassionate analysis," biographer Ronald Steel wrote. "He had a marvelous ability for simplifying the complex." At the end of World War II with many believing that the United States stood supreme

Figure 5.3 Walter Lippman *Source:* Library of Congress Prints and Photographs Division.

in the world, Lippmann warned about being overly ambitious with the new power. "Great as it is, American power is limited," he wrote. "Within its limits, it will be greater or less depending on the ends for which it is used."

Dorothy Thompson's column appeared in the *Herald Tribune* on alternating days as Lippmann. Their views on domestic and foreign affairs often differed, but she was just as popular with many readers. Thompson's father was a Methodist minister, and after graduating from Syracuse University, she worked for a women's suffrage organization for several years. In the 1920s, she traveled in Europe working as a freelance journalist for news organizations in the United States. Although she initially underestimated the rise of Adolf Hitler in Germany, she eventually became an outspoken critic of his fascist leadership. In 1934, the Nazi government expelled her from the country for her stories about Hitler's anti-Semitic campaign and other subjects.

Later that year, Thompson was offered her own column in the *Herald Tribune* that would be titled "On the Record." She provided a fresh political view of many issues, which she referred to as new brand of "liberal conservatism." She warned of what she saw as the seduction of the welfare state and was a consistent critic of President Franklin Roosevelt's New Deal. She continued writing about the dangers posed by Hitler and urged America to prepare for war. Thompson developed a number of fictional alter egos that let her discuss serious subjects in a whimsical manner. The best known was the "Grouse," a bad-tempered breakfast companion, who expressed his opinion on the issues of the day. By 1937, her column was syndicated by more than 150 newspapers in the United States. She also provided weekly commentary on NBC radio and wrote a monthly column for *Ladies' Home Journal*. Thompson was the inspiration for a 1942 hit movie, *Woman of the Year*, which starred Katharine Hepburn as a dazzling newspaper columnist who was a laughable failure as a wife.

DEVELOPMENT OF RADIO

Since the invention of the telegraph, inventors had been looking for a way to take things one step further: to send messages without the use of wires. Radio developed through an evolutionary process that reflected the social, political, economic, and technological environment of the times. Early radio development was pioneered by inventors largely working on their own. A young Italian, Guglielmo Marconi, invented a way to use radio waves to transmit signals carrying Morse code. Marconi moved to England, formed the Wireless Telegraph Signal Company in 1897, and a few years later launched an American division. Several years later, a faculty member at the University of Pittsburgh, Reginald Fessenden, demonstrated that radio signals could transmit more than Morse code. In 1906, he became the first to send music and voice over the air.

The shipping industry recognized the value of sending messages without wires. Accidents were a constant problem, and wireless telegraphy permitted ships in trouble to send messages requesting help. The sinking of the *Titanic* catapulted radio technology into national prominence. As the grand ocean liner made its maiden voyage across the Atlantic in 1912, it struck an iceberg. The crew immediately used the wireless equipment to send an emergency message calling for help. However, some ships in the vicinity had their radios tuned to other bands; others had turned them off for the night. The *Carpathia*, fifty-eight miles away, received the message but took two hours to arrive. By that time, many of the *Titanic*'s 1,522 passengers had drowned in the frigid waters. The tragic sinking of the *Titanic* attracted attention to the role that radio could play in ship safety. Congress quickly adopted legislation requiring that all American ships, and all those entering US ports, be equipped with radios. Moreover, they must be kept on at all times.

World War I also proved to be a boon to radio. When America entered the war, the Department of Defense effectively took control over radio development. Both the army and navy needed hundreds of new wireless sets for the war effort. To boost production, the government suspended all patent claims and poured millions of dollars into research. After the war, big companies moved into the fledgling radio industry. General Electronic bought Marconi's American division and transformed it into a new subsidiary, the Radio Corporation of America, or RCA. American Telephone and Telegraph (AT&T) and Westinghouse put together a cross-licensing deal that allowed them to share many radio patents. AT&T focused on manufacturing transmitters, while RCA and Westinghouse focused on manufacturing receiving sets.

Before and after the war, a few experimental radio stations had begun appearing around the country. The stations broadcast only one or two days a week and most did not last more than a few months. Although there is some disagreement, most agree that KDKA in Pittsburgh was the first commercial radio station to broadcast in the United States. KDKA had been started as an experimental station operated by a Westinghouse engineer, Dr. Frank Conrad. Beginning in 1919, he played music for two hours in the evenings and later supplemented the music with a smattering of news, including sports scores. In the summer of 1920, a Pittsburgh department store, Joseph Horne, began advertising amateur wireless with which to listen to Conrad's station. Westinghouse, which was selling amateur radio units, recognized that a commercial station would be a boon for its new radio manufacturing business and decided to build its own station in the city.

What is often considered to be the first commercial broadcast took place on November 2, 1920, when Conrad broadcast the presidential election returns from a 100-watt transmitter in a small building atop a Westinghouse manufacturing facility in Pittsburgh. In between the election results, Conrad broadcast music played from a hand-wound phonograph. Eager to know who was listening, Conrad at one point asked, "Will anyone hearing this broadcast please communicate with us, as we are anxious to know how far the broadcast is reaching and how it is being received?" Nightly broadcasts followed and soon Westinghouse boosted the station's power with a 500-watt transmitter. With no competition on the airwaves, KDKA often could be heard as far away as Washington, DC.

Up to this time, radio had largely been used simply for one person to reach another. In many respects it was the telegraph without wires and often called "wireless." However, radio had the ability to reach anyone

Figure 5.4 KDKA Source: Austin C. Lescarboura, public domain, via Wikmedia Commons.

with a receiver tuned in to a particular frequency. Casting a radio signal broadly through the airwaves became known as "broadcasting." For the first time, hundreds, thousands, and soon, millions of people could simultaneously hear the same thing. Mass communication was changed forever.

Not surprisingly, requests for radio licenses grew quickly. By 1922 more than five hundred stations were on the air. That same year, Secretary of Commerce Herbert Hoover convened the first of a series of annual national radio conferences. Hoover wanted to stimulate the radio business by bringing corporate leaders to Washington to discuss their needs. One of his first acts was to allocate the radio spectrum by reserving many of the most desirable frequencies to commercial broadcasters while assigning others to the military and amateurs. This was the spur that many investors needed to jump into radio. Within a few years, thousands of new radio stations were on the air.

In 1926, RCA launched the first radio network, the National Broadcasting Company, owned by RCA, General Electric, and Westinghouse. An estimated five million American homes already had radios; the potential market was four times that size. NBC executives put together a group of stations and supplied them with the same programming, produced in New York. The advantage for the affiliates was that each could collect advertising revenue, while letting NBC produce programming that would attract listeners. The inaugural broadcast by NBC aired on the evening of November 15, 1926, from the grand ballroom of the Waldorf-Astoria Hotel in New York City. The number of affiliates grew so quickly that NBC soon had to create two networks: NBC Red and NBC Blue.

The next year, Columbia Phonograph Corporation and another group joined forced to form a new network. Columbia wanted to use the network to sell more records, but the network struggled initially. William S. Paley, the son of a cigar magnate, used his inheritance to purchase the network and renamed it Columbia Broadcasting System, or CBS. Under Paley, the network's fortunes turned around, in part because of the acquisition of stations in many major cities. Other groups tried to create national radio networks, but the only one to have real success was the Mutual Broadcasting System. Founded in 1934, it was different from NBC and CBS in that it had no central ownership. Mutual was cooperatively owned by key stations, including WGN in Chicago, WOR in New York, WLW in Cincinnati, and WXYZ in Detroit. Mutual grew rapidly, but many of its stations were in smaller cities. It could never attract the big stations that already were affiliates of NBC or CBS.

The popularity of radio was posing a major problem in that many areas of the country radio signals were interfering with each other, making listening difficult or impossible. Some believed the government had to step in, but this presented a new issue: Did Congress have the right to regulate broadcasting? After all, the First Amendment to the Constitution guaranteed protection for free speech and a free press. Shouldn't the new medium of radio have the same Constitutional protection as newspapers and magazines? Led by Hoover, officials in the Commerce Department argued there were fundamental differences between radio and the press. Radio operated on the electronic magnetic spectrum, which was a unique public resource and belonged to the American people. Moreover, the spectrum was limited in size, or bandwidth. Not everyone who wanted to broadcast could do so, or there would be chaos. The government was thus able to make the convincing argument that regulation was needed, and broadcasting rules did not violate the Constitution.

The Radio Act of 1927 created a new federal regulatory agency, the Federal Radio Commission. One of its first acts was to revoke all current radio licenses. This forced stations to reapply and gave the commission time to create the administrative law that would govern broadcasting. The Radio Act required broadcasters to operate in the "public interest, convenience or necessity," and this remains the governing principle of electronic media regulation. When the commission began assigning licenses again, each assigned the holder a particular frequency and signal strength. Moreover, the number of licenses was limited. Within a few years, however, it became clear that the Radio Act couldn't adequately deal with the demand for new stations, as well as the many technological and regulatory changes taking place. The Communications Act of 1934 carried forward many of the principles of the Radio Act. However, it expanded the role of the commission—renamed the Federal Communications

Commission—to include oversight of telephone, telegraph, and a new broadcasting technology under development, television.

RADIO NEWS

In the 1930s, the radio was seemingly everywhere in America. When the decade began, about 65 percent of households had a radio, and the number continued to grow. No longer a luxury, the radio had become a family necessity. As the economic depression of the 1930s grew worse, people relied on the radio for information and entertainment. President Roosevelt delivered regular "Fireside Chats," assuring Americans that his administration was doing everything possible to right the country. Most early radio programming was music, either prerecorded or live. A great deal was classical, and some networks even had their own orchestras. Country music was another favorite. One of the most popular early shows was the *Grand Ole Opry*, a barn dance broadcast live by WSM in Nashville, Tennessee, that became a Saturday night tradition for millions of Americans. Dramas and comedies were more expensive and difficult for the networks to produce, but radio audiences loved them. *Amos 'n' Andy* attracted so many listeners that in some places, theaters stopped showing movies when the show was on the air.

Even though the first commercial radio broadcast was of a news event, news on radio was slow to develop. Most stations did not have their own reporters and editors, so any news that listeners heard generally came from announcers simply reading newspaper stories over the air. Some stations tried their hand with on-the-scene coverage of big news events. In 1923, WRC in Washington, DC, broadcast the memorial service of President Harding. Two years later, WGN broadcast the entire trial of J. T. Scopes, who was accused of breaking the law by teaching evolution in his Tennessee high school biology class. The long-distance loops cost the station $1,000 a day, a great deal of money at the time. WGN thought the cost was worth it because Illinois was the home of Clarence Darrow, the popular attorney who was defending Scopes.

Standing in the way of more news on the radio were newspaper owners, who recognized the threat that the new medium posed to their monopoly on daily news. In 1922, newspaper publishers ordered the Associated Press and its member newspapers to stop letting radio announcers read their stories on the air. Radio stations turned to other news agencies, such as the United Press. They also continued covering the news, regularly scooping newspapers on major stories, such as the report that Charles Lindberg had successfully flown solo across the Atlantic Ocean. The conflict grew for years until, in 1933, representatives of publishers, broadcasters, and news agencies met at the Biltmore Hotel in New York. That meeting resulted in an agreement that allowed the radio networks to create a radio bureau that would provide limited news to radio. CBS and NBC agreed to two newscasts a day, each five minutes long. One newscast had to be broadcast in the morning after 9:30 a.m. and in the evening after 9:00 p.m. Additionally, no single news story on radio could be longer than thirty words, and every radio newscast had to sign off encouraging listeners to check their local papers for the latest news.

In effect, news executives agreed to split up the audience, with newspapers concentrating on news and radio on entertainment. The agreement lasted on paper for the next several years, but stations not affiliated with a major network routinely ignored it. Many stations set up their own news teams and broadcast at various times. Moreover, broadcasters refined how they presented the news, with the networks using commentators to interpret events. Analysts such as Lowell Thomas, Walter Winchell, and H. V. Kaltenborn proved to be popular with listeners. Moreover, newspaper companies, many of which already owned radio stations, continued to view radio as lucrative. The number of newspaper-owned or affiliated stations more than doubled between 1933 and 1938.

During this time, the economic crisis in Europe led to the rise of Socialist parties in Germany and Italy, led by Adolf Hitler and Benito Mussolini. Radio commentators in Europe helped keep listeners apprised of the news. NBC initially had the strongest news operation. However, in 1937, CBS hired Edward R. Murrow to be its European director. The twenty-seven-year-old Murrow had no journalism experience, but he put together a talented team of reporters including William Shirer. Soon after Hitler's Nazi troops invaded Austria the following year, Murrow arranged the first radio news roundup that linked CBS correspondents and other journalists in European capitals, who could discuss the news situation in each country. The roundup technique, which required broadcasting feats never used before, became a staple of radio during the war. By 1940, all the networks were regularly broadcasting from Berlin, Rome, Paris, and London.

Murrow made a name for himself with his broadcasts during Germany's bombing of London in 1940 and 1941. Bravely standing on rooftops with bombs dropping in the background, he always began his broadcasts with the dramatic words, "This is London," and then went on to vividly describe the extraordinary destruction that the city bravely endured. Millions of Americans tuned in to listen to Murrow's riveting broadcasts, and he became one of the best-known voices on radio.

In the midst of the tensions in Europe, a radio drama on the evening of October 30, 1938, demonstrated how popular the medium had become. An estimated six million Americans tuned into CBS's *Mercury Theatre on the Air* and got a Halloween trick with the broadcast of H. G. Wells's science fiction novel *War of the Worlds*. Orson Welles and the cast cleverly used popular radio techniques, such as breaking into live programing for news bulletins, to fool many listeners into thinking that the country was under attack from Martians. At the beginning of the broadcast, Welles announced that the drama was a fictional account, but many listeners tuned in late and didn't recognize that it was just made up. Some frightened listeners panicked but probably not as many as news accounts initially reported. Nonetheless, the broadcast showed the remarkable ability of radio to influence views.

REPORTING WORLD WAR II

Many believed that the Committee on Public Information had gone too far in muzzling the press during World War I. That included President Franklin D. Roosevelt, who had served as assistant secretary of the navy. When the United States joined World War II after the Japanese attacked Pearl Harbor on December 7, 1941, he didn't want to establish another federal agency that directed information, censorship, and propaganda. Roosevelt also didn't seek legislation imposing prior restraint by the government. Only six publications had their second-class mail rates revoked, compared to more than one hundred during World War I.

The government created the Office of Censorship, which supervised official censorship in war zones and voluntary censorship of the media at home. Byron Price, a former reporter and the executive editor of the Associated Press, supervised the office. Price avoided heavy-handed censorship and encouraged journalists to censor themselves. He set up a Press Division and a Broadcasting Division, staffing both with journalists who understood what the news media needed. Consulting with the military, his staff published a list of topics that could aid the enemy: movement of troops, ships and planes; information about fortifications and factories; and sensitive maps and photographs. The military revived its newspaper for soldiers and sailors, *Stars and Stripes*. One of its most popular features was "Willy and Joe," a cartoon drawn by Bill Mauldin. Willy and Joe epitomized the foot soldiers who did the heavy fighting during the war.

The Black press had become increasingly critical of the military because of the discrimination that African American soldiers and sailors endured. Black Americans were generally assigned menial duties in the armed services instead of being given combat assignments. The FBI investigated Black publications for the criticism, but no editors were charged with sedition. Nonetheless, publishers recognized they had to walk a fine line between expressing condemnation for what Black individuals faced in the military and being disloyal during a national crisis.

A Black cafeteria worker at a Cessna Aircraft plant had an ingenious solution. In a letter to the *Pittsburgh Courier*, James G. Thompson wrote that while Black Americans should "keep defense and victory in the forefront" but also should not "lose sight of our fight for true democracy at home." He went on, "Let us colored Americans adopt the double VV for a double victory. The first V for victory over our enemies from without, the second V for victory over our enemies from within." The *Courier* soon launched a Double V campaign that featured smiling readers making two Vs with their fingers. The wildly popular campaign spread to feature celebrities, both Black and white.

There were few violations of censorship rules by journalists because the overwhelming majority patriotically believed that World War II must be fought. Unlike in World War I, it was clear that the United States had enemies that had attacked or threatened the country. "We edited ourselves much more than we were edited," wrote John Steinbeck, who reported from Europe. "There was a general feeling that unless the home front was carefully protected from the whole account of what war was like, it might panic." When Lieutenant General George S. Patton slapped two shell-shocked soldiers in a military hospital in 1943, the story quickly spread among the press corps but was not published for three months. The story saw print only when columnist Drew Pearson learned about the incident and wrote about it.

Perhaps the most difficult story to keep secret was the news of the atomic research being conducted by the government. Stories occasionally ran about the research, but they were not damaging. The military even drafted *New York Times* science writer William L. Laurence to chronicle the "Manhattan Project," as the project was known, and keep it a secret. He wrote several press releases to help the military lie about its test explosion in New Mexico. In return, Laurence was allowed to observe the dropping of the first atomic bomb on Nagasaki, Japan, and given access to write follow-up stories on the cataclysmic event.

More than 1,500 American journalists covered World War II. They included reporters from the wire services, daily newspapers, weekly magazines, and the radio networks. For the first time, a sizable number of the correspondents were women. Two of these women—Sigrid Schultz and Anne O'Hare McCormick—gained national reputations for their reporting abroad.

Schultz was hired by the *Chicago Tribune* in 1919, and within seven years became bureau chief in Berlin. She extensively covered the rise and fall of Hitler and interviewed the dictator several times. She became a magazine war correspondent in 1944, covering Normandy, Buchenwald, and the Nuremberg War Trials. McCormick, who worked for the *New York Times*, also interviewed famous dictators including Hitler, Mussolini, and Stalin. Her reporting earned her a Pulitzer Prize in 1937. Carolyn Edy found at least 250 individual women who worked as war correspondents during this period, although they were not formally recognized as a group until 1944, a year before the war ended.

Undoubtedly, the best-known newspaper journalist during the war was Ernie Pyle. Pyle, who grew up on a farm in Indiana, was already a popular newspaper columnist when the war began. He was a roving correspondent for the Scripps Howard chain, crisscrossing the country to write about everyday Americans. Pyle took the same approach as a war correspondent. He didn't want to merely send back battlefield reports. He wanted to experience the war as the common soldier did, so he traveled and lived with the troops, writing about their experiences living in fox-holes, eating bad food, and confronting death.

Pyle grew to have tremendous respect for the GIs, as he wrote in one column: "I love the infantry because they are the underdogs. They are the mud-rain-frost-and-wind boys. They have no comforts, and they even learn to live without the necessities. And in the end they are the guys that wars can't be won without." His best-known column told the story of how soldiers in the one division reacted to the death of their captain, Henry Waskow, near San Pietro, Italy. Pyle described the moving scene of the soldiers tenderly saying their goodbyes. Hundreds of newspapers printed the story, magazines published excerpts, and radio hosts read it on the air.

Pyle spent time in North Africa, Europe, and, finally, the Pacific. In 1945, he was killed by a machine gunner on a tiny island near Okinawa. In his pocket was part of a column he was writing about the unnatural sight of dead men scattered about. President Harry Truman personally announced Pyle's death to the nation and commended his contribution as a war correspondent. As biographer James Tobin has written, "As a practitioner of the craft of journalism, Pyle was perhaps without peer. After him, no war correspondent could pretend to have gotten the real story without having moved extensively among the front-line soldiers who actually fought."

Photographers also had unprecedented access to the battlefield during the war. They accompanied troops on the ground and flew on missions with the air corps. They landed with the troops at Normandy and were present when concentration camps such as Buchenwald were liberated. With its large format and giant circulation, *Life* provided the ideal platform for the telling photos of Bourke-White, Robert Capa,

George Strock, and others. During the first two years of the war, censorship regulations prevented the publishing of news photos showing dead soldiers. News organizations argued that pictures should show the reality of the war, and in mid-1943 the government reversed its policy. Perhaps the most famous photo showing casualties was made by Strock on a beach in New Guinea. It showed three dead US soldiers lying in the sand where they were shot by the Japanese. Their faces and wounds are not visible, but the photograph was still poignant and captured the terrible cost of the war.

The war presented numerous problems for editors in simply getting their publications into the hands of readers. Fuel rationing forced many newspapers to cut motor routes for delivery. Thousands of men and women left their jobs at publications to serve in the military. Many newsrooms operated with skeletal staffs. Newsprint rationing meant that there was less paper on which to publish. Newspapers and magazines took creative steps to cut the amount of paper used. After publishing as a broadsheet for eighty-three years, the *Rocky Mountain News* in 1942 became a tabloid.

DEVELOPMENT OF TELEVISION

Like radio, television was invented over several decades by individuals in the United States and abroad. Philo T. Farnsworth, who had developed an interest in electronics while still in high school, transmitted an image of a simple straight line from his laboratory on September 7, 1927. With backing from two philanthropists, he designed and built the world's first all-electronic television system a year later. Farnsworth went on to file many patents for television. A surprised RCA, which had its own scientists working on the development of television, tried to acquire his patents. Farnsworth initially refused but eventually sold them, allowing RCA to complete their television system.

The development of television moved slowly in the next decade as the FCC grappled with technical and regulatory standards. World War II interrupted the little progress being made, and it was not until after the war that television was widely introduced. CBS and NBC had the organizational structure in place to develop television, but they moved slowly, initially believing it would hurt the popularity of radio. However, when it became clear that people were becoming enamored with the wonder of the medium—sales exploded from 179,000 in 1947 to a million the next year—the networks quickly built television networks. They used the model of radio affiliates, with some stations owned and operated by the networks and other stations under contract. Not surprisingly, radio and newspaper owners were among the first owners of many local television stations. In Minneapolis–St. Paul, radio station owner Stanley E. Hubbard launched KSTP-TV in April 1948. Three months later, the owners of the *Minneapolis Tribune* and the *St. Paul Pioneer Press* jointly founded WTCN-TV (Twin Cities newspapers).

Television proved popular with viewers initially mostly because of its entertainment programming. Many of radio's most popular shows simply moved from radio to television. A 1944 NBC advertisement for "Fibber McGee and Molly" told consumers that well-liked radio programs "could become real visual experiences . . . experiences for you to watch as well as hear." As with radio, a single corporation often sponsored all advertising on a show. The name of the sponsoring company often was incorporated into the name of the television show. That meant viewers could watch programs such as the *Kraft Television Theatre* or Palmolive's *Days of Our Lives*.

News was slower to develop on television. Various types of news and public affairs aired on experimental television stations in the 1930s. Starting in 1941, CBS and NBC broadcast limited news programs, but they ended after America entered the war because of a lack of equipment and manpower. In 1944, the networks began offering news programming on a limited basis. Many of the radio journalism pioneers moved into television news reluctantly. "We felt it was kind of unmanly to go on TV and perform, just as it was in an earlier era somehow unmanly for newspapermen to go on radio," recalled Howard K. Smith of CBS.

With no experience to guide them, the journalists based their plans on what they had been doing in radio. So when Murrow and his colleagues at CBS made plans to cover the 1948 political conventions, they developed a strategy based on their experiences covering World War II. Television news required a far bigger team of journalists to report the news. Whereas a radio reporter could cover most stories by himself simply using a recorder, television news required a reporter, a cameraman, and a soundman to get the story in the field, as well as a producer and editor to put it together in the studio.

CBS aired the first daily newscast in 1948. Douglas Edwards read the news from a desk at the network's news headquarters in New York City. Don Hewitt, who had worked for a newsreel company, produced the fifteen-minute newscast. NBC soon followed with its own fifteen-minute newscast, *Camel News Caravan*. Sponsored by the R. J. Reynolds Tobacco Company, maker of Camel cigarettes, the newscast was anchored by John Cameron Swayze, who was seated at a desk with a map of the world behind him. With its lucrative sponsorship paying for equipment, salaries and rent, R. J. Reynolds wanted to make sure that cigarettes were shown as often as possible on the newscast. At the beginning of the show, Swayze invited viewers to "Sit back, light up a Camel, and enjoy the news."

Television news certainly had its limitations. At fifteen minutes, the evening newscasts couldn't air in-depth stories and generally gave viewers little more than the headlines. The emphasis on the visual meant that important stories often took a back seat to events that provided good pictures. In some cases, television news resembled entertainment more than journalism. NBC's morning show, *Today*, was part newscast and part variety show. One of its stars was a chimpanzee named J. Fred Muggs.

CBS pioneered much of the early television news programming. *See It Now* premiered in 1951 as a blend of news roundup and film documentary. It was hosted by Murrow, who at the beginning of the inaugural show said, "This is an old team, trying to learn a new trade." CBS proudly showed off its new technology, simultaneously broadcasting live pictures of the Atlantic and Pacific oceans. Murrow also hosted another new program, *Person to Person*, a thirty-minute interview show that went on the air in 1953. Murrow often conducted interviews from the studio with the guests speaking from their homes. Early guests included President Dwight Eisenhower and his wife Mamie. *CBS Reports*, which aired occasionally starting in 1959, was a sixty-minute documentary that tackled subjects in depth. Perhaps the best-known *CBS Reports* broadcast

Figure 5.5 Watching TV *Source:* Evert F. Baumgardner, public domain, via Wikimedia Commons.

was "Harvest of Shame," which introduced many Americans to the great hardships that migrant workers in the United States faced.

The *Huntley-Brinkley Report*, which premiered on NBC in 1956, suffered poor ratings initially but overcame them to become the most popular nightly news show for many years. Journalists David Brinkley and Chet Huntley had been paired to cover the 1956 political conventions. The two men worked so well together that NBC tapped them to replace Swayze on the evening newscast. In an unusual arrangement for the time, Brinkley broadcast from Washington, DC, and Huntley from New York City. To provide cues for switching between the two men, they used each other's first names, which also gave viewers the sense they worked together closely. Their sign-off for the broadcast—"Good night, David"; "Good night, Chet"; "And good night for NBC News"—soon became part of the lexicon. Huntley and Brinkley anchored the newscast for the next fourteen years.

By the early 1960s, television was the primary source of news for most Americans. CBS and ABC expanded their evening newscasts to thirty minutes in 1963. That same year the networks provided nonstop coverage of the shocking assassination of President John F. Kennedy during a motorcade in Dallas, Texas. All three networks broke into daytime programming with news bulletins about the shocking news that the popular young president had been shot with his wife seated by him in the open-top car. They later announced the news that Kennedy had died. CBS anchor Walter Cronkite, seated at his desk in the newsroom, struggled to maintain his composure while reading the bulletin.

Two days later, the networks showed the departure of the president's casket from the White House to the Capitol. NBC switched to the Dallas police headquarters where Lee Harvey Oswald, the suspect in the assassination, was being moved. A man wearing a hat, later identified as nightclub owner Jack Ruby, pushed toward Oswald and shot him point-blank in the stomach. NBC correspondent Tom Petit witnessed what happened and shouted, "He's been shot. Lee Oswald has been shot." NBC showed the shooting live, and within minutes the other networks replayed it. At the time, about 40 percent of American households with television sets were watching the news coverage. As word of what happened spread across the country, the number doubled.

An estimated nine in ten Americans watched President Kennedy's funeral procession to Arlington National Cemetery, moved by sights such as the flag-draped caisson and riderless horse, as well as the loving salute by the president's five-year-old son. The network news staffs had worked virtually around the clock for four days to cover the assassination and funeral. Observers praised the networks for the dedication, resourcefulness, and sensitivity they showed in reporting a story that had captivated the country. Television was becoming a maturing medium, one that understood its role in the expanding news scene. As NBC President Reuven Frank wrote, "The highest power of television is not in the transmission of information, but in the transmission of experience."

CHAPTER 6

The Alternative Press

1950 to 1985

DURING THE THREE DECADES AFTER WORLD WAR II, THE PRESS reported on the sweeping changes roiling American society. The lessons learned in covering McCarthyism, the Civil Rights Movement, the Vietnam War, the Pentagon Papers, and Watergate prompted many news organizations to reconsider objectivity as a sacrosanct principle of journalism. The press became increasingly aggressive and adversarial in its reporting, often casting a more critical eye on the country's leaders and institutions.

The conflicts that marked the 1960s and 1970s led some journalists to conclude that alternative methods were needed to report the news in a more complicated world. These groundbreaking journalists chose to investigate deeply in a search for the truth. At the same time, writing in the news media changed in another way. A group of creative and talented journalists adopted some of the practices of fiction writers, including using the first-person, to report and write stories. New publications appeared that became popular with readers of what became known as the "New Journalism."

Public broadcasting gained a foothold in the United States for the first time, thanks to the support of the federal government and citizens who wanted an alternative to commercial broadcasting. Public radio and television started innovative news programs that gained a reputation for excellence. And the first all-news network debuted, providing another option to the three television networks. Cable News Network, better known as CNN, proved there was a market for news all the time.

MCCARTHYISM AND THE PRESS

After the end of World War II, the United States and the Soviet Union engaged in more than four decades of conflict known as the Cold War. In the early years, Congress began investigating alleged communist sympathizers from all walks of life. The House Un-American Activities Committee (HUAC) led the search for "Reds," as those considered to be disloyal Americans were sometimes known. Several high-profile legal cases helped to fuel the anticommunist hysteria. Alger Hiss, a State Department official, was charged with trying to funnel secret government documents to the Soviet Union. He was convicted of perjury and sentenced to five years in prison. Many in the news media supported the hunt for communists in the United States and editorialized about the need to defeat the Soviet Union in the Cold War.

In early 1950, Senator Joseph McCarthy of Wisconsin gave a speech claiming that he had a list of 205 people working in the US State Department who were known to federal officials as being members of the Communist Party. Over the next several weeks, he repeated the claims and argued that the "enemies from within" posed a grave threat to the security of the country. McCarthy went on to hold a series of high-profile Senate hearings, issuing subpoenas for alleged communists and putting them through withering questioning. The interrogation by McCarthy and the committee often was unfair; in one case, a State Department official, Reed Harris, was grilled about something he had written twenty years earlier.

McCarthy's rise was initially aided in some respects by the way journalists reported the news of his charges. By this time, objectivity had become one of the highest ideals of journalists. In most cases, reporters were instructed to simply report what they had seen or been told. They were also instructed to get both sides of a story, but more often than not, the most sensational aspect got the highest billing. For a time, McCarthy was able to take advantage of this kind of reporting to gain wide publicity for his charges and escape criticism. Without credible evidence, he would make charges about alleged communists working in the federal government and then move on to make new charges. The wire services were most vulnerable to his strategy because they often lacked the time to verify the accusations, or even to get a response from the accused, before reporting them.

However, some journalists and news organizations viewed McCarthy with a critical eye. One of his home-state newspapers, the *Milwaukee Journal*, reported as a lie McCarthy's claim that he had been a heroic air crewman during World War II. The *New York Post* published a multipart series that reported the senator's source of power. The *Washington Post*, on its editorial page, repeatedly criticized McCarthy's tactics, and its editorial cartoonist, Herbert Block (better known as "Herblock"), drew devastating illustrations of the senator as an immoral bully. One Herblock cartoon, depicting McCarthy with a barrel of tar, is credited with popularizing the term "McCarthyism" as shorthand for character assassination in the name of anti-communism.

At CBS, Edward R. Murrow and director Fred Friendly began reviewing the film of McCarthy's hearings. They decided to use their show, *See It Now*, to call into question the senator and his unscrupulous methods. On March 8, 1954, Murrow began the program saying, "Good evening, tonight *See It Now* devotes its entire half-hour to a report on Senator Joseph McCarthy, told mainly in his own words and pictures." Film segments showed the senator's bullying tactics, with Murrow occasionally commenting on a point McCarthy made. The show closed with Murrow expressing the view that the senator was a political opportunist who was taking advantage of people's fear of communism. Murrow concluded:

> We must not confuse dissent with disloyalty. We must remember always that accusation is not proof, and that conviction depends upon evidence and due process of law. . . .
>
> The actions of the junior senator from Wisconsin have caused alarm and dismay amongst our allies abroad and given considerable comfort

to our enemies. And whose fault is that? Not really his. He didn't create this situation of fear; he merely exploited it, and rather successfully.

Murrow gave McCarthy the opportunity to respond on the air and he took the newsman up on the offer. The senator said Murrow and Friendly were part of the "jackal pack which is always found at the throat of anyone who dares to expose individual communist and traitors." Undeterred by Murrow's report, the senator went on to investigate alleged communists in the Army. In hearings televised to the nation by ABC in the spring and summer of 1954, McCarthy once again bullied witnesses, including Army Secretary Robert Stevens. It led to a memorable exchange in which the secretary's lead attorney, Joseph Welch, pointedly asked McCarthy, "Have you no sense of decency?" By that time, McCarthy's colleagues had seen enough. They eventually voted to censure him.

The rise of "McCarthyism" led some news organizations to look more closely at the actions of others in positions of authority. Edwin Hoyt, the editor of the *Denver Post*, issued a two-page memo to his staff in 1953 instructing them that they needed to carefully scrutinize "reckless or impulsive officials." It barred reporters from simply parroting officials without considering the truth of what they said, thereby preventing the officials from using the press to manipulate an unknowing public. Hoyt's memo was distributed to newsrooms across the country.

REPORTING CIVIL RIGHTS STRUGGLE

The modern Civil Rights Movement was born in the 1950s as Black and white supporters worked to achieve the equal rights that African Americans had long been denied in the United States. In many respects, the movement began with the 1954 Supreme Court decision outlawing school segregation and the Montgomery, Alabama, bus boycott the following year. Battles over integrating public schools and transportation followed. African Americans protested their treatment and conducted boycotts and sit-ins, sometimes joined by white supporters. The demonstrations culminated with the 1963 March on Washington, DC, at which Martin Luther King Jr. delivered his "I have a dream" speech. The next year, Congress passed the Civil Rights Act of 1964, which outlawed segregation in public facilities, and it was signed into law by President Lyndon Johnson.

The Black press provided some of the best initial reporting of the Civil Rights Movement, even though most publications had been forced to retrench after World War II. The circulation of the *Pittsburgh Courier*, which had reached a high of 348,000 in 1948, was about half that by 1955. The *Chicago Defender* beat other publications in reporting the 1955 murder of Emmett Till in the Mississippi Delta and the subsequent trial of two white men, including the husband of a woman Till had supposedly flirted with. The fourteen-year-old Till, who lived in Chicago, was visiting his mother's uncle in Mississippi when he was beaten, shot in the head, and tossed into a river with a cotton gin fan tied to his neck. The *Defender* poured its limited resources into extensively covering what soon became a national story, especially when the two men accused of killing Till went on trial. More than one hundred reporters from across the country covered the trial, which ended in the acquittal of the men.

For the Southern press, reporting and editorializing about the Civil Rights Movement was a defining moment. Much of the news media in the region covered the story in a cursory fashion for fear of angering readers and advertisers. For the most part, the press of the South "never got hold of the whole story in front of them," Gene Roberts and Hank Klibanoff wrote in the *Race Beat*. "They had no sense of depth of feeling on either side of the racial divide . . . [and] frequently misjudged the commitment and motives of leaders on both sides." However, the best news organizations covered the story aggressively, especially when it happened in their backyards. In Arkansas, where the governor called out the National Guard to block nine Black students from desegregating Little Rock's Central High School in 1957, the *Arkansas Gazette* poured all its resources into the story. On the *Gazette's* editorial page, editor Harry Ashmore forcefully and courageously criticized the governor. As a result, the newspapers lost readers and advertisers.

Editorially, most newspapers in the South opposed the integration of schools and other public facilities. Two of the most outspoken were the *Richmond Times Leader* and its editor, James Kilpatrick, and the *Jackson* (Mississippi) *Daily News* and its editor, Jimmy Ward. Some Southern journalists, however, were not afraid to speak out. Hazel Brannon Smith, the editor of the tiny *Lexington* (Mississippi) *Advertiser*, used her newspaper to oppose the White Citizens' Council, organized to resist integration in the South. Opponents boycotted her newspapers and burned a cross in her lawn. Another fearless editor was Hodding Carter Jr., the editor of the *Delta Democrat-Times* in Greenville, Mississippi. A racial moderate, he was nonetheless critical of the discrimination that Black Southerners faced. When Carter received the Pulitzer Prize for editorial writing, among the editorials cited for the award was one criticizing plans to erect an honor roll for war veterans that left off the names of Black veterans. Carter later described the plight of many journalists in the South like himself:

> It's not hard to sit . . . in New York and say what's wrong with the South. It is hard to do it as an ordinary Southerner. You've got two strikes on you to start. Your fellow white Southerners hate you for it. You're a scalawag . . . in their eyes. Your Northern reformers derided you for not going far enough. And you're suspected by Negroes everywhere because you're Southern and white.

The national media also covered the Civil Rights Movement. The *New York Times*, *Boston Globe*, *Life*, *Time*, and other publications dispatched reporters and photographers to the South to cover the stories. But television news had the greatest impact in riveting national attention to the struggle. In many respects, the Civil Rights Movement was the first major television news story. Television showed how civil rights protesters used nonviolence to press their cases and, when clashes occurred, it was usually police and other white people who caused the violence. Some of the most moving film came from Birmingham, where the police used fire hoses and German shepherds in 1963 to subdue young protesters. NBC produced a three-hour special: *The American Revolution of '63*. Sponsors refused to advertise on the show, fearing segregationists would boycott their products, but NBC did not buckle to the pressure. Journalists who covered the civil rights activities were sometimes victims of violence.

Richard Valeriani of NBC News was beaten by white segregationists who also sprayed his crew's camera lens with paint.

During the Civil Rights Movement, a historic Supreme Court ruling gave journalists the room to report on the performance of public officials. It originated in an unlikely way. In 1960, a group of civil rights activists purchased a full-page advertisement in the *New York Times* decrying the "unprecedented wave of terror" in Montgomery, Alabama, against protesters including Reverend King. The ad alleged "grave conduct" by Montgomery city officials. Although neither he nor any official was named in the ad, L. B. Sullivan, the police commissioner of Montgomery, Alabama, sued the *Times*, claiming that newspapers had published damaging falsehoods about him. The advertisement, in fact, contained several false statements, some of them minor and some more serious. The case went to the circuit court in Alabama, where Sullivan was awarded $500,000 in damages. Afterward, other public officials in the South filed libel suits against various news media.

The Sullivan case eventually made its way to the US Supreme Court, and on March 9, 1964, the justices voted unanimously to reverse the Alabama court. Public officials who sought office must be willing to take criticism, the court ruled. To win a libel suit, public officials must not just prove that the published material was false and defamatory. They must meet a higher burden of proof and show that the material in dispute was published with the knowledge it was false or published with "reckless disregard" for the truth. Writing for the court, Justice William Brennan Jr. said that "debate on public issues should be uninhibited, robust, and wide-open, and that it may well include vehement, caustic, and sometimes unpleasantly sharp attacks on government and public officials." The Sullivan ruling meant that public officials would have a more difficult time winning libel lawsuits. It allowed the press to report the news aggressively but not recklessly.

Black journalists provided two of the most memorable news accounts of the assasination and funeral of Reverend King, certainly one of the most important stories of 1968. Earl Caldwell was just the second Black journalist at the *New York Times*. He had grown up in rural Pennsylvania and studied business at the University of Buffalo. But Caldwell wanted to be a writer, and he moved from one newspaper to another, often breaking the race barrier in the newsrooms. In the spring of 1968, Caldwell traveled to Memphis, Tennessee, to cover a strike by the city's sanitation workers for the *Times*. King spoke at a rally supporting the strikers and afterward was staying at the Lorraine Motel. Caldwell was the only journalist at the scene when King was hit by bullet fire as he was standing on an outside balcony talking to friends. He immediately called the newsroom and dictated the shocking event he witnessed.

As a photographer for *Ebony* magazine, Moneta Sleet Jr. had been covering King for more than ten years, oftening accompanying him on marches in the South. Sleet was assigned to cover King's funeral at the Ebenezer Baptist Church in Atlanta. A small pool of photographers was selected to take pictures of the service. However, when King's widow noticed that no Black photographers were in the pool, she insisted that Sleet be allowed in the church and given a good vantage point. He took advantage of his position to photograph a mourning Coretta King sitting in the pew with her five-year-old daughter laying across her lap and staring poignantly at the camera. The powerful image captured the tragedy of King's assassination and the Associated Press distributed it to newspapers around the world. For his work, Sleet became the first Black journalist to win a Pulitzer Prize.

Paradoxically, the Civil Rights Movement hurt the Black press. Mainstream publications began hiring African American reporters to cover the news of Black communities, so the Black press lost many of its top journalists. The increased attention to news of African American communities, in turn, led Black Americans to begin buying mainstream newspapers, so Black publications lost circulation. During the next three decades, many Black newspapers cut back and or closed, but some of the largest Black newspapers managed to hang on. One was the *Defender*, whose best-known reporter was Ethel Payne. A Chicago native, she began working at the newspaper in the early 1950s and eventually took over the *Defender*'s one-person bureau in Washington, DC. Payne covered the Montgomery bus boycott and the integration of the University of Alabama, all the while facing racism herself. When traveling in the

South covering stories, she could not find hotels to accommodate her and often had to stay in private homes.

Payne was not afraid to ask tough questions. In the midst of the uproar over the Supreme Court's 1954 *Brown v. Board of Education* decision, she asked President Dwight Eisenhower whether his administration supported further integration. Eisenhower considered the question unreasonable. Payne later traveled to Vietnam to write about the Black troops who made up a large part of US Army contingent in the country. While working on the CBS program *Spectrum* from 1972 to 1978, she also became the first Black female radio and television commentator. Payne was, unapologetically, an advocate for Black Americans. She once explained, "I stick to my firm, unshakeable belief that the black press is an advocacy press, and that I, as a part of that press, can't afford the luxury of being unbiased . . . when it comes to issues that really affect my people, I plead guilty, because I think that I am an instrument of change."

VIETNAM WAR

At the same time the Civil Rights Movement was taking place, America was becoming increasingly embroiled in the Asian nation of Vietnam. The war between a bitterly divided North Vietnam and South Vietnam began in 1955. The army of North Vietnam was supported by the Soviet Union, China, and other communist allies, while the army of South Vietnam was supported by the United States, South Korea, and other anti-communist allies. The United States, which feared that victory in South Vietnam would be followed in domino fashion by communist takeovers of other Asian countries, initially served only as military advisers. US participation escalated in the early 1960s and American ground troops began fighting in 1965.

The press corps in Vietnam grew in tandem with US involvement in the war. One of the first correspondents to be assigned to the conflict was David Halberstam, the Saigon bureau chief for the *New York Times*. Before joining the *Times*, Halberstam had been a reporter with the *Nashville Tennessean*, where he covered the Civil Rights Movement. He was only twenty-eight years old when he arrived in Vietnam in 1963, but in many respects he was already a veteran reporter. He was joined in the early years by Malcolm Browne of the Associated Press and Neil Sheehan of United Press International. Both Browne and Sheehan had served with the army in Korea, so they had valuable experience with the military, experience that came in handy in Vietnam.

The three men—and the other journalists who followed them— initially enjoyed great freedom in Vietnam. Officially, there was little censorship. The military issued basic guidelines, but because the United States was helping to fight an undeclared war, officials could not impose official censorship. In fact, the military often obliged journalists, allowing them to get on board jeeps, helicopters, and ships to report the fighting. At the same time, military officials believed they had to sell the war, and skeptical reporters were encouraged to "get on the team," as an admiral once told Browne. When that didn't work, officials tried to convince journalists that South Vietnam and its allies were winning.

An incident on June 11, 1963, dramatized the difficulties the allies faced in Vietnam. Vietnam's large Buddhist population wanted to celebrate the birthday of the Buddha, but the South Vietnamese government said no. Buddhists protested across the country, and the government cracked down. Browne had been writing about the protests, and on June 10 he got a phone call saying there would be a major event outside a pagoda in Saigon the next day. Browne and Halberstam went there, but only Browne carried a camera. They found hundreds of monks ringed around a seventy-three-year-old monk sitting in the middle of the street. Several monks doused the elderly man with gasoline. Then he struck a match, engulfing himself in flames as a protest against the South Vietnamese regime. Browne photographed the gruesome scene. His story and the photographs were published around the world.

During Vietnam, the press for the first time showed the horrors of war: American troops wounded and killed; villages being destroyed; and civilians fleeing for their lives. One of the most controversial stories was the 1965 CBS News broadcast by Morley Safer of American troops burning a village using Zippo cigarette lighters. Safer described the destruction, including the death of a baby, and added his commentary. President Lydon Johnson was outraged by the report and called CBS

President Frank Stanton to protest. The Pentagon demanded that CBS remove Safer from Vietnam, but the network refused.

During the Tet offensive in 1968, the North Vietnamese launched simultaneous assaults on more than one hundred sites, including the US Embassy. The news media, especially television, gave a great deal of attention to the offensive, showing all the carnage. Tet shocked Americans who believed that victory was imminent, and the news media wrongly concluded that it was a major tactical victory for the North Vietnamese and Viet Cong. Seymour Hersh, a former Associated Press reporter, published another controversial story: the slaughter by American troops of hundreds of civilians in the village of My Lai. Hersh learned that the army was secretly court-martialing a lieutenant named William L. Calley Jr. for the incident. Working independently, Hersh found Calley's lawyer and then the lieutenant himself. He persuaded Calley to talk about what happened and then sold the story to about thirty newspapers in the fall of 1969. Hersh investigated further and learned that more than five hundred civilians had been killed in what had come to be known in the press as the "My Lai Massacre." He also reported that army officers had tried to cover up the deaths.

As the Vietnam War dragged on, distrust grew between the military and the press, as military leaders presented an optimistic picture of what was happening on the battlefield while correspondents were seeing a far different scene. Contributing to the distrust were the daily afternoon press briefings, which reporters found to be so misleading that they dubbed them the "Five O'Clock Follies." A scholar of the era wrote, "Optimism without results would only work for so long. After that, it would produce the credibility gap." For example, President Richard Nixon, who followed Johnson in the White House, in an April 26, 1972, television address, announced that twenty thousand more US troops would be pulling out of Vietnam "without detriment to our overall goal of ensuring South Vietnam's survival as an independent country." Around the same time, CBS correspondent Bill Simon painted a far different picture. Covering brutal fighting during North Vietnam's Easter offensive, Simon showed images of South Vietnamese refugees—including children—who had been killed or maimed by a land mine that destroyed their truck. Concluding the report, Simon said, "There's nothing left to say about this war. There's just nothing left to say."

The credibility gap could be traced to growing distrust in the US government and Central Intelligence Agency (CIA) after the failed Bay of Pigs invasion of Cuba in 1961 by anti-Castro fighters supported by the CIA. The debacle sparked critical media attention, and the press increasingly was seen as adversarial by many in government. The administration of President Nixon, in particular, viewed journalists with suspicion. Nixon had received editorial support early in his career, but in an emotional news conference after losing the 1962 California gubernatorial race, he blamed the press. Nixon accused the news media of a liberal bias and claimed that reporters were "delighted" that he lost. After winning the presidency in 1968, Nixon told prospective cabinet members, "Always remember, the men and women of the press approach this as an adversary relationship."

The president and his aides became increasingly furious with the news media for portraying Vietnam as a failure. Vice President Spiro Agnew vehemently criticized the press and turned the term "credibility gap" around, saying "a widening credibility gap . . . exists between the national news media and the American people." News executives disputed the administration's claims. Just a few weeks after Agnew's remarks, CBS anchor Walter Cronkite, in a speech, charged the Nixon administration with orchestrating "a grand conspiracy to destroy the credibility of the press."

The view became popular that news media coverage of the war and the antiwar protest movement contributed to the US decision to withdraw from Vietnam in 1973. Samuel Huntington, writing in the 1975 Trilateral Commission study of the war, noted: "The most notable new source of national power in 1970, as compared to 1950, was the national media . . . There is . . . considerable evidence to suggest that the development of television journalism contributed to the undermining of governmental authority." Although there is disagreement that the news media were as powerful as the study suggested, future government policy on military–press relations would be influenced by the belief that the press had played a major role in turning public opinion against the

Vietnam War. In future combat, the press wouldn't have the freedom to report as they pleased. Censorship and control became facts of life.

PENTAGON PAPERS

The troubling nature of the Vietnam War led many to raise questions about how the United States had become so embroiled in what essentially was a civil war in a small Asian country. In 1967, Secretary of Defense Robert McNamara commissioned a top-secret history of American involvement in the war. The study, known as the Pentagon Papers, concluded that the Truman, Eisenhower, Kennedy, and Johnson administrations had often misled American citizens and Congress about the aims of the war. Daniel Ellsberg, a contractor recruited to work on the report, became convinced that the war was a mistake and decided that the American people must know what was in the Pentagon Papers. He began secretly photocopying the massive study and decided to turn over copies to the press.

Ellsberg contacted Neil Sheehan, who, after working for the UPI during Vietnam, had joined the *New York Times*. Ellsberg gave a copy of the Pentagon Papers to Sheehan, and the *Times* staff set about deciding how to report it. Four reporters and two editors were assigned to work on what was dubbed "Project X." Hidden away in a New York hotel, they spent weeks reading and analyzing seven thousand pages of documents. Because the report had been classified as top secret, anyone in possession of it could face charges of stealing government property and, possibly, treason. The lawyers for the *Times* disagreed about whether the newspaper could be prosecuted, but publisher Arthur Ochs Sulzberger decided to keep the staff working on the project. Ultimately Sulzberger gave the go-ahead to publish.

On June 13, 1972, the *Times* broke the story of the Pentagon Papers. The lead story, written by Sheehan, reported that the study showed that "four presidential administrations had progressively developed a sense of commitment to a non-communist Vietnam, a readiness to fight the North to protect the South, and an ultimate frustration with this effort— to a much greater extent than their public statements acknowledged at the time." The *Times* said more stories would be forthcoming. However, two days later, government lawyers asked a federal court to stop the *Times* from publishing any more stories based on the Pentagon Papers. It was the first time in American history that the government had sought to impose prior restraint on the press on the grounds of national security.

The judge assigned to the case granted the government a temporary restraining order and set a hearing for later in the week. The *Times* obeyed the order and suspended the series. Meanwhile, the *Washington Post* was trying to get the story, too. Ellsberg, who was concerned that the government would be successful in blocking the *Times*, contacted an editor at the *Post* and said he could provide the documents. The *Post*'s reporters and editors dug into the Pentagon Papers, rushing to get stories out. It was a big risk because the court had already issued a restraining order, and the newspaper's executives could not argue they didn't know the judge's stance. Editors contacted Katharine Graham, the *Post*'s publisher, who was hosting a dinner party at her home. She gave the okay, and on the same day of the court hearing, the *Post* published a front-page story about the Pentagon Papers. Lawyers for the government immediately sought a restraining order against the newspaper, and it was granted. But in a shocking decision issued the next day, the judge ruled against the government, saying the Justice Department had failed to provide compelling reasons for continued secrecy. He did allow the restraining order to remain in place until the government had a chance to appeal.

On June 25, the Supreme Court agreed to review the cases against the *Times* and *Post*. The following day, in a rare Saturday session, the justices heard arguments from lawyers for the government and the two newspapers. Then, on June 30, the court by a vote of 6–3 ruled that the *Times* and *Post* could resume publication of the Pentagon Papers. The majority said that the government had a heavy burden of proof in questions of prior restraint; it had to show that publications would present an immediate, serious, and irreparable harm to national security. In the case of the Pentagon Papers, the court said, the government had not met the standards. It was a landmark legal victory, one that taught journalists important lessons. As Sanford J. Ungar has written, the press learned that it "should be more bold and outspoken in digging behind official policy, both domestic and foreign." The Pentagon Papers also intensified the battle between the Nixon administration and the press.

WATERGATE CRISIS

President Nixon became increasingly fixated on news leaks that made his administration look bad in the press. During his first two years in office, he ordered the wiretapping of numerous officials in the federal government, including the State Department, National Security Council, and even the White House. Taps were put on phones, and the taped conversations were sent to his chief of staff, H. R. Haldeman. A wary FBI and CIA refused to carry out all the surveillance that Nixon wanted, so he ordered the creation of the White House's own espionage unit. That unit, which was supposed to stop leaks, would become known as the "Plumbers." One of the unit's first targets was newspaper columnist Joseph Kraft, who had criticized Nixon's foreign policy. Kraft and more than fifty other journalists were put on an "enemies list" that eventually included more than two hundred people considered disloyal to the administration.

As protests against the Vietnam War continued, Nixon became worried about his reelection. Polls in mid-1971 showed the president trailing Democratic contenders Edward Kennedy and Edmund Muskie. By the end of the year, leaders of the Committee for the Re-election of the President had devised a plan to disrupt the Democratic election effort through espionage and sabotage. Early on the morning of June 17, 1972, five men that included some of the Plumbers broke into the offices of the Democratic National Committee in the Watergate office complex in Washington. They planned to place phone taps and photograph documents, but a security guard noticed they had placed tape on a basement door to keep it unlocked while they worked. Police summoned by the guard arrested the intruders in the Watergate offices. Bob Woodward, a young reporter who had worked at the *Washington Post* for less than a year covered their arraignment later in the day. Woodward and Carl Bernstein were assigned the next day to do a follow-up story about James McCord, one of the men arrested.

Their front-page story was the first of many that Woodward and Bernstein would write over the next two years as the two reporters unraveled the story of what became known as "Watergate." They were helped by other reporters at the *Post* who worked on the story at various times and by supportive editors who gave them the time needed to work on the story. They were also aided by an anonymous adviser who gave Woodward what the *Post* later described as "confirmation and context" for some of the most explosive stories. The managing editor of the *Post* jokingly dubbed him "Deep Throat" after the title of a popular pornographic movie character at the time, and his identity was a secret for more than thirty years. In 2005, Mark Felt, formerly the second-ranking official at the FBI, announced he was the source.

The dogged Woodward and Bernstein soon discovered that the Nixon campaign had a special account for espionage activities and that campaign officials had ordered the destruction of records after the break-in. It was the first piece of a puzzle that turned out to be the biggest abuse of power in the history of the American presidency at the time. Woodward and Bernstein made mistakes in some of their stories. One of the biggest was reporting that Haldeman was one of the five people who approved payments for espionage activities. Woodward and Bernstein also violated ethical principles, if not the law, in talking to grand jury members at one point. All in all, however, their reporting was on the mark. In the end, twenty-one members of the administration were convicted of various crimes, and all but two served time in prison. In early 1974, the House of Representatives voted overwhelmingly to begin an investigation of Nixon's role in the conspiracy. Facing certain impeachment, the president resigned on August 9, 1974.

Woodward and Bernstein won the 1973 Pulitzer Prize for public service. They wrote a best-selling book, *All the President's Men*, that was made into a popular movie. The *Post* reporters and their editors don't deserve all the credit for exposing the scandal. The *New York Times*, *Los Angeles Times*, and other news organizations also contributed important reporting. However, the full extent of the criminal conspiracy probably wouldn't have been exposed without the relentless digging of the *Post*. The *Post's* reporting of the Watergate story showed what a news organization could accomplish in the face of enormous political pressure. It also led journalists to a greater reliance on anonymous sources—who are people anonymous to the public, but not to the journalist reporting the story. And it started a new wave of "investigative reporting" by news organizations throughout the country. Investigative reporting, of course, was not new; the muckrakers and others had done outstanding investigative work for decades. Yet, the "watchdog role" of the news media was increasingly emphasized by many news organizations in the decades that followed. The *Post's* aggressive reporting of the Watergate crimes also was a stark example of how the relationship between the press and politicians had changed over two centuries. Two groups that for decades had been willing political partners now often viewed one another with suspicion and distrust.

WOMEN REPORTERS AND THE WOMEN'S MOVEMENT

Journalism has been a male-dominated field since words were first printed in ink. While a few women were able to break gender barriers and have successful careers, historically, men have always outnumbered women in newsrooms across America. Some women thrived during World War I and II. But, as men returned home from the war, most newswomen were expected to give back their reporting positions to men. Yet, over the mid-twentieth century, conditions improved for women as they fought for society and the newsroom to change.

Traditionally, women working at news organizations were expected to cover social matters. At newspapers, this gendered coverage was considered "soft news" and went in a section often known as the "Women's Pages." While men were typically assigned "hard news" topics covering politics, law enforcement, finance, international affairs, and science, the average newspaperwoman would write articles about food, fashion, family, and furnishings. A typical "Women's Page" story would cover a prominent new marriage, parenting advice, or housekeeping tips. Moreover, it was difficult for women to maintain long-term journalism careers, as many were fired if they became pregnant. With no laws protecting them, new mothers generally did not have jobs waiting for them after the arrival of a baby. In many cases, women were expected to quit journalism after they got married.

While gender barriers were present in all areas of the news media, it was especially troublesome at news magazines. Popular publications, including *Newsweek, Time,* and *Reader's Digest,* hired women to assist male reporters as researchers. The researchers would often report, fact-check, interview sources, and even write news articles. However, only their male counterpart would receive a byline. Additionally, women were paid extremely low wages, which financially benefited the news organizations. Many women asked for promotions and the opportunity to become a reporter. In response, they were told, "Women do not write here."

As the country became embroiled in civil rights marches and Vietnam War protests, a new movement evolved which demanded equal rights for women. What is often called the women's liberation movement slowly began in the 1930s when working-class labor feminists fought for equal pay, support for working mothers, and livable wages. Yet it was during the 1960s that the movement gained traction. Women began reading literature about women's second-class standing in society and attended consciousness-raising groups where they shared stories about the sexism they experienced. They also marched in protest, formed professional organizations, and gained press coverage by protesting events like the Miss America pageant.

As women marched for equal rights in the streets of New York City, newswomen also began to demand change inside newsrooms. In the spring of 1970, a large group of women commandeered the editor-in-chief's office at *Ladies Home Journal* and staged a sit-in. The popular women's magazine was founded in 1883, and by the mid-twentieth century, it boasted a circulation of 6.8 million. However, the magazine was run and edited by men. The protestors—in addition to smoking the editor's cigars—stayed for eleven hours and asked that women hold more editorial control at the conventional magazine. While the protest resulted in incremental change, it marked an important kick-start to a decade-long battle for equal rights at news organizations.

Newswomen found another way to protest. After the passage of the 1964 Civil Rights Act, sex discrimination in the United States became illegal. As a result, during the 1970s women organized class-action sex discrimination lawsuits and sued for equal pay and promotion. Lawsuits were filed against the *Washington Post*, Associated Press, *New York Times*, *New Haven* (Connecticut) *Journal-Courier*, *Detroit News*, *Reader's Digest*, *Time*, *Life*, *Fortune*, *Sports Illustrated*, *Newsweek*, and CBS. Alongside a changing society at large, the lawsuits resulted in the hiring and promotion of more women inside news offices across the country.

As more women entered newsrooms, news coverage also changed. Women began writing stories about the women's liberation movement, the birth control pill, sex discrimination, and abortion. As a result, stories that were once buried inside the "Women's Pages" were often placed on the front page. Additionally, women were given greater access to physical spaces where they were once denied, including the locker rooms of male sports teams. They forced professional organizations to admit women members while also forming associations of their own.

The women's liberation movement helped women to enter journalism in larger numbers, but it certainly did not stop discrimination inside America's newsrooms. The 2019 Women's Media Center released a disparaging report that detailed gender inequities in all aspects of US media, particularly regarding employment, promotion, and representation. The report found that most newspaper and magazine editors are white men who earn more than women. Men also still dominate hard-hitting news beats. This is happening at a time when female college students dominate enrollment in journalism programs across the country. Organizations, many of which were formed during the 1970s, continue to fight on behalf of women working in the news.

LITERARY JOURNALISM

The societal upheavals in the 1960s and 1970s affected journalism. Some believed that the traditional practices of gathering and reporting the news were inadequate to report on an increasingly complex world. Talented writers who borrowed the techniques of fiction—while not making up stories—had always worked in journalism. The *New Yorker* magazine, for one, regularly published the work of such literary journalists as A. J. Liebling, Rachel Carson, John Hersey, Lillian Ross, and Truman Capote. But in the 1960s and 1970s, literary journalism became increasingly popular, led by magazines such as *Esquire*, *Rolling Stone*, and the *Saturday Evening Post*. Some newspapers followed suit, encouraging more creative approaches to reporting and writing.

Esquire was a hotbed for boundary-pushing writers such as Tom Wolfe, Joan Didion, and Gay Talese. The magazine, founded in 1933 and aimed at men, had a bawdy reputation for years. However, by the 1960s it had shifted gears to focus on culture, society, and politics. Wolfe, who had been a newspaper reporter, championed what he called "saturation reporting," in which a writer spent days, and sometimes weeks, with a subject. He used the technique in writing *The Right Stuff*, an account of the military pilots who went on to become America's first astronauts. Didion became known for a series of stories about her experiences in California during the 1960s. They were collected in a popular book, *Slouching Towards Bethlehem*. Talese often wrote profiles of well-known figures, including popular singer Frank Sinatra and baseball star Joe DiMaggio. He provided perhaps the best summary of what some called "Literary Journalism" or "New Journalism":

> The new journalism, though often reading like fiction, is not fiction. It is, or should be, as reliable as most reliable reportage, although it seeks a larger truth than is possible through the mere compilation of verifiable facts, the use of direct quotations, and adherence to the rigid organization style of the older form. The new journalism allows, demands in fact, a more imaginative approach to reporting, and it permits the writer to inject himself into the narrative if he wishes.

An important new publication launched during this time, *Ms.*, addressed the issues of feminism, while also emphasizing literary journalism. Gloria Steinem, a journalist and political activist, founded the magazine in 1972. She had started as a freelance magazine writer in New York City, and, for one story, she went undercover as a Playboy bunny, writing about the exploitation of the waitresses who dressed in strapless corsets, collars, cuffs, and bunny ears at the New York Playboy Club. Along the way, Steinem became a political activist, protesting on behalf of the civil rights, antiwar, and feminist movements. In 1968 she wrote a review of the book *Born Female* for the *New York Times*. In the review she lamented that female journalists were "supposed to be specialists on themselves, and little else." She added, "Newspapers and magazines are generous with assignments on fashion, beauty and childbirth. (Would men like to write about hunting, shaving and paternity?) But scientific or economic or political stories have a way of gravitating somewhere else."

Steinem and a group of women had been kicking around the idea of a national women's magazine. Several liked the name *Sisters*, but Steinem wanted it to be *Ms.*, a title that suggested a woman was not defined by her relationship to a man. *New York* magazine editor Clay Felker proposed to insert a sample issue of *Ms.* into *New York*'s year-end issue in 1971 to see if *Ms.* would be popular with readers. The magazine was not just popular—it was a runaway hit. The first regular monthly issue of *Ms.* appeared on newsstands in July 1972. The cover issue explored what it would mean to have a serious female candidate for president. Other features included a review of sex manuals, advice on how to fix a car by yourself, and a story about body hair. The staff of *Ms.* had said the magazine would not solicit

Figure 6.1 Gloria Steinem on the *Phil Donahue Show Source:* Gloria Steinem (left) on the *Phil Donahue Show* (NBC), Photofest.

or accept ads that were "insulting to women." Among the ads in the first issue were those for deodorant, nail polish, cigarettes, and liquor.

During its first year, *Ms.* showed it was not afraid to court controversy. It published a list of women who admitted having undergone an abortion when the procedure was still illegal in the United States. Steinem was on the list. In 1976, *Ms.* published a story examining the issue of domestic violence, and the cover photo featured a woman with a battered face. Over the years, *Ms.* also has published investigative stories about sex trafficking, the wage gap, the glass ceiling, and date rape. Although *Ms.* enjoyed great popularity during the 1970s, it struggled to reconcile its ideological goals with commercial success. For a time, the magazine didn't run ads because the owners believed that advertisers asserted too much control over the stories published in women's magazines. *Ms.* has gone through several ownership changes since its founding. In 2001, the magazine was sold to the Feminist Majority Foundation, a nonprofit organization whose mission is to advocate for women's equality. *Ms.* switched from publishing monthly to bimonthly in the 1990s. Since 2001, it has been published quarterly.

Public Broadcasting

In the early 1940s and 1950s, the Federal Communications Commission reserved space—first on the FM band and, later, on the television band—for local nonprofit stations that emphasized educational programming. Many of the stations were associated with a local university or school board. Ten years later, hundreds of public radio and television stations were on the air across the United States. However, most operated on bare-bone budgets and produced little high-quality programming. At the same time, there was a growing concern about the value of programming on the three commercial networks. The concern was summed up by FCC Chairman Newton Minow, who, in a speech, described commercial television programming as a "vast wasteland." During his stint at the FCC, Minow called for more children's, public affairs, and cultural programming. Network officials and some members of Congress fought him, arguing that ratings should determine what the public wanted.

In 1967, the Carnegie Commission on Educational Television published a report, "Public Television: A Program for Action." It recommended that a Corporation for Public Television be created with three missions: to receive and disburse funds from the government and other sources to produce programming; to support national production agencies; and to encourage the interconnection of public radio and television stations. The report received wide support, and later that year, with the encouragement of President Johnson, Congress passed the Public Broadcasting Act. The act created the Corporation for Public Broadcasting to oversee the development of programming. Two years later, the Public Broadcasting System, better known as PBS, was created to oversee the interconnection of public broadcasting stations.

On the radio side, National Public Radio helped launch such popular shows as *Car Talk, Fresh Air*, and *Wait, Wait . . . Don't Tell Me*. On the television side, PBS helped start such shows as *Sesame Street, Mr. Rogers's Neighborhood, Nature, American Experience, Masterpiece Theatre, Great Performances*, and *Austin City Limits*. Many of the shows were the brainchild of member stations, such as WQED in Pittsburgh, WGBH in Boston, WETA in Washington, and WNET in New York. Arguably, the most successful public television show has been *Sesame Street*. Produced by the Children's Television Network, *Sesame Street* was pioneering in its use of modern commercial television techniques. Set on a city street and broken into numerous rapidly moving parts, it was quickly successful much to the chagrin of the commercial networks, which turned down the show before it was offered to public television.

National Public Radio's flagship radio news show is *All Things Considered*. The late-afternoon show went on the air in 1971 and soon developed a loyal group of listeners. Despite low salaries and cramped offices, the show attracted outstanding journalists who loved the medium of radio. Without a comparable morning show, for years NPR lacked any potential audience during the "morning drive," the time of day when most people listened to radio. That problem was solved in 1979 with the addition of *Morning Edition*, and within a year 90 percent of NPR's more than two hundred affiliated stations were carrying the program. *Morning Edition* also helped to seal NPR's reputation for outstanding journalism.

The *PBS NewsHour* is known for its in-depth coverage of news and issues. The show has a more deliberate pace than the evening newscasts on the commercial networks. News segments run six to twelve minutes, providing a deeper examination of subjects. The show began in 1975 as the *Robert McNeil Report*, hosted by the former NBC correspondent and produced by WNET. Journalist Jim Lehrer soon joined the broadcast, and it was renamed *The MacNeil/Lehrer Report*. In 1983, the show became America's first one-hour evening network newscast. Later, the name of the show was changed to the *PBS NewsHour*. In 2013, Gwen Ifill and Judy Woodruff became the first female-only anchor team on a nightly national news broadcast. Ifill, who died in 2016, had been a reporter for the *New York Times* and NBC. Woodruff had also worked at NBC News before joining PBS.

Because public broadcasting is noncommercial, it relies on a combination of public, private, and government funding. The public funding is most evident in the pledge drives that local stations hold several times a year. Companies and foundations help to underwrite most programs with spots acknowledging the contributions airing at the beginning and end of shows. Government funding of public broadcasting has always been controversial with conservative leaders arguing that free enterprise should dictate what is broadcast on radio and television. Some have also argued that the public-affairs programming on public radio and television has a liberal bias. Defenders of public broadcasting maintain that the federal funds are only a tiny part of the federal budget and that the government has a responsibility to support high-quality programming.

CABLE TELEVISION AND CNN

As public broadcasting was hitting its stride, the Cable News Network, better known simply as CNN, was launched in 1980 as another alternative for viewers. The idea of a full-time news network had precedents. Several major cities had all-news radio stations, and both the AP and UPI had been operating text-based cable news feeds for more than ten years. However, a twenty-four-hour television news operation would be an enormous undertaking, and nobody knew if the public would watch in sufficient numbers to make it feasible. At the time, ABC, CBS, and

NBC still broadcast only a thirty-minute evening newscast, as they had done since the early 1960s. The three networks also had morning shows that were a mix of news and entertainment. Most local television stations broadcast three news shows, one at noon, one in the early evening, and one in the late evening.

Ted Turner, a brash Southerner who took over his family's outdoor advertising company and made a fortune, was one of the first to see the potential of satellite television. He turned a struggling Atlanta station, WTCG, into a so-called SuperStation by using satellite technology to broadcast movies, sports, and old situation comedies across the country. Turner felt pressure to create a cable TV news network while the field was open, but he was an unlikely figure to do so. Turner had once declared that he disliked news because it made people "feel bad." The only news on WTCG aired at 3:00 a.m. and was more comedy than real news. The show was hosted by Bill Tush, who once read the news while holding a picture of Walter Cronkite in front of his face.

When Turner pitched the idea of all-news channel to cable operators, he found little enthusiasm. But Turner, an astute businessman, was also a maverick, and he decided to forge ahead. "Business is like a chess game and you have to look several moves ahead," he once remarked. "Most people don't. They only think one move at a time. But any good chess player knows that when you're playing against a one-move opponent, you'll beat him every time." Turner hired Reese Schonfeld, a TV news veteran, to head the operation. The two men disagreed initially about the network's philosophy. Turner wanted a soft approach that featured more entertainment, while Schonfeld wanted to emphasize breaking news. Schonfeld's vision eventually prevailed. The network was headquartered in Atlanta with bureaus in New York, Washington, Chicago, and other cities. To keep costs down, the staff consisted mainly of young journalists with little experience. The network's best-known correspondent was Daniel Schorr, who had been a reporter at the *New York Times* and later CBS.

On June 1, 1980, CNN debuted from its headquarters in a renovated former country club in Atlanta. Turner gave a short speech, a military band played the national anthem, and a graphic, "CNN, The News Channel," appeared. Anchors Lois Hart and Dave Walker said, "Good evening" and read the news. The network struggled initially, with just 1.7 million viewers its first year, well below Turner's projection. Critics called CNN "Chicken Noodle News" for its sometimes-amateurish operation. Once, while correspondent Bernard Shaw was on the air, a cleaning lady walked across the set and emptied his wastebasket. "Here is news, alive with all its wonderful technical warts and missed cues," a writer for *Variety* magazine observed, "and it all worked."

CNN didn't turn a profit until 1985, but by the end of the decade it had become a respected news operation, in large part because of its coverage of live events. While the other three networks could only cover the biggest news stories live, CNN could do so regularly. "We want to go live with breaking stories as much as possible," Schonfeld said. "Our philosophy is live, live, and more live." One of its first tests took place in 1981, when President Ronald Reagan was shot by a gunman after giving a speech in Washington, DC. Shaw went on the air to report the news several minutes before the other networks. CNN had the only video of the president walking into the emergency room with his arm over a Secret Service agent's shoulder. Shaw steadfastly refused to report the unconfirmed rumor that Reagan's press secretary, James Brady, had been killed. Finally, the news came that Brady was alive, although seriously injured. Shaw and Schorr stayed at the anchor desk for more than seven hours. Two anchors flew to Washington from Atlanta to take over from them. Later that evening, when ABC, CBS, and NBC signed off, local stations across the country picked up CNN's coverage. Over time, CNN became the go-to network for viewers who wanted to watch breaking news. The popularity of CNN forced the three broadcast networks to offer more news programming.

In 1985, Turner purchased the Metro-Goldwyn-Mayer/United Arts film studio. Turner spun off United Artists, but the purchase left him heavily in debt. He later sold a minority share of Turner Broadcasting System (the parent company of CNN) to Time Inc. and a group of cable operators. CNN expanded overseas, and in 1987 *CNN World Report* began airing in more than seventy-five countries. By the time CNN celebrated its ten-year anniversary in 1990, it had 1,800 employees at nine US bureaus and eighteen international bureaus. The network could be seen in 53 million homes in the United States, as well as eighty-four other countries.

The success of CNN was another example of how television had eclipsed newspapers as the dominant news medium for Americans. Most newspapers still enjoyed healthy circulations, but the number of newspapers began to shrink as it became apparent that most places couldn't support more than one publication. Many newspapers that had published in the afternoon switched to morning publication so as not to compete with the evening news broadcasts. And many big-city newspapers that had always enjoyed a statewide readership retreated to their local circulation areas.

In 1982, the Gannett Company took television news head on when it launched *USA Today*, the country's first national newspaper in decades. Gannett conducted extensive market research in planning *USA Today*. Readers said they wanted news and information that could be digested quickly. *USA Today* consciously adapted various aspects of television news with its emphasis on short stories, photographs, charts and graphs, weather, and the use of color. Even *USA Today*'s news stands were different. Instead of the traditional newspaper "box," they resembled a television set on a stand. Critics were not impressed. They said *USA Today* emphasized packaging and appearance over enterprising and hard-hitting journalism. However, *USA Today* developed a devoted national following, and its circulation eventually grew to more than two million. As a result, many daily newspapers adopted its practices, especially printing in color.

The alternative ways of reporting the news would expand during the modern era, thanks to digital technology and the popularity of the internet. CNN, *USA Today*, and other traditional media outlets would wrestle with the changes. They would be joined by new digital-only sources of news.

CHAPTER 7

The Digital Press

1985 to 2023

As the twenty-first century approached, the news business had become big business. Many local news properties enjoyed fat profits and were snapped up by the growing number of big media companies. Some of the largest companies, in turn, were bought and sold at astounding prices. The corporatization of the press affected the way journalism was practiced in the United States. In some cases, the new owners poured resources into their new properties, making it possible to produce better journalism. In other instances, the new owners seemed interested only in wringing more profits from their properties.

At the same time, studies found the American public increasingly lacked trust in the press and believed it too often was hostile to the country's best interests. Conservatives argued that the news media was too liberal and didn't reflect the views of many Americans. The talk-radio format that became popular in the 1980s gave conservative commentators a platform to express their views directly to listeners. The conservative media was bolstered in 1996 when the Fox network launched an all-news TV competitor to CNN. Despite the criticism, the press did some of its finest work, including the reporting of the 2001 terrorist attacks on the United States. Journalists provided exhaustive coverage of the shocking events, while also helping families cope with their losses.

The internet overturned the ways the traditional media operated, and news organizations for years struggled to adapt to the digital world.

As a new technological platform for the press, online news competed with both print and broadcast news. Moreover, in the new century, many readers and viewers abandoned the traditional media for new, and often free digital-only sources of news. With their economic model battered, some established media properties have sold or closed. Virtually all have been forced to make painful cuts, including the number of journalists they employ. However, the digital press continues to report the news in impactful ways, giving observers hope for the future of journalism, albeit one that will look far different.

ECONOMICS OF NEWS BUSINESS

The value of many news media properties increased in the 1970s and 1980s. Local media still were scarce commodities in most places. As a result, they attracted plenty of advertising and enjoyed fat profit margins. This, in turn, made them appealing targets for purchase by big media companies. At the same time, many of America's best-known news organizations became public companies whose shares were sold on the stock exchanges. By the late 1980s, at least fifteen publicly traded companies owned newspapers, including the New York Times Company and Washington Post Company. Newspaper chains such as Gannett, Knight Ridder, Times-Mirror, and Newhouse acquired more local newspapers, while broadcasting giants such as Meredith, Viacom, and Clear Channel bought local stations from coast to coast. Chain ownership was nothing new for the news media. Scripps Howard, Hearst, and others had built large chains since early in the century. However, the size and reach of the new media companies was extraordinary. By the early 1980s, chains owned one-half of the nation's daily newspapers and accounted for two-thirds of the circulation. At the end of the century, Clear Channel alone owned more than one thousand radio stations.

During a period of about fifteen years, a series of acquisitions and mergers pointed to how big the news media had become. The flurry of activity started in 1985 when Capital Cities Communication bought ABC for $3.5 billion. The same year, General Electric bought RCA and NBC for $6.3 billion. In 1989, Time Inc. merged with Warner Brothers in a $14 billion deal, and several years later, Turner Broadcasting System merged with the new Time Warner Inc. In 1995, Westinghouse bought CBS for $5.4 billion, and the next year the Disney Company purchased the new Cap Cities/ABC for $19 billion. Westinghouse did not hang on to CBS for long, selling the network in 1999 to Viacom. In 2000, Time Warner merged again, this time with America Online. The deal was valued at about $145 billion, an indication of how big the two companies had become.

The acquisitions and mergers were part of a general business trend that placed a growing part of the American economy in the hands of large, publicly owned companies. However, the trend had an impact on the practice of journalism. As corporations bought media properties, local ownership decreased. By 2005, the largest twenty-one newspaper chains owned 40 percent of the daily newspapers and controlled 70 percent of the daily circulation. Moreover, fewer cities had competing daily newspapers. In 1945, 117 cities had competing daily newspapers; by 2005 only forty-one cities had more than one newspaper. As public companies, the big media corporations were answerable to shareholders instead of simply readers, listeners, or viewers. Shareholders expected returns on their investment, increasing the pressure on news organizations to be more profitable.

In some cases, the acquisitions meant communities got improved journalism. With greater financial resources, big media companies were in a better position to support enterprising and aggressive journalism—provided they wanted to. An example was in Philadelphia, where the *Philadelphia Inquirer* for decades had been an undistinguished newspaper in one of the nation's largest cities. The *Inquirer* began a remarkable turnaround after being purchased in 1970 by Knight Newspapers, which became Knight Ridder in a 1974 merger with Ridder Publications. The new owners were willing to absorb short-term losses in a successful gamble that they could win the battle for survival with the locally owned *Evening Bulletin*. They brought in top talent, including executive editor Gene Roberts, who had been a reporter and editor at the *Detroit Free Press* and the *New York Times*. Under the leadership of Roberts and others, the *Inquirer* became one of the most admired and respected newspapers in the country, winning eighteen Pulitzer Prizes over the next two decades.

However, in other places corporate ownership hurt the quality of journalism. For decades, the Louisville *Courier-Journal* had been the largest news organization in Kentucky. Under the ownership of the Bingham family, the newspaper was known for its exhaustive coverage of news and its fearless editorial page. While the family owned the newspaper, the *Courier-Journal* won seven Pulitzer Prizes, and it was consistently ranked as one of the best newspapers in America. A series of family disagreements led the Binghams to sell the *Courier-Journal* to Gannett in 1986. The *Courier-Journal* won another Pulitzer Prize, but the giant chain didn't devote the same amount of resources into the newspaper, and the quality suffered. For example, in 2005, editorial cartoonist Nick Anderson won the Pulitzer Prize, but when he left the *Courier-Journal*, the newspaper didn't replace him.

Corporate ownership also meant that conflicts of interest were more likely. Journalists always prized their independence, but they could find that more difficult when their reporting might make the parent company look bad. An example was at ABC, where investigative reporter Brian Ross learned that Walt Disney World in Orlando was so hard-pressed to find security guards that they sometimes hired convicted sex offenders to work at the popular theme park. Worried about angering their superiors at Disney, Ross's editors at ABC decided to hold the story. In fact, Disney executives had never told ABC editors what to do, and the editors were just anticipating their reaction. The ethics issue did not come to light until Ross later spoke about it. ABC eventually reported the story and Walt Disney World changed its hiring practices.

Declining Trust and Increasing Criticism

Beginning in the 1980s, national surveys documented the public's declining trust in the press. Critics charged that too many journalists "were out of control and out of line with the dominant social values" and "had come to constitute a separate and subversive class." The news media responded by creating or strengthening codes of ethics. In 1973, the Society of Professional Journalists adopted an ethics code. Two years later, the American Society of Newspaper Editors adopted a revised statement of principles. Many newspapers and broadcast stations followed suit and created their own written policies on newsroom standards and policies. The initial codes sought to improve credibility by eliminating conflicts of interest, such as accepting gifts ("freebies," as they were commonly known) and avoiding engaging in political activity other than voting. Later, codes of ethics sought to define best practices for journalists, such as being fair and accurate, protecting sources, minimizing harm, and deciding when, if ever, deception is justified.

As Gene Foreman has written, several factors prompted the growth in ethical awareness by journalists. A new generation of journalists, better educated and more idealistic, had joined the profession in the years after social responsibility became a driving force for the news media. Journalists were covering government and society more critically and responsibly than ever. In 1988 alone, the *Alabama Journal* investigated the state's unusually high infant mortality rate. The *Chicago Tribune* reported on the self-interest and waste that plagued the Chicago City Council. The *Charlotte Observer* revealed misuse of funds by the popular PTL Christian television ministry. And the *St. Paul Pioneer Press Dispatch* published a moving series about the life and death of an AIDS victim in a rural Iowa community.

However, several high-profile ethics scandals rocked journalism. The most notable was at the *Washington Post*, where reporter Janet Cooke admitted that she made up her Pulitzer Prize–winning story of an eight-year-old heroin addict. The child was not real, but a composite figure created from what Cooke had learned about heroin addiction. The *Post* immediately fired Cooke and returned the Pulitzer Prize, but the damage to its credibility had already been done. As a result of the scandals, the media came under increased scrutiny by media watchdogs such as the *Columbia Journalism Review* and alternative weeklies such as the *Village Voice*.

The sex scandal that enveloped President Bill Clinton absorbed the press and led to more criticism. The *Drudge Report* learned in 1998 that *Newsweek* magazine was investigating an affair that Clinton had with a White House intern. When *Newsweek* balked at printing the story before it could be confirmed, the website reported it. The rest of the press jumped on the story, in some cases relying on rumors and anonymous sources. Clinton initially denied having a sexual relationship with the intern, but after being called to testify before a federal grand jury, the president admitted he had lied. "The country is awash in the muck of White House nastiness, and dirty with the cynicism that flows from it," *New York Times* columnist A. M. Rosenthal wrote. Independent counsel Kenneth Starr released a 445-page report that included charges of perjury and obstruction of justice, as well as explicit descriptions of sexual acts committed in the White House. Some newspapers published the entire report, and cable television networks gave it continuous coverage. Critics said press coverage of the scandal often was excessive and, in some cases, irresponsible.

The news media was embroiled in another controversy during the 2000 presidential election between Republican George W. Bush and Democrat Albert Gore. The reporting on election night was punctuated by a series of mistakes that many in the press later agreed should have been avoided. By 7:55 p.m. Eastern Standard time, CBS, NBC, CNN, and the Associated Press declared Gore the winner of the pivotal state of Florida and thus the election. The networks based their calls on exit polling of voters conducted by the Voter News Service, a consortium funded by the networks and the Associated Press. Officials with the Bush campaign immediately complained about the calls, arguing that it discouraged voters in Florida's panhandle, which is in the central time zone, as well as other states, from going to the polls. Two hours later, the networks changed Florida from a win for Gore to "too close to call." Early the next morning, with Bush holding a small lead and 98 percent of the votes counted, the networks declared Bush the winner. Many newspapers published headlines saying, "Bush Wins," but others said the race was too close to call. The Gore campaign contested the results, and challenges were heard by the Florida and US Supreme Courts. Thirty-six days after the election, Gore conceded the race.

Some pointed to the Voter News Service as the cause of the reporting debacle. However, many others said the news media, especially the networks, bore responsibility by declaring a winner so early. A report by three veteran journalists said, "Television interfered with the electoral process and the election results" and that constituted "an abuse of power, if unintentionally so." A congressional committee held hearings in 2001 to determine how the election results were reported and what could be done to prevent the mistake from happening again. The committee played tapes of the coverage, including *CBS Evening News* anchor Dan Rather declaring that viewers could "take it to the bank" that Gore had won the race in Florida. The television networks later announced they were changing their methods of declaring election winners.

Even as the news media sought to fulfill an obligation of social responsibility, the public became increasingly antagonistic. The Project for Excellence in Journalism, in its 2004 report, *The State of News Media*, concluded: "Americans think journalists are sloppier, less professional, less moral, less caring, more biased, less honest about their mistakes, and generally more harmful to democracy than they did in the 1980s." The Pew Research Center for the People and the Press noted a growing partisan divide in the way the public perceived the news media. Democrats were generally more trusting in the press than Republicans and independents. Moreover, the Pew Research Center found that a growing number of citizens believed the news media were "too critical of America."

CONSERVATIVE MEDIA

Conservatives increasingly believed that the press too often reflected the views of only liberals. The criticism was not new. For decades, leaders on the right had argued that many in the news media pushed a liberal political agenda. William F. Buckley Jr. founded the conservative magazine *National Review* in 1955. Starting with the first issue, the magazine has regularly published essays on the "delinquencies of the Liberal press." Buckley later began hosting the nationally televised interview program *Firing Line*. He and his guests regularly argued about the issue of media bias; some shows were solely devoted to the subject. In 1969, a group led by economist Reed Irvine formed Accuracy in Media (AIM) designed to identify and publicize errors in reporting by national news organizations. AIM maintained that it was nonpartisan but promoted an alternative news view favoring the right. That same year, Vice President Spiro Agnew complained in a nationally televised speech that the national media too often was unfairly hostile to the conservative Nixon administration. Some news media leaders said the criticism was intended to stifle the press. However, many on the right, including conservative publications, cheered.

When he took office, President Ronald Reagan wanted to deregulate the American economy. Since the 1940s, the FCC had sought to ensure diversity and local control in the ownership of radio and television stations by limiting the number of broadcast stations a company could own. Reagan believed that free-market forces better served the public than the government. In 1985, the FCC relaxed the rules limiting how many radio stations a single entity could own. Large broadcasting companies began snapping up as many local stations as they could. In 1987, the FCC repealed the so-called Fairness Doctrine, which since 1949 had required broadcast stations to seek people with different views and provide them equal airtime for free to express their views. Congress tried to restore the Fairness Doctrine by enacting it into law, but Reagan vetoed the bill and Congress failed to override it.

The two FCC decisions spurred the "talk" format on radio. Hosts and stations no longer had an obligation to provide balance on topics or give opposing views airtime. Talk radio emerged at the ideal time for many AM stations. Since the 1970s, FM had been the preferred radio band, because it provided a clearer signal and stereo sound. As a result, AM stations floundered. Talk radio provided new programming for the struggling AM stations. In the five years after the repeal of the Fairness Doctrine, the number of talk radio stations grew from about 240 to about 900. They were not only on the AM dial, but FM too.

A former disc jockey became the most influential—and most controversial—talk radio host. Rush Limbaugh was an unlikely candidate to be a leading voice of modern conservatism. The native of Cape Girardeau, Missouri, dropped out of college to become a full-time disc jockey and over the years held a series of jobs in radio. By the mid-1980s, Limbaugh was working in Sacramento, California, where he experimented with hosting a talk program without guests, inviting listeners to call in and give their opinions. A syndication executive liked what Limbaugh was doing and hired him in 1988 to start a national daily talk show. Limbaugh expressed his conservative viewpoint on the show, and listeners who dared to call in to disagree more often than not were told by Limbaugh they were wrong. Unlike other talk-show hosts, Limbaugh didn't invite experts to express their opinions. The show was all Limbaugh.

The format flew in the face of other radio programming, but that didn't matter. Listeners who shared Limbaugh's outspoken conservative views loved it. *The Rush Limbaugh Show* became the most-listened to talk show on radio, and its host became one of the highest-paid figures in the American media. Over time, many Republicans acknowledged Limbaugh's role as a party leader. Some even credited him with helping their party recapture the House of Representatives in 1994. The provocative Limbaugh was never afraid of controversy. He accused Hillary Clinton of covering up a murder, a rumor he read from a fax sent to his office. He regularly used provocative musical props to introduce his monologues. He maintained that the props were meant to be entertaining, but critics said they were insulting and distasteful. Limbaugh made disparaging comments about feminists, African Americans, environmentalists, and others. The most controversial comments led some commercial sponsors to stop advertising, but that didn't stop radio stations from broadcasting his show. Limbaugh was heard on more than six hundred stations and by up to twenty-seven million people each week. One of his most popular targets was the news media, or the "drive-by media," as he liked to say. Limbaugh argued that the national media was part of the liberal elite that is at the root of many of America's problems. "The media is now considered just part of the arrogant, condescending elite, and out-of-touch political structure . . . engaging in the abuse of power," he said.

Conservatives gained another ally when Rupert Murdoch, the Australian and British media titan, decided to create an all-news channel to compete with CNN. Murdoch had bought the historic *New York Post* in 1976 and turned it into sensational, conservative tabloid. Although the *Post* lost money every year, it allowed Murdoch to express his right-wing views. In 1986, he launched Fox Broadcasting, a cable television channel that featured such shows as *The Simpsons* and *American Idol*. Fox Broadcasting didn't have a news division, but instead of creating one inside the network, Murdoch launched a separate channel, Fox News, in 1996. Murdoch hired Roger Ailes to run Fox News. Ailes had worked in broadcasting before joining the staff of Vice President Richard Nixon, who was gearing up for the 1968 presidential campaign. He devised Nixon's television strategy and became a Republican consultant. Ailes later joined NBC, helping to oversee the launch of CNBC, the network's all-business cable channel. Murdoch and Ailes had long believed that the national press had a liberal bias, and the two men wanted to create an all-news conservative alternative. From the start, Fox was unabashedly ideological in most of its news programming. Ailes declared that the network would be "fair and balanced," implying that the other television networks were not. In 2016, Ailes resigned when prominent female Fox staffers accused the executive of sexual harassment.

Fox initially struggled against an entrenched CNN. The network spent an enormous amount of money to open bureaus and hire staff. It also had to pay cable operators to carry the network. Time Warner initially resisted Murdoch's plans and the mogul claimed the cable company was trying to protect CNN from competition. When Murdoch filed a breach of contract suit against Time Warner, Turner called Murdoch a "scum-bag." Murdoch used the *New York Post* to respond. One headline in the tabloid read, "Is Ted Turner Nuts? You Decide." Fox provided traditional news programming during the day but interspersed it with more partisan opinion shows than CNN in the evening prime time. The most popular show for years was *The O'Reilly Factor*, hosted by veteran television anchor Bill O'Reilly. The show was infused with the host's unbridled patriotism and his scorn for liberals. During the run-up to the 2003 invasion of Iraq, O'Reilly declared, "Once the war against Saddam Hussein begins, we expect every American to support our military, and if they can't do that, to shut up. Americans, and indeed our allies who actively work against our military once the war is underway will be considered enemies of the state by me." Many people were outraged, but fans of the show couldn't get enough. For years, *The O'Reilly Factor* was the highest-rated show on the cable news networks. O'Reilly was the inspiration for comedian Stephen Colbert's Comedy Central show *The Colbert Report*, in which he parodied a conservative television commentator. O'Reilly was forced to resign in 2017, and his popular show went off the air after several female staff members at Fox accused him of making unwanted sexual advances.

REPORTING MODERN CONFLICTS AND TERRORISM

The reporting of the Vietnam War led some military and government leaders to argue that the press had contributed to the quagmire. They were determined to impose tight controls on news media coverage of future conflicts. In 1983, when US military forces invaded Grenada to protect students from a purported takeover of the island by communist forces, journalists were kept far away during the initial days of action. The news media widely protested the move, arguing that Americans had a right to know what was happening. The military responded by creating "press pools," a small group of journalists selected to report on fighting and serve as surrogates for those not selected. Military leaders reasoned that the pools allowed them to keep track of the reporters and concentrate on winning the fighting. The press would have access to the military action, albeit in far fewer numbers.

However, when the US military invaded Panama to capture Manuel Noriega in 1989, the press pool didn't work, at least as far as the news media was concerned. The pool journalists were taken to Panama after the initial action and did not have a chance to observe what took place. As a result, questions about what actually happened in Panama, including the disputed number of Panamanian civilians killed during the invasion, were not answered. During the Persian Gulf War of 1991 (known as "Operation Desert Storm"), the military maintained its tight control of the press. More journalists were permitted to cover the brief conflict, but the restrictions imposed again limited what Americans could read or see. Critics said the military wanted to be the first to provide the most important news. General Norman Schwarzkopf provided press briefings, showing sanitized versions of the fighting, especially the "smart bombs" being dropped without the realistic destruction and casualties that they caused. Frustrated by the press controls and determined to do his own reporting, CBS newsman Bob Simon broke away from the pool only to be captured by Iraqi forces. And CNN correspondent Peter Arnett managed to broadcast from Baghdad.

The press distinguished itself in reporting the terrorist attacks of September 11, 2001, when nineteen Islamic terrorists hijacked four passenger airliners and targeted the World Trade Center Towers and the Pentagon. The first plane crashed into the North Tower of the World Trade Center in New York City at 8:46 a.m. Sixteen minutes later, a second plane slammed into the South Tower. A third plane hit the Pentagon in Washington, DC, about thirty minutes later, and later in the morning, the fourth crashed in rural Pennsylvania after passengers bravely fought with the hijackers. In all, 2,996 people died and more than six thousand were injured in the shocking attacks that became known simply as "9/11."

Within minutes of the first attack, journalists rushed to the scene and television was providing live video. Photographers in Washington had to walk to the Pentagon because all of the bridges in the city were closed. The coverage of the disaster was so fast-paced that new footage was shown on TV before being screened and the images often were graphic. Jim Murphy of *CBS Evening News* said his team would "mark the tape" if the footage was too graphic and not show it again. "Some of them were incredibly gruesome. . . . There is just no reason to, there is just no reason to give it to people over and over, there is just no reason." Around 10:00 p.m. on September 11, NBC reporter Rehema Ellis and her crew had passed security guards to enter ground zero and give a description of the scene: "It's like going inside a disaster. . . . There's an eerie light

Figure 7.1 View of Lower Manhattan from the Manhattan Bridge, September 11, 2011 *Source:* Library of Congress Prints and Photographs Division.

that's cast over the entire area. . . . It takes your breath away to stand in what was the center of America's financial area, and now it doesn't exist anymore."

Many newspapers initially were slow to use their websites to provide coverage. Instead, more than 150 morning newspapers published extra editions later in the day, the first time many had done that in years. The *New York Times* and other newspapers published graphic photos of people falling or jumping from the towers to their death in its morning paper the next day. Many other newspapers published similar photos. One editor defended the use of the images: "The horror of the event and the magnitude just demanded that you get that across in a very forceful and powerful way. . . . You can't not run a picture like that." The television networks provided around-the-clock coverage for days. Much of the coverage ran without commercials. Explaining the decision for the exhaustive coverage, NBC president Neil Shapiro said, "This is the most important story of my lifetime. I think it's our job to stay on the air."

The news media in the New York area provided exhaustive coverage of the victims and their families, most of whom lived in the metropolitan area or surrounding states. Two days after the attack, *Newsday* began publishing a daily two-page feature profiling the victims and posted the stories on its website. *Newsday* called it "a commitment to our neighbors." The *New York Times* also published profiles of all the victims, under the headline "Portraits of Grief." With no actual list of the dead, the *Times* began assigning reporters to write short vignettes, each with a photo, which captured some aspect of the life of the victim. More than ten reporters were assigned to write the mini-profiles, and by the end of the year, they had published about 1,900. Wrote one reader: "I live in San Francisco, and though I did not personally know anyone whose life was taken, your portraits bring to every reader a sympathy for the surviving families and friends."

The press soon began devoting increasing attention to stories about how the terrorists managed to pull off such devastating attacks and what they meant to the security of Americans. Less than a month after the attacks, the United States military went on the offensive against al Qaeda, the terrorist organization responsible for masterminding them.

At the request of the White House, the six major TV networks agreed to edit a videotaped statement that terrorist leader, Osama bin Laden, made that might inspire his followers or might contain coded messages to other terrorists. It marked the first time the networks agreed to a joint arrangement to limit coverage. CBS news president Andrew Heyward defended the move, saying America was facing "a new kind of enemy" and that it was appropriate to consider "new ways of fulfilling our responsibility to the public." However, other journalists objected to cooperating with the government and said news organizations should make their own decisions about what should be broadcast or published.

The controversial issue of whether the news media should cooperate with the government was raised again during the US–Iraq war. The White House maintained that Iraq might be supporting al Qaeda and that it possessed "weapons of mass destruction" that could be targeted against America. The United States began bombing Iraq in March 2003, and a ground attack started soon afterward. Journalists were permitted to accompany troops as "embedded reporters," attaching them to units. The system gave them more opportunities for on-the-scene reporting but limited where they could go. Some journalists said they were forced to rely too heavily on American soldiers for protection in combat, and that made objectivity difficult. However, most considered the tradeoff to be worthwhile.

After the fighting began, critics said the press didn't fully investigate the Bush administration's argument for going to war. Some news organizations later acknowledged that the reporting relied heavily on erroneous information and was not as rigorous as it should have been. The last American troops left Iraq in 2011, but thousands of advisers remained. The next year, bin Laden was tracked down and killed by American forces while he was hiding in Pakistan. When President Barack Obama went on national television to announce the news, network and cable TV channels interrupted programming to carry the statement. Newspapers blared the news in headlines the following day.

THE INTERNET AND ITS IMPACT

Technological developments at the end of the twenty-first century had a profound impact on the news media. Beginning in the 1970s, computers changed the way all journalists did their jobs. First, word processors and later personal computers replaced typewriters in newsrooms, making it possible to write and edit stories faster and more efficiently. Computers were also used to design and assemble the pages of newspapers and magazines, transmitting them directly to the printing press in a process called pagination. In the transition, publishers eliminated lead type—so-called hot metal—along with the jobs of the printers who had put together pages with the type. In broadcast news, the introduction of mobile electronic news gathering (ENG) equipment permitted television to more easily report live from the field using microwave technology. Both the television networks and local stations increasingly used ENG trucks to report from the site of breaking news events and they became ubiquitous.

With the development of data networks in the 1970s, communications companies experimented with ways to send news and information over telephone lines. The most ambitious undertaking in the United States was Viewtron, launched in 1983 and funded largely by the Knight Ridder newspaper chain. Viewtron provided a continuously updated news report and other features via a modified color terminal equipped with a typewriter-like keyboard. The news, provided by Knight Ridder newspapers and the Associated Press, was text and graphics with no video. However, Viewtron was expensive and the technology cumbersome. It never caught on with subscribers, and in 1986 Knight Ridder shuttered Viewtron after losing tens of millions of dollars.

Media companies continued to test ways to deliver news to consumers digitally. At the same time, the popularity of personal computers grew, particularly with the popularity of the user-friendly Macintosh manufactured by Apple. Visionaries saw an opportunity for computers users to share information with one another. The internet had been born in the 1960s through research by the federal government's Advanced Research Projects Agency (ARPA) as a means of allowing computers to share information. Telephone network technology was inefficient for computers because it required companies to lease dedicated telephone lines to ensure that circuits were available when information was being transferred between computers. Known as ARPANet, the internet initially was limited to research, government, and education uses. It was a complex system and, a result, used only by computer-savvy scientists and engineers.

In the 1970s, Vincent Cerf and Bob Kahn developed the TCP/IP protocol (transmission control protocol/internet protocol) that meant computers manufactured by different companies to exchange information. The ease of use improved with the development of email, electronic mail that allowed users to send messages to one another instantaneously. Thousands of researchers used email and it generated a majority of the traffic on ARPANet. (They also developed "emoticons" by using a combination of keyboard symbols to express feelings.) As personal computers became popular in the 1980s, commercial information services like CompuServe and Prodigy began to offer information from telephone dial up services. Later in the decade, America Online (AOL) began to mass market online access to information along with services such as email, chat rooms, and Instant Messaging. AOL and similar services prepared consumers and sparked an appetite for the internet.

Then, in 1990, Tim Berners-Lee, a software engineer working at CERN, the European particle physics laboratory, introduced a "hypertext" system of linking information on computers everywhere. Working with others, he developed the hypertext markup language (HTML) that allows any computer to read any document or content using the language. They also created the hypertext transport protocol (HTTP) that made it possible to communicate over the internet. The World Wide Web was born. By 1993, the internet became readily accessible to ordinary computer users when the Mosaic browser was introduced by the National Center for Supercomputing Applications (NCSA) at the University of Illinois. Mosaic was the first point-and-click web browser with the ability to display text and images together. The graphical interface made the internet more appealing to ordinary computer users. Soon, thousands of free copies of the Mosaic software were being downloaded each month from the NCSA website. Netscape was launched as a commercial company to market Mosaic, which was renamed Netscape Navigator.

Initially, many in the news media didn't know what to make of the new technology. In a memorable exchange in January 1994, the hosts of NBC's *Today* show discussed the @ symbol that was part of email addresses. "What is the Internet anyway?" Bryant Gumbel asked. "Do you write to it like mail?" To which cohost Katie Couric replied, "A lot of people use it and communicate." Indeed, they were doing just that, and gradually the press began to recognize the internet's enormous potential for reporting the news. By creating websites and posting stories as soon as they were ready, newspapers found they could get news on the web as quickly as television, no longer constrained by publication schedules. In mid-1995, fewer than one hundred newspapers had their own websites. A year later, the number had jumped to more than four hundred. Television stations also launched sites, providing more depth for stories than was permitted with the traditional thirty- or sixty-minute newscasts. Initially, the news media simply dumped content onto their websites, but over time they began providing additional material, including charts, sidebars, audio, and video.

The "digital revolution," as it has become known, had a profound effect on journalism. With the digital media, computers take words, sounds, and images and turn them into codes (strings of two digits, 1 and 0). Digital media replaced the physical media that used to be needed to put out a newspaper or a news broadcast. And thanks to the internet, the digital media can be transmitted to anyone with a connection. As Christopher Daly has noted, one of the most significant impacts of the digital revolution was in the definition of the press. Before the internet, newspapers, magazines, radio, and television were distinguished by the way they delivered news to their customers. Newspapers and magazines were "print," while radio and television were "broadcast." However, on the Web, those old ways of sharing the news were no longer delineated. Although the traditional media still delivered the news the way they always had, they increasingly poured more resources into delivering news via the internet.

The digital revolution has meant the tasks that two or three journalists working together once accomplished now can often be done by just one person. A reporter with a laptop computer, digital camera, and smartphone can report almost any kind of story from almost anywhere. The Web and the technological tools have also given journalists new ways to report the news and tell stories. Some of the most compelling are in the form of multimedia packages that combine text, audio, video, and graphics.

However, the internet has posed a significant issue for the "legacy" media, as some call the press that existed before the internet. Newspapers and magazines could not simply abandon their print products, nor could radio and television stations give up their over-the-air broadcasts, in favor of going all-in with the Web. Many people still wanted to get their news in paper form or over the air on sets. And many companies also liked these traditional means of advertising their products and services. Over time, however, more and more people were getting their information from the internet, in part because it was easier but also because for a long time it was all free.

As the number of news websites grew, some became "aggregators," collecting news that originated from other sites, provided a summary, and then linked to the original source. Aggregation sites such as Yahoo! News had no original reporting but simply offered a simple way for users to find news. This presented problems for the traditional media that were reporting the news. If aggregation sites provided the news for free, how could news sites charge for their product? Aggregators maintained that in the online economy value is created by the number of visitors drawn to a site. They argued that they were doing news sites a favor by providing links to their sites.

At the same time, new "dot-com" companies cut into one of the traditional revenue sources of the news media. Newspapers had long relied heavily on the income from classified advertisements. Many classified ads were bought by businesses looking for employees or individuals selling items. New internet companies, such as Monster.com and Craigslist, made it possible to list thousands of jobs in one place and bypass newspaper classifieds. eBay and other online auctions allowed people to post items for sale and buyers to bid on them online, once again bypassing classified ads. (In 1998, three years after it was founded, eBay went public; the company sold 3.5 million shares and raised $63 million.)

The internet also made it possible to easily start new sources for news and information. Whereas it had always taken a great deal of money and resources to start and operate a newspaper, magazine, radio, or television station, creating a news website cost relatively little. Suddenly almost anyone could become an information provider—and many people jumped at the opportunity. One of the first was Matt Drudge, a Washington, DC, native who moved to Los Angeles in 1989 and was working in the gift shop at CBS Studios. He bought a personal computer and began passing along gossip to friends via email. He eventually started a website for his newsletter, which he called the *Drudge Report*. *Drudge* emphasized conservative political news and opinion, mostly by providing links to the work of other writers. The *Drudge Report* became an internet sensation, especially among conservatives, during the Clinton–Lewinsky sex scandal in 1998. And it has remained a popular site for many readers who have disdain for the traditional news media. Even so, it has maintained the spare look of its home page that has only one big headline and many smaller headlines, all in the same typewriter font.

In 2005, Ariana Huffington launched the *Huffington Post* as a liberal alternative to the *Drudge Report*. Whereas the *Drudge Report* mainly uses content from its own sources, the *Huffington Post* offers original reporting, along with commentary, analysis, and blogging. *HuffPo* became one

DRUDGE REPORT

WASH POST Ignatius Calls on Biden to NOT Run Again...

SCARBOROUGH: Every Dem Off Air Admits He's Too Old!

Hunter Sues Ex-Trump Aide Over Accessing Laptop...

Don embraces Putin's sympathetic comments to claim political persecution...

UPDATE: France Orders iPhone 12 Sales Halted Over Radiation...

Users bash new 15...

Iran President to Hold Secret Powwows in NYC...

Shocker: TV Season Faces Cancellation if Strikes Not Resolved in 2 Weeks...

Biden faces moment of peril as UAW threatens broad strike...

Members feel abandoned by Dems...

AOC Married? Her Office Says No. Her Legal Filings Say Otherwise...

MLB star Alex Rodriguez ratted out PED users.

Scientists unveil 'mummified alien' corpses to Mexico Congress...

Three-fingered hands, unknown DNA, eggs inside...

Found in Peru mines...

El Chapo's beauty queen wife released from US custody in Long Beach...

Singer Threatened By Cartel Over Songs...

Authors Sue META, OpenAI Alleging Infringement...

Figure 7.2 Drudge Report Homepage *Source:* Drudge Report, homepage: https://drudgereport.com.

of the most popular news sites on the internet because of its wide variety of content. *Huffington* did not pay most of its contributors, but for years there were few complaints because of the site's large readership. In 2011, American Online purchased the *Huffington Post* for $315 million, proving that online journalism could be profitable for entrepreneurs. In 2012, the *Huffington Post* became the first commercial media site to win a Pulitzer Prize for its ten-part series on American troops severely wounded in Afghanistan and Iraq.

Others used the internet to create hybrid forms of the news media, part print and part broadcast. That was the idea behind *Slate*, a daily online magazine (or e-zine) founded in 1996. *Slate* was the brainchild of Michael Kinsley, a veteran journalist, and leaders of Microsoft, the computer software giant. Kinsley wanted to start his own magazine, and Microsoft wanted to expand its presence on the Web. *Slate* covers news, politics, arts, and sports with the goal of helping readers understand the world through entertaining writing. Although *Slate* runs traditional long-form magazine pieces, many of the articles are short and argument-driven. *Slate* was also one of the first news sites to embrace "podcasts," episodic audio or video series that are downloaded onto computers and phones. Some of the most popular *Slate* podcasts have been roundtable discussions of various topics. Helped by the popularity of the podcasts, which are attractive to advertisers, *Slate* became profitable in 2007.

The internet also spawned a new form of online journalism, the web log or "blog," as it is more commonly known. Blogs are written in diary form and generally contain snippets of news or commentary. News sites embraced blogs and many staff writers used them to report on politics, business, health, sports, arts, and other subjects. Some of the most popular bloggers were not attached to any particular news organization but attracted wide readership because of their creativity, initiative, and salesmanship. Nate Silver, a statistician, created the *FiveThirtyEight* blog to report on a variety of subjects, including politics, sports, economics, and popular culture. It became so popular that in 2010, it became a licensed feature of the *New York Times* online.

Journalism in the New Century

By the turn of the century, the internet had disrupted the traditional press in profound ways. As the cost of personal computers came down and the speed of internet transmission improved, more people got news online. Many readers and viewers left traditional newspapers, magazines, radio, and television for new sources of news that often were free. So-called digital natives embraced news on the Web because that is the way they had always gotten it. Digital natives are considered people born after about 1980, who came of age when the internet was born. Many in this age-group have never regularly read a newspaper or watched an evening newscast. As Elliott King has written, "The question was whether an economic model that would support online journalism would emerge. News, it seemed, had become a commodity, and a free commodity at that."

The internet crippled the newspaper business model by decimating its advertising. Entrepreneurs like those who founded Google, Monster.com, eBay, and Craigslist were more innovative and nimble than the established communications industry was. The old business model was based on using news coverage to attract an audience of consumers, who then were collectively rented out to advertisers. The advertising revenue effectively underwrote the cost of news coverage. In contrast, as digital-age consumers go to their computers to find the product they want to buy, and news only gets in the way of their search. As advertising revenues declined, print media began revisiting their decisions to offer their reporting free on the Web. Although some national publications such as the *New York Times* and *Wall Street Journal* saw success in their efforts to market their news coverage, it remains to be seen whether regional and local publications can earn enough money from Web subscriptions to support the quality and quantity of news coverage that consumers had come to expect in the pre-digital age.

Social media has also played a large role in taking both readers and advertising dollars away from the traditional press. Ads that once went inside newspapers and were read aloud on radio stations are now seen digitally as eyeballs scroll on social media sites. Prior to the internet, newspapers received 80 percent of their revenue from advertising. While Craigslist took away most classified advertisements, Facebook and

Google then took much of the rest. By 2021, large technology companies controlled 86 percent of the online advertising market and readership followed suit. Social media sites became a dominating news source in 2018, beating out newspaper readership. By 2021, 86 percent of Americans were receiving their news digitally, outranking television and radio.

In addition to revenue changes, social media has played a large role in changing news coverage. Social media helps average citizens generate and produce news stories to which the traditional press often responds. In many ways, traditional gatekeeping where reporters and editors set the news agenda has significantly lessened. This was especially evident during social justice movements like #MeToo and #BlackLivesMatter when millions of citizens called attention to sexual violence and demanded racial justice.

Certainly, social media became a useful tool for many reporters looking for sources, story ideas, and photos. Additionally, reporters and news organizations use social media to promote readership. However, misinformation on social media can play a dangerous role. In 2007, after a gunman killed thirty-three people on Virginia Tech's campus, Fox News wrongly reported the gunman's identity due to a rumor spread on Facebook. Then in 2013, when two religious extremists bombed the Boston Marathon, a manhunt spread across the city and on social media. False information was spread over several sites and then was repeated on the front pages of newspapers and broadcast on television news.

The struggles that the legacy media have encountered has been exemplified by the *New York Times*. The country's foremost news organization made its initial foray into online delivery in 1994 with *@times*, arts and entertainment stories that it licensed to America Online. The service had little success, so two years later the *Times* launched a web version, nytimes.com. The site provided all the newspaper's content free to readers. However, it attracted few advertisers and siphoned off many of the paying subscribers. In 2005, the *Times* introduced Times Select, in which certain content was put behind a pay wall, so readers who wanted to read the work of some of its most popular writers had to pay a monthly fee. That experiment lasted two years before it was abandoned. In 2011, the *Times* tried another tack, this time giving readers free access to a limited number of stories. If they want more than that number, they have to pay a monthly fee. That system has enjoyed far more success. In 2018, the *Times* had more than 2.5 million digital subscribers, and by early 2023, that number grew to 9.6 million. The organization has also invested heavily in podcasting. Its premier show, *The Daily*, along with other podcasts on politics, opinion, and culture boasts over one hundred million downloads a month.

Declining readership and the loss of advertising have led longtime print-media owners to sell their properties, shift to online exclusively, or close them entirely. Knight Ridder, the second-largest newspaper chain and owner of such respected newspapers as the *Miami Herald*, *Philadelphia Inquirer*, *Kansas City Star*, and *Charlotte Observer*, sold its publications to McClatchy Company in 2006. The *Los Angeles Times*, *Chicago Tribune*, *Minneapolis Star Tribune*, and *San Diego Union Tribune*, went through bankruptcy proceedings and acquired new owners. Denver's *Rocky Mountain News*, which had begun publication in 1859 and won four Pulitzer Prizes since 2000, closed in 2009. The *Seattle Post-Intelligencer*, founded in 1863, became an online-only publication the same year. The New Orleans *Times-Picayune*, which had published during Hurricane Katrina and its aftermath despite its staff being evacuated from its office, began publishing a print edition only three times a week. Time Warner sold its portfolio of magazines, including *Time*, *Sports Illustrated*, and *Fortune*, to Meredith Publishing. Many local radio and television stations changed hands several times. "It's certainly not anything you did," the *Rocky Mountain News* publisher told the newsroom staff in announcing the newspaper was closing. "You all did everything right. But while you were out doing your part, the business model and economy changed, and the *Rocky* became a victim of that."

Faced with declining revenues, news organizations at the national and local levels have cut the number of journalists on their staffs. Major newspapers, as well as the television networks, shuttered foreign bureaus. Many news organizations substantially reduced their coverage of state government. Between the years 2006 and 2021, the number of local newspaper employees—reporters, photographers, videographers, and editors—in the United States fell about 70 percent from 375,000 to

104,000. Although digital news organizations have hired ten thousand employees from 2008 to 2022, it does not account for the number of traditional news journalists who have lost their employment. With fewer resources, newspapers have also been unable to report on local police, government, and education as they once did, not to mention produce the kind of human-interest stories that delight readers and viewers. The woes have led some observers to caution that journalism is facing an existential crisis.

The press also faced a challenge with the relentless—and some argue dangerous criticism—by President Donald Trump, who was elected in 2016. Since his early days as a real estate developer, Trump sought media coverage, believing that it helped his business interests. When he was strictly a real estate developer, the news reporting about him was generally positive, focusing on his gleaming skyscrapers and flamboyant lifestyle. The New York tabloids, led by the *New York Post*, often flattered Trump and gave him the kind of headlines he wanted. During the 2016 primary, Trump often received more news attention than other candidates, in large part because he was not a typical presidential candidate but also because he made himself widely available to the press. Critics said journalists gave Trump an unfair advantage over his Republican rivals with what they said was essentially free publicity.

However, after Trump became the Republican nominee, the reporting of him became more critical. The most sensational story was the revelation of a 2005 audiotape in which Trump bragged about groping women, using crude language that many found abhorrent. Trump denied that he had ever assaulted women and called his words merely "locker room talk." He also fired back at the news media for reporting the story and argued the press favored his Democratic opponent, Hillary Clinton. News organizations defended the coverage, saying the American people had a right to know the character of a presidential candidate. The aggressive reporting continued after Trump was elected president. Led by the *New York Times*, the *Washington Post*, the *Wall Street Journal*, and CNN, the press scrutinized many of the administration's policies as well as his personal conduct.

The hard-hitting news coverage of an administration was not unusual. Every American president has complained about how he has been treated by the press. However, Trump responded like no other chief executive before. He repeatedly called the reporting of his presidency "Fake News" and declared the press to be the "Enemy of the People," knowing that he was tapping into the views that many of his core supporters held about the news media. In a 2018 tweet, Trump wrote: "The Fake News is working overtime. Just reported that, despite the tremendous success we are having with the economy & all things else, 91% of the Network News about me is negative (Fake). Why do we work so hard in working with the media when it is corrupt? Take away credentials?" To many, the president equating "negative" news with "fake" news showed that he believed—and, importantly, wanted others to believe—they mean the same thing, even though they do not.

Observers have noted that Trump's co-opting of the term "fake news" makes the problem of real "fake news" more difficult to combat. The term "fake news" been used for decades to describe news intentionally made up to deceive or entertain. Disinformation or hoaxes spread by the news media goes back to the earliest days of the press. In many cases, the fake news was intended to drive up readership, listenership, or viewership. (The Moon Hoax and the "War of the Worlds" broadcast discussed in previous chapters are just two examples.) Usage of the term became more widespread in the twentieth-first century, especially with the popularity of so-called fake news satirical shows and publications like *The Daily Show* and *The Onion*.

But whereas *The Daily Show* and *The Onion* were created to entertain, news that is intentionally made up with the goal of damaging—politically, socially, or financially—is far more troublesome. Moreover, news that is made up to mislead undermines accurate and honest news coverage, because the public may not know what to believe or what not to believe. Fake news spreads far more quickly and easily on the internet, especially social media platforms such as Facebook and Twitter (now X), where it's far more difficult to challenge. It was a major issue during the 2016 presidential election. One study found that the top twenty fake news stories about the election received more engagement on social media than the top twenty news stories from legitimate news sources. This issue worsened during the 2020 presidential election when Trump denied the election results against his democratic opponent Joe Biden. Tensions reached a head on January 6, 2021, when a mob of Trump supporters attacked and entered the US Capitol in an effort to halt Congress from certifying the election results, which showed Biden defeating Trump. The news dominated the news cycle and resulted in several social media sites banning Trump, who continued to falsely claim that he won the election.

A COMPLICATED FUTURE

The digital revolution continues to transform the press. Journalists are reporting the news and telling stories in ways that were not possible in the past. With the popularity of smartphones, more people are getting the news on their phones instantaneously. TikTok and other social media, including Facebook and Instagram, have become an increasingly important means of reporting the news and driving followers to stories. Podcasting has grown to become enormously popular. However, the digital environment also presents a host of challenges. Thanks to the internet, the walls that existed between the print and broadcast media have crumbled. As a result, every media organization—big and small—is searching for the best ways to reach news consumers. The press also continues to search for ways to monetize a business in which print advertising has collapsed. Newspapers and magazines understand that readers will have to pay to get access to their favorite publications.

Perhaps the greatest crisis facing journalism is with local news, particularly local newspapers. Since 2005, about 2,500 newspapers in the United States have closed, most of them weeklies. During the COVID-19 pandemic alone, 360 newspapers stopped publishing. Total weekday circulation has fallen from 122 million to twenty-six million. The closing of newspapers has been felt especially in rural areas. Hundreds of communities across the country have become isolated "news deserts" with little or no reporting of the events taking place. But even in most larger American towns and cities, news that was once routinely covered by publications—law enforcement, government, education, business, sports, and cultural affairs—is often ignored because there is not adequate staff.

To make up for the shortfall in reporting by the traditional press, new Web-based news sites have been launched. The sites take different forms, and they rely on various sources of revenue. They include independent, nonprofit news organizations that focus on public service and investigative reporting, such as *Minn Post*, *Chicago Reporter*, *PublicSource*, *Carolina Public Press*, and *Texas Tribune*. ProPublica is the most ambitious of the investigative reporting sites. Founded in 2007 and based in New York City, it has a staff of more than one hundred reporters and editors. Investigative stories by ProPublica are reported by its staff and published on its website. They are also distributed to news partners for publication or broadcast. In some cases, reporters for ProPublica and its partners work on stories together. ProPublica has won six Pulitzer Prizes, including the 2011 national reporting prize for an in-depth series on the questionable practices of Wall Street financiers that contributed to the economic recession, and the 2020 public service prize for its partnership with the *Anchorage Daily News* that found one-third of Alaskan villages had inadequate law enforcement.

The digital-first model also allows organizations outside of the mainstream press to reach wider audiences. This is especially evident in

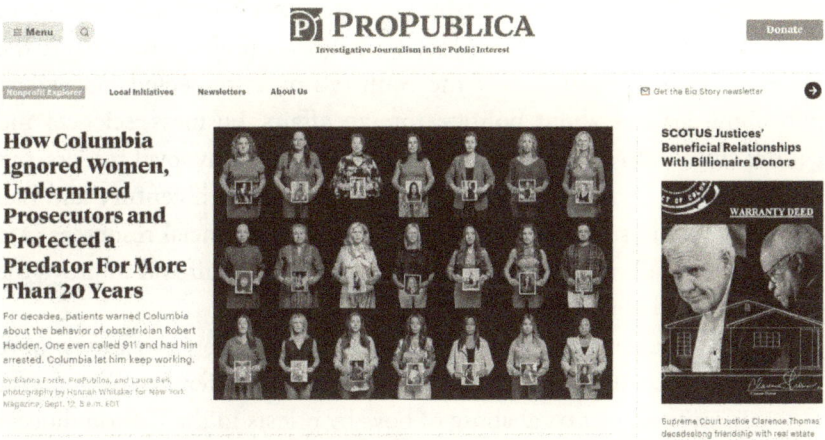

Figure 7.3 ProPublica Homepage

Indigenous media. According to Victoria and Benjamin Rex LaPoe, digital media provides an "extension" of oral storytelling traditionally found in Native cultures. Many Native American newspapers have transitioned to online platforms and former journalists, like Jodi Rave Spotted Bear, have started their own nonprofit digital news sites. Buffalo's Fire is a nonprofit run by the Indigenous Media Freedom Alliance and covers national Native stories. Similarly, Indian Country Today is another digital nonprofit news site. Yet, just like Indigenous newspapers from the nineteenth century, these digital media sites vary in their scope and ownership. Some publications are tribal-owned, while others are independent or nonprofit organizations. Additionally, national organizations help Indigenous reporters stay connected. In 1983, Tim Giago, owner of the *Lakota Times*, brought a group of Native journalists together at Penn State University to create a group now known as the Native American Journalists Association. The group's mission is to create fair coverage of Native people and support tribal media.

Financial backers also have stepped up to support some of the best-known legacy media to ensure they continue their work. In 2013, Jeff Bezos, the founder of Amazon, purchased the *Washington Post* from the Graham family, the longtime owners. Under the ownership of Bezos, the *Post* has more of a digital focus, while still emphasizing aggressive, responsible reporting. The *Post* has a new slogan, "Democracy Dies in Darkness." A group headed by Laurene Powell Jobs (the widow of Apple Company founder Steve Jobs) purchased the *Atlantic* in 2017. The *Atlantic* has long been one of the country's most respected magazines, publishing articles about politics, foreign affairs, business, science, and culture since 1857. The magazine has always had many loyal readers, but it experienced financial problems in the late twentieth century and had a series of owners. The new owners have poured financial resources into the magazine, allowing it to increase the size of the staff and improve the printed magazine and the website.

In the challenging press environment, news organizations have continued to produce reporting that has made a difference. The *Boston Globe* uncovered the sexual abuse of boys by priests in the Boston diocese that was covered up for years by the Catholic Church. The *Minneapolis*

Star-Tribune reported on the high number of infant deaths at poorly regulated day care centers. The Associated Press examined the labor abuses tied to the supply of seafood of American supermarkets and restaurants. National Public Radio (NPR) reported on the toxic culture inside banking giant Wells Fargo, including employees being fired after filing complaints. The *Charleston Gazette-Mail* exposed the flood of opioids flowing into depressed areas of West Virginia. CBS reported on the misleading and false claims of some genetic testing companies. The *New Yorker* and *New York Times* exposed powerful and wealthy men who sexually abused women in the workplace, sparking the #MeToo movement.

The important work by both the old and new forms of the news media in fulfilling their role in serving the country gives hope for the future of journalism. Undoubtedly, some of the traditional ways in which people have gotten their news eventually will come to end. However, the practice of journalism will continue as long as people need and want news. American journalism will simply take a different shape.

Bibliography

Chapter 1: The Founding Press

The Public Prints: The Newspaper in Anglo-American-Culture (New York: Oxford University Press, 1994) by Charles E. Clark examines the formative era of newspaper publishing in America. *The Early American Press, 1690–1783* (Westport, CT: Greenwood Press, 1994) by W. David Sloan and Julie Hedgepth Williams is a comprehensive examination of the early press. *Colonial American Newspapers: Character and Content* (Newark: University of Delaware Press, 1997) by David Copeland is a study of the first newspapers and what they published. *Printers and Press Freedom: The Ideology of Early American Journalism* (New York: Oxford University Press, 1988) by Jeffrey A. Smith is an essential study of the views of early American publishers. *Benjamin Franklin: An American Life* (New York: Simon & Schuster, 2004) by Walter Isaacson is an outstanding biography of the printer, inventor, and statesman. Richard Kluger's *Indelible Ink: The Trials of John Peter Zenger and the Birth of America's Free Press* (New York: W.W. Norton, 2016) is a narrative account of the famous trial. Marion Marzolf, "The Woman Journalist: Colonial Printer to City Desk," *Journalism History* 1, no. 4 (Winter 1974): 100–7 and Ellen M. Oldham, "Early Women Printers in America," *Boston Public Library Quarterly* 10 (1958): 6 offer groundbreaking work on women publishers in colonial America.

Other useful works are Richard D. Brown, *Knowledge is Power: The Diffusion of Information in Early America, 1700–1865* (New York: Oxford University Press, 1989*)*; Louis B. Wright, *The Cultural Life of the American Colonies 1607–1763* (New York: Harper & Row, 1957); Ralph Frasca,

Benjamin Franklin's Printing Network (Columbia: University of Missouri Press, 2006); David Freeman Hawke, *Everyday Life in Early America* (New York: Harper & Row, 1988); Wm. David Sloan, ed., *Media and Religion in American History* (Northport: Vision Press, 2000); Patricia Bradley, "Forerunner of the 'Dark Ages': Philadelphia Tradition of a Partisan Press," *American Journalism* 13, no. 2 (Spring 1996): 126–40; David Copeland, "In All the Papers: Reporting on Religion in Colonial America," *American Journalism* 13, no. 4 (Fall 1996): 390–415; David Paul Nord, "Teleology and the News: The Religious Roots of American Journalism, 1630–1730," *Journal of American History* 77, no. 1 (June 1990): 9–38; A. Franklin Parks, *William Parks: The Colonial Printer in the Transatlantic World of the Eighteenth Century* (State College: Penn State University Press, 2012); Lisa Smith, *The First Great Awakening in Colonial American Newspapers: A Shifting Story* (Lanham, MD: Lexington Books, 2012); Rosalind Remer, *Printers and Men of Capital: Philadelphia Book Publishers in the New Republic* (Philadelphia: University of Pennsylvania Press, 1996); and Lisa M. Parcell, "Early American Newswriting Style: Who, What, When, Where, Why, and How," *Journalism History* 37, no. 1 (2011): 2–11.

CHAPTER 2: THE POLITICAL PRESS

Bernard Bailyn and John B. Henck, *The Press and the American Revolution* (Boston: Northeastern University Press, 1981); Carol Sue Humphrey and David Copeland, *The American Revolution and the Press: The Promise of Independence* (Evanston, IL: Northwestern University Press, 2013); Carl Berger, *Broadsides and Bayonets: The Propaganda War of the American Revolution* (Philadelphia: University of Pennsylvania Press, 1961); Jordan E. Taylor, *Misinformation Nation: Foreign News and the Politics of Truth in Revolutionary America* (Baltimore, MD: Johns Hopkins University Press, 2022); Arthur M. Schlesinger, *Prelude to Independence: The Newspaper War on Great Britain* (New York: Knopf, 1957); and Janice Hume, *Popular Media and the American Revolution: Shaping Collective Memory* (New York: Routledge, 2014) are useful studies about the role that the press played in the Revolutionary War. Eric Foner, *Tom Paine and Revolutionary America* (New York: Oxford University Press, 1976) examines the life and work of the famous propagandist. Culver H. Smith, *The Press, Politics and Patronage: The American Government's Use of Newspapers, 1789–1875* (Athens: University of Georgia Press, 1977) examines the importance of government patronage to the early press. Jeffrey L. Pasley, *The Tyranny of Printers: Newspapers Politics in the Early American Republic* (Charlottesville: University Press of Virginia, 2001) explores the influence of editors in the early 1800s. Richard B. Kielbowicz, *News in the Mail: The Press, Post Office, and Public Information, 1700–1860s* (Westport, CT: Greenwood Press, 1989) is a useful study of the important role of the post office.

Other helpful works for understanding this period include Leonard W. Levy, *Emergence of a Free Press* (New York: Oxford University Press, 1985); Ira Stoll, *Samuel Adams: A Life* (New York: Free Press, 2008); Edmund S. Morgan and Helen M. Morgan, *The Stamp Act Crisis: Prologue to a Revolution* (Chapel Hill: University of North Carolina Press, 1953); Francis G. Walett, *Massachusetts Newspapers and the Revolutionary Crisis* (Boston: Massachusetts Bicentennial Commission, 1974); Carol Sue Humphrey, *The Press of the Young Republic, 1783–1833* (Westport, CT: Greenwood Press, 1996); Richard R. John, *Spreading the News: The American Postal System from Franklin to Morse* (Cambridge, MA: Harvard University Press, 1995); Winifred Gallagher, *How the Post Office Created America: A History* (New York: Penguin Press, 2016); Paul Starr, *The Creation of the Media: Political Origins of Modern Communications* (New York: Basic Books, 2004); Marcus Daniel, *Scandal & Civility: Journalism and the Birth of Democracy* (New York: Oxford University Press, 2009); Jerry W. Knudson, *Jefferson and the Press: Crucible of Liberty* (Columbia: University of South Carolina Press, 2006); Roger P. Mellen, "The Colonial Virginia Press and the Stamp Act," *Journalism History* 38, no. 2 (2012): 74–85; Robert K. Steward, "The Exchange System and the Development of American Politics in the 1820s," *American Journalism* 4, no. 1 (1987): 30–42; and Wm. David Sloan, "The Early Party Press, The Newspaper Role in American Politics, 1798–1812," *Journalism History* 9, no. 1 (1982): 18–24.

CHAPTER 3: THE PUBLIC PRESS

William E. Huntzicker, *The Popular Press, 1833–1865* (Westport, CT: Greenwood Press, 1999) is a useful overview of the penny press period. Henry L. Stoddard, *Horace Greeley: Printer, Editor, Crusader* (New York: G. P. Putnam's Sons, 1946) is a valuable biography of the influential New York editor. Andie Tucher, *Froth and Scum: Truth Beauty and, Goodness, and the Ax Murder in America's First Mass Medium* (Chapel Hill: University of North Carolina Press, 1994) and Patricia Cline, *The Murder of Helen Jewett: The Life and Death of a Prostitute in Nineteenth-Century New York* (New York: Alfred A. Knopf, 1998) examines the famous Helen Jewett murder. Henry Mayer, *All on Fire: William Lloyd Garrison and the Abolition of Slavery* (New York: St. Martin's Press, 1998) is an outstanding biography of the controversial abolitionist editor and leader. Donald E. Reynolds, *Editors Make War: Southern Newspapers in the Secession Crisis* (Nashville, TN: Vanderbilt University Press, 1966) surveys the views of Southern editors in the years leading up to the Civil War. The most valuable works on reporting of the Civil War are two books by J. Cutler Andrews, *The North Reports the Civil War* (Pittsburgh: University of Pittsburgh Press, 1955) and *The South Reports the Civil War* (Princeton, NJ: Princeton University Press, 1970). For an overview of magazine illustrations during the Civil War, see W. Fletcher Thompson Jr., *The Image of War: The Pictorial Reporting of the American Civil War* (New York: T. Yoseloff, 1960). Bob Zeller, *The Blue and Gray in Black and White: A History of Civil War Photography* (Westport, CT: Praeger, 2005) is the best single source on the role of photography. Ford Risley, *Civil War Journalism* (Santa Barbara, CA: Praeger, 2012) is an overview of the reporting, editorializing, photography, and illustrations during the war.

Other useful works are John D. Stevens, *Sensationalism and the New York Press* (New York: Columbia University Press,1991); Victor Rosewater, *History of Cooperative Newsgathering in the United States* (New York: D. Appleton, 1930); Menaheim Blondehim, *News Over the Wires: The Telegraph and the Flow of Information in America, 1844–1896* (Cambridge, MA: Harvard University Press, 1994); James McPherson, *Struggle For Equality: Abolitionist and the Negro in the Civil War and Reconstruction* (Princeton, NJ: Princeton University Press, 1964); Russell

B. Nye, *Fettered Freedom: Civil Liberties and the Slavery Controversy, 1830–1860* (East Lansing: Michigan State University Press, 1963); Ford Risley, *Abolition and the Press: The Moral Struggle Against Slavery* (Evanston, IL: Northwestern University Press, 2008); John Nerone, *Violence Against the Press: Policing the Public Sphere in US History* (Oxford: Oxford University Press, 1994); Dan Schiller *Objectivity and the News: The Public and the Rise of Commercial Journalism* (Philadelphia: University of Pennsylvania Press, 1981); David Mindich, *Just the Facts: How "Objectivity" Came to Define American Journalism* (New York: New York University Press, 1998); David W. Bulla and Gregory A. Borchard, *Journalism in the Civil War Era* (New York: Peter Lang, 2010); Matthew J. Shaw, *An Inky Business: A History of Newspapers from the English Civil Wars to the American Civil War* (London: Reaction Books, Limited, 2021); and David B. Sachsman, Gregory A. Borchard, Dea Lisica, *The Antebellum Press: Setting the Stage for Civil War* (New York: Routledge, 2019); Carter R. Bryan, "Negro Journalism in America Before Emancipation," *Journalism Monographs* 12 (1969): 38; Kathleen L. Endres, "Jane Grey Swisshelm: 19th Century Journalist and Feminist," *Journalism History* 2, no. 4 (1975): 128–32; and Richard B. Kielbowicz, "The Law and Mob Attacks on Antislavery Newspapers, 1833–1860," *Law and History Review* 24, no. 3 (2006): 559–600.

CHAPTER 4: THE COMMERCIAL PRESS

Louis Filler, *The Muckrakers: Crusaders for American Liberalism* (Chicago: Regnery, 1964) is an essential study of the muckraking journalists. Garna L. Christian, *El Paso's Muckraker: The Life of Owen Payne White* (Albuquerque: University of New Mexico Press, 2015), Stephanie Gorton, *S. S. McClure, Ida Tarbell, and the Magazine that Rewrote America* (New York: HarperCollins, 2020), and Harold S. Wilson, *McClure's Magazine and the Muckrakers* (Princeton, NJ: Princeton University Press, 1970) each examine key figures and publications during the height of muckraking reporting. Works helpful for understanding the frontier press include James E. Mueller, *Shooting Arrows and Slinging Mud: Custer, the Press and Little Big Horn* (Norman: University of Oklahoma Press, 2013); John M. Coward, *The Newspaper Indian: Native American Identity in the*

Press 1820–90 (Urbana: University of Illinois Press, 1999); Hugh J. Reilly, *The Frontier Newspapers and the Coverage of the Plains Indian Wars* (Santa Barbara, CA: Praeger, 2010); William H. Lyon, *The Pioneer Editor in Missouri* (Columbia: University of Missouri Press, 1965); Barbara Cloud, *The Coming of the Frontier Press: How the Press was Really Won* (Evanston, IL: Northwestern University Press, 2008); and Ken J. Ward, *Last Paper Standing: A Century of Competition Between the Denver Post and the Rocky Mountain News* (Boulder: University of Colorado Press, 2023).

Helpful texts for understanding Native American presses include Sharon Murphy, "Neglected Pioneers: 19th Century Native American Newspapers," *Journalism History* 4, no. 3 (October 1, 1977): 79–100; Melissa Greene-Blye, "Great Men, Savages, and the End of the Indian Problem," *Journalism History* 46, no. 1 (January 2020): 32–49; Meta G. Carstarphen and John P. Sanchez, eds. *American Indians and the Mass Media* (Norman: University of Oklahoma Press, 2012); Cristina Azocar, "Native People," in *The Diversity Style Guide*, edited by Rachele Kanigel (Hoboken: Wiley & Sons, 2018), 61–83; John M. Coward, *Indians Illustrated: The Image of Native Americans in the Pictorial Press* (Champaign: University of Illinois Press, 2016); and Jacqueline Emery, "Mining Boarding School Newspapers for Native American Women Editors and Writers," *American Periodicals* 27, no. 1 (2017): 11–15. Important biographies for key figures of the era include: David Nasaw, *The Chief: The Life of William Randolph Hearst* (Boston: Houghton Mifflin, 2000); Brooke Kroeger, *Nellie Bly: Daredevil, Reporter, Feminist* (New York: Times Books, 1994); Gerald J. Baldasty, *E. W. Scripps and the Business of Newspapers* (Urbana: University of Illinois Press, 1999); James McGrath Morris, *Pulitzer: A Life in Politics, Print and Power* (New York: Harper, 2010); Arthur Lubow, *The Reporter Who Would Be King: A Biography of Richard Harding Davis* (New York: Scribner, 1992); and Steve Weinberg, *Taking on the Trust: The Epic Battle of Ida Tarbell and John D. Rockefeller* (New York: W. W. Norton & Company, 2008).

Other helpful works for understanding this period include Mark Wahlgren Summers, *The Press Gang: Newspapers and Politics, 1865–1878* (Chapel Hill: University of North Carolina Press, 1994); Mitchell Stephens, *A History of News* (New York: Oxford University Press, 2007),

Richard Hofstadter, *The Age of Reform* (New York: Vintage, 1955); Susan Tift and Alex S. Jones, *The Trust: The Private and Powerful Family Behind The New York Times* (Boston: Little, Brown, and Company, 1999); Harrison E. Salisbury, *Without Fear or Favor: The New York Times and its Times* (New York: Times Books, 1980); Thomas C. Leonard, *The Power of the Press: The Birth of American Political Reporting* (New York: Oxford University Press, 1986); Michael Schudson, *Discovering the News: A Social History of American Newspapers* (New York: Basic Books, 1978); Victor Rosewater, *History of Cooperative News-Gathering in the United States* (London: D. Appleton, 1930); Hazel Dicken Garcia, *Journalistic Standards in Nineteenth-Century America* (Madison: University of Wisconsin Press, 1989); W. Joseph Campbell, *Yellow Journalism: Puncturing the Myths, Defining the Legacies* (Westport, CT: Praeger, 2001); Bernell Tripp, *Origins of the Black Press: New York, 1827–1847* (Northport, AL: Vision Press, 1992); Joyce Milton, *The Yellow Kids: Foreign Correspondents in the Heyday of Yellow Journalism* (New York: Harper & Row, 1989); Linda Steiner, "Finding Community in Nineteenth-Century Suffrage Periodicals," *American Journalism* 1, no. 1 (Summer 1983): 1–15; Stanley K. Schultz, "The Morality of Politics: The Muckrakers' Vision of Democracy," *Journal of American History* 52, no. 3 (1965): 527–47; Randall S. Sumpter, "'Practical Reporting': Late Nineteenth-Century Journalistic Standards and Rule Breaking." *American Journalism* 30, no. 1 (Winter 2013): 44–64; Jinx Coleman Broussard, *African American Foreign Correspondents: A History* (Baton Rouge: Louisiana State University Press, 2013); and Autumn Lorimer Linford, "'They'll Never Make Newspaper Men': Early Gendering in Journalism, 1884–1889." *American Journalism* 38, no. 3 (2021): 342–63.

CHAPTER 5: THE EXPANDING PRESS

Leonard Ray Teel, *The Public Press, 1900–1945* (Westport, CT: Praeger, 2006) is an overview of the period. Two books by Erik Barnouw—*A Tower in Babel: A History of Broadcasting in the United States to 1933* (New York: Oxford University Press, 1966) and *Tube of Plenty: The Evolution of American Television* (New York: Oxford University Press, 1990)—examine the history of radio and television, respectively. Stanley

Cloud and Lynne Olson, *The Murrow Boys: Pioneers on the Front Lines of Broadcast Journalism* (New York: Houghton Mifflin, 1996) examines the work of Edward R. Murrow and his colleagues at CBS. Alan Brinkley, *The Publisher: Henry Luce and His American Century* (New York: Knopf, 2010) is an outstanding biography of the founder of *Time, Life,* and other important magazines. Mike Conway, *The Origins of Television News in America: The Visualizers of CBS in the 1940s* (New York: Peter Lang, 2009) explores the early years of television news at CBS. Patrick Parsons, *Blue Skies: A History of Cable Television* (Philadelphia, PA: Temple University Press, 2008) is the standard account of the subject. Patrick S. Washburn, *The African American Newspaper: Voice of Freedom* (Evanston, IL: Northwestern University Press, 2006) is a valuable survey of the Black press. Chris Dubbs, *American Journalists in the Great War* (Lincoln: University of Nebraska Press, 2017) and Michael S. Sweeney, *The Military and the Press: An Uneasy Truce* (Evanston: Northwestern University Press, 2006) are accounts of the reporting of World War I and II. Steven Casey, *The War Beat, Europe: The American Media at War against Nazi Germany* (New York: Oxford University Press, 2017) is an account of the reporting in World War II.

For information on the women's suffrage press, see Linda Steiner, Carolyn Kitch, Brooke Kroeger, *Front Pages, Front Lines: Media and the Fight for Women's Suffrage* (Champaign: University of Illinois Press, 2020); Faye E. Dudden, *Fighting Chance: The Struggle over Woman Suffrage and Black Suffrage in Reconstruction America* (Oxford: Oxford University Press, 2011); Carla LaRoche, "Black Women and Voter Suppression," *Boston University Law Review* 102, no. 7 (December 2022): 2431–95; Teri Finneman, *Press Portrayals of Women Politicians, 1870s–2000s: From "Lunatic" Woodhull to "Polarizing" Palin* (Lanham, MD: Lexington Books, 2015); and Jane Rhodes, *Mary Ann Shadd Cary: The Black Press and Protest in the Nineteenth Century* (Bloomington: Indiana University Press, 1999).

Other useful works are Armistead S. Pride and Clint C. Wilson II, *A History of Black Press* (Washington, DC: Howard University Press, 1997); Rodger Streitmatter's *Raising Her Voice: African-American Women Journalists Who Changed History* (Lexington: University of Kentucky Press, 1994); Linda O. McMurray's, *To Keep the Waters Troubled: The*

Life of Ida B. Wells (New York: Oxford University Press, 1998); Ronald Steel, *Walter Lippmann and the American Century* (Boston: Little, Brown and Company 1980); Peter Kurth, *American Cassandra: The Life of Dorothy Thompson* (Boston: Little, Brown and Company 1990); Susan J. Douglas, *Listening In: Radio and the American Imagination* (New York: Times Books, 1999); Tom Lewis, *Empire of the Air: The Men Who Made Radio* (New York: Edward Burlingame Books, 1991); Ashley Walter and Karlin Andersen Tuttle, "All the President's Media: How the Traditional Press Responded to New Communications Technology Adopted by US Presidents," *American Journalism* 40, no. 1 (2023): 4–25; Robert W. McChesney, *Telecommunications, Mass Media, and Democracy, 1928–1935* (New York: Oxford University Press, 1993); Donald Godfrey, *Philo T. Farnsworth: The Father of Television* (Salt Lake City: University of Utah Press, 2001); Christopher Sterling and John M. Kitross, *Stay Tuned: A History of American Broadcasting* (Belmont, CA: Wadsworth, 1978); Craig M. Allen, *News is People: The Rise of Local News and the Fall of News from New York* (Ames: Iowa State University Press, 2001); James Tobin, *Ernie Pyle's War: America Eyewitness to World War II* (New York: Free Press, 1997); Vicki Goldberg, *Margaret Bourke-White: A Biography* (London: Heinemann, 1987); Carolyn M. Edy, *The Woman War Correspondent and US Military, 1846–1947* (Lanham, MD: Lexington Books, 2017); Richard Fine, "The Ascendancy of Radio News in Wartime Charles Collingwood and John McVane in French North Africa, 1942–43," *Journalism History* 40, no. 1 (2014): 2–14; Shelia Webb, "The Tale of Advancement: *Life* Magazine's Construction of the Modern American Success Story," *Journalism History* 32, no. 1 (2006): 2–12; Agnes Hopper Gotlieb, "Grit Your Teeth, Then Learn to Swear: Women in Journalism Careers, 1850–1926," *American Journalism* 18, no. 1 (2001): 53–72; Will Mari, *The American Newsroom: A History, 1920–1960* (White River Junction: University of Missouri Press, 2021); and Gwyneth Mellinger, *Chasing Newsroom Diversity: From Jim Crow to Affirmative Action* (Champaign: University of Illinois Press, 2013).

CHAPTER 6: THE ALTERNATIVE PRESS

James Brian McPherson, *Journalism at the End of the Century, 1965–Present* (Westport: Praeger, 2006) is an outstanding overview of the period. Daniel C. Hallin, *Introduction to Uncensored War: The Media and Vietnam* (New York: Oxford University Press, 1986) is an important study of news reporting of the war. Gene Roberts and Hank Klibanoff, *The Race Beat: The Press, the Civil Rights Struggle, and the Awakening of a Nation* (New York: Vintage Press, 2006) is essential for understanding how the press covered the civil rights movement. Edwin R. Bayley, *Joe McCarthy and the Press* (Madison: University of Wisconsin Press, 1981) is a valuable study of how journalists covered the controversial senator, while James Aronson, *The Press and the Cold War* (New York: Bobs-Merrill, 1970) examines the larger period. Carl Bernstein and Bob Woodward, *All the President's Men* by (New York: Simon & Schuster, 1974) tells the story of how the two *Washington Post* reporters unraveled the Watergate story. Katherine Graham, *Personal History* (New York: Vintage, 1997) has insightful chapters on the Pentagon Papers and Watergate. Jon Marshall, *Watergate's Legacy and the Press: The Investigative Impulse* (Evanston: Northwestern University Press, 2011) explores the reporting of Watergate and what it meant to do investigative reporting. Sanford J. Ungar, *The Papers & The Papers* (New York: E. P. Dutton, 1972) is a valuable account of the legal and political battle over the Pentagon Papers. Marc Weingarten, *The Gang that Wouldn't Shoot Straight: Wolfe, Thompson, Didion and the New Journalism Revolution* (New York: Crown Publishers, 2006) provides insight into the important journalists of the so-called New Journalism period.

For an exhaustive look at women's media history, see Brooke Kroeger, *Undaunted: How Women Changed American Journalism* (New York: Knopf, 2023); Kay Mills, *A Place in the News: From the Women's Pages to the Front Pages* (New York: Dodd, Mead & Company, 1988); and Maurine H. Beasley and Sheila J. Gibbons, *Taking Their Place: A Documentary History of Women and Journalism*, second edition (State College, PA: Strata Press, 2003). Useful texts for understanding the women's liberation movement and women's media, include Kathleen L. Endres and Therese L. Lueck, *Women's Periodicals in the United States: Social and Political Issues* (Westport,

CT: Greenwood Publishing Group, 1996) and Pamela Newkirk, *Within the Veil: Black Journalists, White Media* (New York: New York University Press, 2000). For more about the class-action sex discrimination lawsuits, see Lynn Povich, *The Good Girls Revolt: How the Women of Newsweek Sued Their Bosses and Changed the Workplace* (New York: Public Affairs, 2012) and Elaine Auerbach, *Dirty Linen: How Women Sued the Reader's Digest and Changed History* (Los Angeles, CA: Wildcat Press, 2021).

Other useful works for understanding the period are James L. Aucoin, *The Evolution of American Investigative Journalism* (Columbia: University of Missouri Press, 2005); Matthew Pressman, *On Press: The Liberal Values that Shaped the News* (Cambridge, MA: Harvard University Press, 2018); Kevin M. Lerner, *Provoking the Press: (MORE) Magazine and the Crisis of Confidence in American Journalism* (Columbia: University of Missouri Press, 2019); Douglas Brinkley, *Cronkite* (New York: Harper, 2012); Susan E. Tift and Alex S. Jones, *The Patriarch: The Rise and Fall of the Bingham Dynasty* (New York: Summit Books, 1991); Richard Kluger, *The Paper: The Life and Death of the* New York Herald Tribune (New York: Knopf, 1986); Anthony Lewis, *Make No Law: The Sullivan Case and the First Amendment* (New York: Random House, 1991); Michael P. McCauley, *NPR: The Trials and Triumphs of National Public Radio* (New York: Columbia University Press, 2005); Nan Robertson, *The Girls in the Balcony: Women, Men and* The New York Times (New York: Random House, 1992); Maurine H. Beasley, *Women of the Washington Press: Politics, Prejudice, and Persistence* (Evanston: Northwestern University Press, 2012); Gloria Steinem, *Outrageous Acts and Everyday Rebellions* (New York: Holt, Rinehart and Winston, 1983); Tom Wolfe, *The New Journalism* (New York: Harper & Row, 1973); Robert S. Draper, *Rolling Stone Magazine: The Uncensored History* (New York: Doubleday, 1990); Ron Powers, *The Newscasters: The News Business as Show Business* (New York: St. Martin's Press, 1977); Hank Whittemore, *CNN: The Inside Story* (Boston: Little, Brown and Company 1990); Clarence R. Wyatt. "'At the Cannon's Mouth': The American Press and Vietnam War," *Journalism History* 13, no. 3 (1986): 104–13; Pamela E. Walck and Emily Fitzgerald, "Finding the 'Cullud' Angle: Evelyn Cunningham, 'The Women,' and Feminism on the Pages of the Pittsburgh Courier,"

Journalism History 46, no. 4 (2020): 339–57; David Wallace, "Piercing the Paper Curtain: The Southern Editorial Response to National Civil Rights Coverage," *American Journalism* 33, no. 4 (2016): 401–23; Joe Hagan, *Sticky Fingers: The Life and Times of Jann Wenner and Rolling Stone Magazine* (New York: Alfred A. Knopf, 2017); and Ashley Walter, "On the Cover of the Rollin' Stone: How *Rolling Stone* Magazine Frames Politics and News," *Journal of Magazine Media* 19, no. 2 (2019): 25–49.

CHAPTER 7: THE DIGITAL PRESS

Leonard Downie Jr. and Robert G. Kaiser, *The News about the News: American Journalism in Peril* (New York: Alfred A. Knopf, 2002) explores the impact of economic, technological, demographic, and social changes on modern journalism. David R. Davies, *The Postwar Decline of Newspapers* (Westport, CT: Praeger, 2006) looks at how after World War II newspapers were slow to react to threats to its existence. James B. McPherson's *The Conservative Resurgence and the Press: The Media's Role in the Rise of the Right* (Evanston, IL: Northwestern University Press, 2008) and Anthony Nadler and A. J. Bauer, *News on the Right: Studying Conservative News Cultures* (New York: Oxford University Press, 2019) examine the relationship between conservatism and the media. Elliot King's *Free for All: The Internet's Transformation of Journalism* (Evanston, IL: Northwestern University Press, 2010) looks at how the Internet has changed the news media. For studies on reporting of 9/11, see Brian A. Monahan, *The Shock of the News* (New York: New York University Press, 2010); Elinor Kelley Grusin and Sandra H. Utt, eds. *Media in an American Crisis: Studies of September 11, 2001* (Lanham, MD: University Press of America, 2005); and Ralph Izard and Jay Perkins, eds. *Lessons from Ground Zero: Media Response to Terror* (New Brunswick, NJ: Transaction Publishers, 2011).

For additional readings on the digital spread of fake news, see Brian McNair, *Fake News: Falsehood, Fabrication and Fantasy in Journalism* (New York: Routledge, 2018); Donald A. Barclay, *Fake News, Propaganda, and Plain Old Lies: How to Find Trustworthy Information in the Digital Age* (Lanham, MD: Rowman & Littlefield, 2018); Ed Madison and Ben DeJarnette, *Reimagining Journalism in a Post-Truth World: How Late-Night Comedians, Internet Trolls, and Savvy Reporters are Transforming*

News (Santa Barbara, CA: Praeger, 2018); David Sumpter, *Outnumbered: From Facebook and Google to Fake News and Filter-Bubbles—The Algorithms That Control Our Lives* (London: Bloomsbury Publishing, 2018); and Andie Tucher, *Not Exactly Lying: Fake News and Fake Journalism in American History* (New York: Columbia University Press, 2022).

Other useful works for understanding the period are Ben Bagdikian, *The News Media Monopoly* (Boston: Beacon Press, 2004); Ken Auletta, *Backstory: Inside the Business of News* (New York: Penguin Press, 2003); Gene Foreman, *The Ethical Journalist: Marking Responsible Decisions in the Pursuit of News* (New York: Wiley-Blackwell, 2010); Christopher B. Daly, *Covering America: A Narrative History of a Nation's Journalism* (Amherst: University of Massachusetts Press, 2012); Mette Mortensen, *Journalism and Eyewitness Images: Digital Media, Participation, and Conflict* (New York: Routledge, 2015); Michael Schudson, *Why Journalism Still Matters* (Cambridge: Polity Press, 2018); Victoria L. LaPoe and Benjamin Rex LaPoe, *Indian Country: Telling a Story in a Digital Age* (East Lansing, MI: Michigan State University Press, 2017), Jon Marshall, *Clash: Presidents and the Press in Times of Crisis* (Lincoln, NA: Potomac Books, 2022); and Teri Finneman and Erika Pribanic-Smith, *Social Justice, Activism and Diversity in US Media History* (New York: Routledge, 2023).

American Journalism Timeline

1704   Postmaster John Campbell publishes the first successful newspaper in the American colonies, the *Boston News-Letter*.

1729   Benjamin Franklin takes over the *Pennsylvania Gazette* and turns it into the best-looking and best-written newspaper in the American colonies.

1735   New York newspaper publisher John Peter Zenger is found not guilty of seditious libel, a victory for press freedom.

1738   Elizabeth Timothy becomes the first women to publish a newspaper in America, the *South Carolina Gazette*, when her husband dies.

1765   Colonial press protests the Stamp Act, which taxed the paper used to print newspapers and other publications.

1776   Thomas Paine publishes *Common Sense*, an appeal for American independence.

1787–1788   The Federalist Papers, a group of political essays, appears in the *New York Independent Journal*.

1791   The Bill of Rights, comprising the first ten amendments to the US Constitution, is ratified. The First Amendment guarantees freedom of the press.

1798   President John Adams signs the Alien and Sedition Acts, and they are used to indict leading Republican newspaper editors.

1827	John Russwurm and Samuel Cornish establish *Freedom's Journal*, the first newspaper published by Black journalists in the United States.
1828	Elias Boudinot establishes the *Cherokee Phoenix*, published partly in English, partly in Cherokee.
1830	*Godey's Lady's Book*, the first successful women's magazine, is launched in Philadelphia.
1833	Benjamin Day starts publishing the *New York Sun*, the first "penny paper."
1837	Louis Daguerre invents a practical method of photography.
1844	Samuel Morse demonstrates the telegraph.
1847	Frederick Douglass establishes the *North Star*.
1848	The Associated Press, a national cooperative news service, begins operation.
1850	Jane Grey Swisshelm is the first woman admitted to the congressional press gallery.
1861	Journalists for Union and Confederate newspapers report the beginning of the Civil War with the attack on Fort Sumter in Charleston, South Carolina.
1870	*Woman's Journal* is founded to advocate women's right to vote and other rights.
1871	Cartoonist Thomas Nast helps expose the corrupt Tweed Ring in New York.
1883	Joseph Pulitzer purchases the *New York World* and brings his "new journalism" to America's largest city.
1887	Nellie Bly writes "Ten Days in a Mad-House" to expose condition at Blackwell's Island Asylum.
1892	A mob wrecks the office of the *Memphis Free Speech*, for which Ida B. Wells investigated the lynching of Black businessmen.
1896	Adolph S. Ochs purchases the *New York Times* and establishes it as one of the most influential newspapers in the United States.

1902	*McClure's Magazine* publishes investigations of political corruption and the Standard Oil monopoly, launching the era of muckraking journalism.
1907	The *Pittsburgh Courier*, one of the leading Black newspapers, is founded.
1919	The *New York Illustrated Daily News*, the first successful tabloid newspaper in the United States, is launched. The name is later shortened to the *Daily News*.
1920	KDKA in Pittsburgh begins operation as the first commercial radio station, broadcasting the results of the presidential election.
1923	Henry R. Luce and a partner launch *Time*, a weekly newsmagazine. Luce later starts *Life*, *Sports Illustrated*, and *Fortune*.
1926	NBC, the first radio network, is launched.
1945	Popular war correspondent Ernie Pyle is killed by a Japanese sniper in the closing months of World War II.
1947	The Hutchins Commission issues "A Free and Responsible Press."
1949	The newscast *CBS TV News* with Douglas Edwards debuts, later followed by NBC's *Camel News Caravan* with John Cameron Swayze.
1954	The CBS News documentary *See It Now* shows the abusive tactics used by Senator Joseph McCarthy's "red scare."
1962	Rachel Carson publishes "Silent Spring" as a series in the *New Yorker*.
1964	In *Sullivan v. New York Times*, the Supreme Court rules that a public official may only win a libel suit by proving the story was published with "actual malice."
1967	Congress approves the Public Broadcasting Act, creating the Corporation for Public Broadcasting.
1970	Women at *Newsweek* file a sex discrimination class action lawsuit kicking off a decade-long movement at US news organizations.

1971	The *New York Times* and *Washington Post* begin publishing the Pentagon Papers.
1973	*Washington Post* reporters Carl Bernstein and Bob Woodward are assigned to cover the Watergate scandal.
1980	CNN, a cable news network featuring twenty-four-hour news coverage, is started.
1982	The Gannett Co. begins publishing *USA Today*, the first national newspaper in decades.
1993	The *News & Observer* (Raleigh, NC) and *San Jose* (CA) *Mercury News* become the first newspapers published on the World Wide Web.
1995	Walt Disney Co. purchases ABC, setting off a string of purchases of television networks that establishes giant US media conglomerates.
1998	The *Drudge Report* breaks the news that President Bill Clinton was having an affair with White House intern Monica Lewinsky.
2006	Twitter is launched.
2007	ProPublica is founded as an investigative, nonprofit news organization.
2013	Gwen Ifill and Judy Woodruff of the *PBS NewsHour* become the first female-only anchor team on a nightly national news broadcast.
2016	Claims of fake news escalate during the US presidential campaign.
2018	Americans consume more news via social media than newspapers.
2020	Many news outlets scale back or close during the COVID-19 pandemic.
2023	Fox News settles a defamation suit by Dominion Voting Systems in the wake of the 2020 presidential election.

INDEX

Author Bios

Ford Risley is a distinguished professor in the Bellisario College of Communications at Penn State University. He is the author or editor of four books, including *Civil War Journalism* (Praeger, 2012) and *Abolition and the Press: The Moral Struggle Against Slavery* (Northwestern, 2008).

Ashley Walter is an assistant professor of journalism and media at Saint Louis University. She is an expert in women's media history. Her work has been published in *Journalism History*, *American Journalism*, and The Women's Media Center.